Police Program Evaluation

Edited by
Larry T. Hoover
Sam Houston State University

Larry T. Hoover, Director
Police Research Center
Sam Houston State University
Huntsville, TX

Gerald L. Williams, Executive Director
Bill Blackwood Law Enforcement Management Institute of Texas
Sam Houston State University
Huntsville, TX

Chuck Wexler, Executive Director
Police Executive Research Forum (PERF)
Washington, DC

This anthology was produced by the Police Research Center and the Bill Blackwood Law Enforcement Management Institute of Texas at Sam Houston State University, Huntsville, Texas. Publication is by a cooperative agreement with the Police Executive Research Forum. The views expressed in this publication are those of the authors and do not necessarily represent those of PERF's members.

Police Executive Research Forum
1120 Connecticut Ave. NW, Suite 930
Washington, DC 20036

Contents

Preface

My law enforcement career began with enrollment at Michigan State University in what was then the School of Police Science and Administration (now, of course, Criminal Justice). We have come a long way in the ensuing years, but not far enough. There is still not enough police science in police administration. This book is intended to contribute to our empirically defined knowledge base regarding "what works."

As I argue in Chapter One, the police do indeed make a difference. Structured, proactive, tightly focused response can reduce the incidence of a wide range of offenses. But careful evaluation is essential to document what interventions truly work. Evaluation efforts to date have established that crime-specific policing works. But evaluative efforts have been too meager to provide police managers with anything but vague guidelines for generic approaches. Specificity with regard to both tactics and the environmental context in which those tactics are applied is needed.

This is the third in a series of joint publications by Sam Houston State University and the Police Executive Research Forum. The first, *Police Management: Issues and Perspectives* (1992), addressed endemic issues in law enforcement administration. The second, *Quantifying Quality in Policing* (1996) provided a comprehensive review of the application of total quality management to policing. Like the previous two books, this work is designed to fill a significant gap in the literature base of law enforcement administration. Each chapter was individually commissioned and written for this anthology.

Larry T. Hoover

Acknowledgments

First and foremost, I want to acknowledge the irreplaceable assistance of Ms. Jamie Tillerson, program manager for the Police Research Center at Sam Houston State University. She not only managed development, but contributed to the copy edit and layout. Second, I wish to thank Ms. Kay Billingsley, who did copy layout. Each of the authors provided works of insight and originality. The core of the anthology is, of course, theirs.

As director of the Bill Blackwood Law Enforcement Management Institute of Texas, Dr. Gerald Williams provided the largely invisible administrative support that makes the production of publications such as this possible. Additionally, staff of the Texas Commission on Law Enforcement Officer Standards and Education helped foster the development of the original program evaluation packages that were the genesis of this book. Fred Toler (now retired), Jack Ryle (now director of the Texas Police Association), Craig Campbell, Ed Laine, and Joe Gonzalez (now retired) all had a hand in the process of development.

Finally, I want to acknowledge the assistance of PERF staff, particularly Ms. Martha Plotkin, PERF's communications director, for her management of the endeavor; and Ms. Suzanne Fregly who did a thorough and superb copy edit/revision.

Chapter 1

Rationale for Police Program Evaluation

Larry T. Hoover

Introduction

One of the most common misconceptions pervading modern criminology is that the police make no difference. Engendered by two early research studies on nondirective approaches, i.e., the Kansas City Preventive Patrol Experiment and the RAND Criminal Investigation Study, the axiom was born that nothing the police do has an appreciable effect on crime rates. Myths that have some basis in scientific fact die hard. And analyses of *macro* law enforcement approaches indeed have indicated nominal police effectiveness. Bolstering the findings of the Kansas City and RAND studies is the fact that no correlation exists between police-citizen ratios in major U.S. cities and crime rates. Thus, if one tends to believe that the police make no difference, a quick glance at generic correlation between police staffing levels and overall crime rates can quickly confirm one's bias.

However, there is consistently accumulating evidence that focused police efforts to reduce particular crimes committed by particular offenders at particular times and places are effective. In this chapter, we refer to such approaches as *crime-specific policing*. Virtually every controlled experiment entailing crime-specific interventions has yielded positive results, i.e., crime went down. In other words, when the police concentrate resources on a particular crime, the incidence of that crime drops.

Several well-known national studies illustrate the point. Over 20 years ago, the San Diego Field Interrogation Experiment (Boydstun 1975) demonstrated the efficacy of proactive stop-and-question techniques. Eck and Spelman's evaluation of problem-oriented techniques in Newport News, Va., launched an approach almost universally regarded as having the potential not only to reduce calls for service, but also to reduce crime. The Minneapolis Recap

Experiment confirmed the short-term effect of problem-oriented approaches directed toward problem locations. More recently, the Kansas City Gun Reduction Experiment illustrated the effectiveness of focusing street enforcement on a specific problem.

There are other examples of the efficacy of crime-specific policing. In both Illinois and Texas, the creation of auto theft task forces led to immediate and dramatic reductions in the incidence of that crime. Along the Texas border with Mexico, theft rates fell to one-third of their previous level in a year. (Nationally, auto theft rates had decreased only slightly over the same time frame.)

Perhaps more than any other research study, the 1993 Kansas City Gun Reduction Experiment demonstrates the very narrow effect of a particular police strategy (Sherman, Shaw and Regan 1995). One might reasonably expect that with additional units aggressively patrolling target areas, overall crime in those areas would drop. But while there was a very dramatic effect on the targeted gun crimes, there was no measurable impact on other offenses. Police efforts targeted at particular offenders committing particular crimes produced results in the Kansas City Gun Reduction Experiment, as it did in Newport News, San Diego and Texas. But unfocused strategies have produced few results. Directed patrol in Pontiac, Mich., and New Haven, Conn., targeted various offenders committing a variety of various crimes at various times of the day—and no definitive results materialized. The same held true for the Wilmington Split-Force Patrol Experiment.

Nevertheless, we must be cautious about dismissing broad proactive arrest efforts. Dramatically increased enforcement activity in Houston and New York City recently produced considerable drops in crime. The most likely explanation is that the effectiveness of particular police strategies depends on environmental circumstances. When enforcement is lacking for long periods and there is a sudden and dramatic turnaround in general enforcement effort, results are measurable. At the same time, merely assigning added patrol units to an area apparently has little impact.

Crime Rates in the 1990s

In the United States, we now find ourselves in the midst of a historically unprecedented drop in crime rates. For several years, virtually every type of crime has decreased. Granted, there is some unevenness. While crime is dropping precipitously in cities such as Houston and New York, it has actually increased in a few others. But the exceptions are indeed few. There are five possible explanations for the decrease:

Social-Demographic Trends Criminologists generally regard social-demographic trends as the strongest influence on crime rates—more important than structured social response (police-courts-corrections). A high proportion of 14- to 25-year-olds equals a high overall crime rate. Factors such as migration patterns also influence crime. Mobile, disrupted groups tend to commit more crimes than settled, stable groups.

Economic Conditions The economy is recognized as influencing the rate of both violent and property crime. Extreme economic stress, for example, breeds social violence, particularly spouse abuse. Obviously, property crime is likewise influenced by changing economic conditions. However, the relationship is not necessarily a straightforward one. Property crime may increase in an improving economy, particularly if increases in wealth are unevenly distributed.

Drug Use Prevalence Crime is linked in complicated ways to the supply of illicit drugs. Scarce supplies raise street prices, potentially increasing crime, but may also mean fewer users, thus decreasing crime. Drug supply and drug use prevalence interact.

Incarceration Rates For the last 10 years, most states have built new prisons at record rates. Incapacitation rates appear, at least on the surface, to offer one of the best explanations for decreasing street crime.

Police Programs Decreases in crime have not been evenly distributed. Where agencies have implemented aggressive intervention styles, crime has dropped precipitously. Clearly, the police make a difference.

There is no way to determine which of these factors is causing the current downward trend. However, one may certainly argue that of the five, two have had the greatest effect—incarceration rates and police programs. The others tend to have longer-term effects on crime rates. When crime drops in a particular city by 30 percent in one year, it is not likely that changes in demographics are the explanation. And indeed, there have been no dramatic shifts in the nation's demographics during the 1990s. The shifts that are occurring are, by and large, part of longer-term trends present for the last 25 years. Changes in economic conditions also do not appear to have had a dramatic effect. With the exception of two or three very mild recessions, the nation has experienced slow but steady economic growth since 1970. Unemployment rates have varied within a range of 2 percent. In fact, if one were to look to economics for any type of explanation, one might argue that changes in the distribution of wealth in the 1990s would beget more crime, not less. Additionally, one cannot point to any dramatic economic changes in cities like Houston or New York that would account for the decreases in crime.

Like trends in demographics and economics, trends in drug use do not offer any apparent explanation for the decrease in crime. While the use of some drugs decreased in the late 1980s and early 1990s, the use of others remained steady. Further, in the mid-1990s, drug experimentation surveys of high school students indicate increases in use, or at least in experimentation. Statistics on drug seizures indicate that trafficking continues unabated. The war on drugs has not caused the dramatic decreases in crime.

Unlike demographics, economics and drug use prevalence, incarceration rates should be considered as a possible explanation for the recent drop in crime. Over the past 10 years, prison capacity has increased dramatically in some states. For example, in Texas, prison capacity has tripled. Fed up with persistent high crime rates, the public has demanded that chronic offenders, particularly violent offenders, be locked up for long periods. Thus, a building boom has accompanied changes in sentencing laws.

Some cautionary notes are in order. In some states where incarceration has increased, there has not been a dramatic decrease in crime. Further, it is unlikely that incarceration would have a sudden and dramatic effect on crime rates in individual large cities. To better understand the possible mixed effect of incarceration and police programming, the author and Tori Caeti (1994) compared the sharp drop in crime in Houston in 1992 with the crime rate in other major Texas cities. While incarceration affected all of the state's major cities, a sudden and dramatic drop in crime occurred only in Houston. This drop correlated month by month with dramatically increased arrests.

The argument that most of the drop in crime in Houston was the product of police agency proactivity rather than offender incarceration was bolstered by a similar drop in New York City two years later. Like Houston, New York elected a new mayor who brought in a new police chief determined to use different approaches to crime. As in Houston, both the mayor and the police chief dismissed the fluff elements of community policing. Instead, they mandated that precinct commanders take personal responsibility for crime rates in their area. In turn, commanders ordered patrol officers to make arrests. Long-standing policies prohibiting patrol officers from enforcing vice and narcotic offenses were lifted (those policies were meant to control corruption at the beat level). Crime started dropping immediately.

College students are taught in their first research methods class that correlation does not equal cause and effect. Indeed, instructors usually go out of their way to find historical accounts of the misinterpretation of correlation as cause and effect. The experimental design is, of course, offered as the ultimate solution to isolating cause and effect from correlation. Unfortunately, many criminologists who have spent their careers cautioning undergraduates about this phenomenon have allowed their own perspective to become distorted. They can no longer accept the obvious link between phenomena in the real world. Absent an experimental design, nothing should be accepted as causal. It is true that we can always find absurd examples of correlation. The viscosity of asphalt on a given day in a beach community correlates with the number of drownings. Obviously, there is no cause-and-effect linkage between these phenomena—more people swim on a warm day. But the link between increasing enforcement efforts and a drop in crime is not *prima facie* absurd; indeed, it is *prima facie* logical. And when several major cities dramatically increase enforcement efforts, and the crime rate drops precipitously, it is illogical to dismiss the relationship as spurious.

An analogous international problem may be relevant here. The 1990s saw a different kind of violence in Bosnia. In an effort to stop the killing, U.N. troops were dispatched. However, commanders were hamstrung—ordered not to use force unless in immediate danger. The killing went on. Finally, fed up with the genocide, NATO took over—dispatching troops with orders to shoot to stop the killing. And the killing stopped. It is perhaps stretching the point a long way, but the parallel between the crime in major U.S. cities and the situation in Bosnia is striking. When the police are merely present, but passive, crime continues. When the police suddenly and decisively change their approach to one of proactive intervention, crime starts dropping.

Our Research Legacy: A Brief Synopsis

Kansas City Preventive Patrol Experiment. The granddaddy of all police research is the Police Foundation's Kansas City Preventive Patrol Experiment. Conducted in Missouri from 1972 to 1973, the research is also the most frequently misinterpreted.

To understand this misinterpretation, a quick review of the research design is necessary. The south patrol district contained 15 beats. Five of these beats were designated as controls, where the level of routine preventive patrol for a year was to remain constant with past practice. Five of the beats were designated reactive. On these beats, patrol units would enter to handle calls for service, then immediately leave. In effect, routine preventive patrol was withdrawn. Five of the beats were designated proactive. The patrol units on the reactive beats were instructed to conduct routine preventive patrol in the proactive beats, in effect doubling the amount of patrol in these areas. Additional patrol officers were assigned to the south district, such that the patrol level on the proactive beats was two to three times what it had been. Everyone in the police field knows the results. Over the course of a year, no change was detected in reported crime, crime as measured by victimization surveys, citizen satisfaction with the police, or several other efficiency measures. Researchers, chief among them George Kelling, appropriately and conservatively concluded that routine preventive patrol as practiced in Kansas City had no effect on crime   (Kelling et al. 1974).   Unfortunately, the very conservative conclusions drawn were inappropriately and grossly overgeneralized in subsequent years.   The conservative conclusion that "routine preventive patrol within the limits tested in Kansas City has no measurable effect on crime" became "the police don't make a difference."

To fully appreciate just how wrong such an overgeneralization is, one must carefully consider what was tested in Kansas City. In 1972, routine preventive patrol was not a sharp, focused tactic. Typically, in urban areas, between 40 and 60 percent of patrol time is uncommitted (as opposed to committed to responding to calls for service). Analysis in several jurisdictions indicates that of the uncommitted patrol time, only about half is spent cruising through a beat. The other half is spent on administrative matters or breaks. Thus, for a typical beat, about two hours out of every eight are spent on nondirected cruising. This was the case in Kansas City.

There could not be a more generic approach to policing than routine preventive patrol. The patrol officer decides what merits attention. If an officer likes to engage in traffic enforcement, or is under pressure to do so, then that will occupy a substantial portion of routine preventive patrol time. If an officer is inclined to make a round of visiting on the beat, then that becomes routine preventive patrol. And so it goes. The individual patrol officer accounts for most of the variation in the specific activities conducted during routine patrol. However, patterns also vary by the nature of the beat, the time of the day, and the day of the week. No police strategy could be more diffuse. One must truly believe that the mere occasional presence of a patrol car cruising by deters crime to believe that routine patrol makes any difference.

Further, one must visualize the design of the Kansas City experiment. On the one hand, the decision to concurrently test decreases in routine preventive patrol and increases in adjoining beats had its strengths, particularly in an era when there was virtually no research on police strategy. In withdrawing and increasing routine preventive patrol in the south district, the researchers assumed that citizens perceive the amount of preventive patrol, and react to it, within the confines of beat boundaries. In other words, someone living in a designated reactive beat would hypothetically conclude there was less preventive patrol based solely on the fact that there was less preventive patrol on that beat. Similarly, someone in an adjoining proactive beat would hypothetically conclude there was more preventive patrol based solely on the increase on that beat, ignoring adjacent beats. With rare exception, citizens do not know where the boundary lines are drawn. So our assumption is that most south district citizens would perceive more or less preventive patrol, and alter their behavior accordingly, within a living/working area bounded by a single beat.

However, someone residing in one beat and working and/or playing in another would in effect live in both a proactive and a reactive area. Indeed, any mobility at all would result in citizens' experiencing all three levels of patrol. Thus, a necessary assumption is that most citizens would perceive variation, if it were to be perceived, independently and without overlap within the boundaries of the 15 police beats. No one would propose that *every* citizen perceived the levels of preventive patrol exclusively within the boundaries of a single beat. Kansas City is a horizontal municipality. The south district contains a range of residential, business and shopping/ recreation areas. Everyone recognizes that a lot of citizens routinely crossed beat boundaries. The issue is perceptual effect. Would a lack of preventive patrol in a particular area, or an increase in another area, be perceived by enough people to change their behaviors?

Now, from one perspective, that was the whole point of the experiment. It was designed to test such perception. But is it not possible that the perception of withdrawal was canceled by the perception of enhancement? In other words, is it possible that most citizens could not detect any difference in preventive patrol because, overall, in the south district there was no difference in the level?

This is not to suggest that the experiment was flawed. It was well conceived and carefully designed and monitored. The researchers drew conservative conclusions The issue is overgeneralization of results. Like any good piece of research, the experimental variable in Kansas City was very narrowly drawn. It demonstrated that citizens did not perceive variation in routine preventive patrol across beats. It did *not* demonstrate that police activities directed at particular targets made no difference. It did *not* demonstrate that withdrawal of patrol across a broadly defined area made no difference. It did *not* demonstrate that increasing routine preventive patrol across a broad area made no difference. It says nothing about potential patrol saturation effect, regardless of the nature of the patrol activity (given the size of police beats in Kansas City's south district, two to three patrol units in one of those areas is hardly saturation). Most importantly, the Kansas City Preventive Patrol Experiment says nothing about the efficacy of planned, focused police field intervention. One must be very conservative drawing conclusions about police effectiveness from this study.

San Diego Field Interrogation Experiment. Following close on the heels of the Kansas City experiment is the San Diego Field Interrogation Experiment (Boydstun 1975). The contrast in results is striking, and it supports the principle that proactive patrol interventions reduce crime. To the extent that the Kansas City Preventive Patrol Experiment demonstrated that a passive police presence made no difference, the San Diego Field Interrogation Experiment demonstrated that an active police presence made a dramatic difference. Conducted in 1973, the experiment involved varying the intensity of police stop-and-question activities. Three areas in San Diego were compared. One group of beats was designated control, where field interrogations during the experimental period were maintained at the same intensity as before. In a second group of beats, officers were trained to conduct field interrogations with more courtesy (it was felt that an increase in the already high levels of field interrogations would infringe upon civil rights). A third group of beats was designated as "no field interrogations." Actually, field interrogations were allowed on these beats, but officers were to conduct them only when extreme suspicion existed. The level of field interrogations in the experimental beats dropped tremendously. Suppressible street crime was measured for seven months before the experiment, for nine months during which experimental conditions were maintained, and for five months as follow-up. Suppressible crime was defined as robbery, burglary, auto theft, street theft, street rape, other sex crimes, malicious mischief, and disorderly conduct.

There was no change in crime in the control beats and in those where officers were specially trained. However, on the beats where field interrogations were withdrawn, the average number of suppressible crimes jumped from 75 to 104 per month. When field interrogations were reestablished, suppressible crime dropped down to 81 offenses per month. There was about a one-month lag time between the change in the number of field investigations and the change in crime rates.

While the passive police activity characterized as routine preventive patrol had no effect in Kansas City, the proactive activity characterized by field interrogation had a dramatic effect in San Diego. Interestingly, officers conduct most field interrogations after observing suspicious behavior while on routine preventive patrol. But some officers may engage in routine preventive patrol and never initiate a field interrogation. Thus, researchers must test these activities independently.

Directed Patrol in New Haven and Pontiac. As a result of the Kansas City Preventive Patrol Experiment, many agencies implemented directed patrol programs in the late 1970s. The idea was to use uncommitted patrol time to focus on particular problems, e.g., thefts from autos in shopping area parking lots. Evaluations of directed patrol efforts were conducted in New Haven and Pontiac (Cordner 1996). Little crime reduction was noted. However, it must be observed that the evaluators did not employ experimental designs. Further, the evaluators noted that implementing directed patrol was problematic.

Split-Force Patrol in Wilmington. Another effort to use uncommitted patrol time in a structured strategy was launched by the Wilmington, Del., Police Department in 1975 (Kenney 1992). The department divided its patrol division into a basic patrol force, about 70 percent of the officers, and a structured patrol force, about 30 percent of the officers. The structured patrol force was not to respond to calls for service except in emergencies, allowing them to conduct proactive crime intervention activities. The structured patrol force spent their time on problem areas and initial follow-up investigations of all crime-in-progress calls. The patrol division's overall arrest rate increased by 4 percent, charges per arrest by 13 percent and clearances by 105 percent. However, the detective division's clearance rate dropped by 61 percent, producing an overall drop of 28 percent for the department. The agency abandoned the split-force approach partially for the statistical reasons, and partially because of disillusionment in the patrol force. In particular, the officers in the basic patrol force deeply resented the freedom given the other officers.

Problem-Oriented Policing in Newport News. Nearly 15 years after the Kansas City Preventive Patrol Experiment, the first truly innovative alternative use of uncommitted patrol time was developed in Newport News. Darrel Stephens, then chief of the police department, implemented problem-oriented policing. Refined by Herman Goldstein, the technique involves making patrol officers responsible for finding longer-term solutions to recurrent police problems. Eck and Spelman (1987) documented the success of problem-oriented policing in Newport News with regard to three issues: thefts from autos in the parking lots adjoining the shipyards, robberies associated with a deteriorating downtown area, and burglaries and other problems associated with the New Briarfield housing project. For all three problems, patrol officers attacked underlying conditions and substantially reduced crime rates. Problem-oriented policing is still one of the most popular patrol strategies.

Minneapolis Repeat Call Address Policing (Recap or Hot Spots). In 1988, the city of Minneapolis determined that 3 percent of the city's 115,000 addresses accounted for 50 percent of police calls for service. Five percent of those addresses generated 64 percent of the calls, and during the time frame analyzed, nearly 60 percent of the city's addresses generated no calls. Minneapolis formed a special unit of five officers who were assigned 125 residential and 125 commercial addresses. They were to use problem-oriented techniques to reduce the calls for service coming from those addresses. After six months, the target addresses had 15 percent fewer calls for service (Sherman 1990). However, after one year, all the gains were erased; indeed, the residential addresses were actually producing more calls for service. The conclusion was reached that target rotation may be the best police strategy when dealing with problematic addresses.

Kansas City Gun Experiment. From July 1992 to January 1993, patrol overtime hours from 7 to 10 p.m. were directed at detecting concealed weapons in beat 144 of Kansas City. A total of 4,512 officer hours (2,256 patrol car hours) were concentrated in the beat during the six months. Typically, two extra patrol units were in the beat each evening. Beat 144 is an 8-by-10-block area with a 1991 homicide rate of 177 per 100,000, about 20 times the national average. The beat is 92 percent nonwhite, and 66 percent own homes.

Police gun seizures in the target area increased by more than 65 percent while gun crimes declined by 40 percent (Sherman, Shaw and Regan 1995). Neither gun seizures nor gun crimes changed significantly in a similar beat several miles away, where directed patrol was not used. Further, there was no measurable displacement of gun crimes to patrol beats adjacent to the target area. While drive-by shootings dropped from seven to one in the target area, they doubled from six to 12 in the comparison area. Again, there was no displacement to areas adjacent to the target beat. Homicide showed a statistically significant reduction in the target area, but not in a comparison area. The investment of 4,512 police officer-hours was associated with 29 more guns seized and 83 fewer gun crimes, or about 55 patrol hours per gun crime and almost three gun crimes prevented per gun seized. Traffic stops were the most productive way to find guns, with an average of one gun found for every 28 stops. Interestingly, two-thirds of the people arrested for carrying guns lived outside the target area. Only gun crimes were affected by directed patrols, with no changes in the number of calls for service or the total number of violent and nonviolent crimes reported.

The Unexplored Wilderness of Criminal Investigation. In a typical police department, 50 percent of personnel are assigned to patrol, 30 percent to investigative units, and the remaining 20 percent to traffic, records, custodial, planning and research, and various other functions. While from one perspective there is little research on the effectiveness of various patrol strategies, compared with research on the effectiveness of investigations, the catalog of patrol research reports looks like a Library of Congress listing. There is literally almost no research on the relative efficacy of the strategies used by one-third of the personnel in a typical urban police agency.

Like the patrol function, the criminal investigations function suffers from an early macroanalysis with overgeneralized results. In 1975, the RAND Corp. tried to ascertain if any broad approaches to criminal investigation worked better than others by analyzing approaches used in major urban police departments (Greenwood and Petersilia 1975). A written questionnaire was sent to the 300 agencies employing more than 150 personnel that year, inquiring about investigative training, staffing, workload, and procedures. RAND received 153 responses. Researchers then made site visits to 25 of the responding agencies to gather more detailed information.

RAND concluded that the investigative divisions' organization and staffing could not be significantly related to variations in arrest or clearance rates, as reported by participating police departments to the FBI Uniform Crime Reports. The ancillary conclusions the researchers drew were perhaps as important as the primary one. They noted that (1) 65 percent of all serious crimes received no more than superficial attention from investigators; (2) the single most important factor in whether a case will be solved is the information the victim supplies to the responding patrol officer; (3) in cases that are solved, the investigator spends more time on post-clearance processing than on identifying the perpetrator; and (4) of cases ultimately cleared in which a perpetrator was not identified during the initial police incident-reporting processes, almost all were solved as a result of "routine police procedures" (fingerprinting, obtaining tips from informants, etc.). The RAND study attacked the Sherlock Holmes image of investigators, implying that instead of super sleuths, detectives were, in effect, clerks for the district attorney—helping to prepare solved cases for courtroom presentation. For those inclined to believe that the police are by and large ineffective, the RAND report was music to their ears. While the preventive patrol experiment "demonstrated" that uniformed officers make no difference, the RAND study similarly "demonstrated" that plainclothes officers are equally useless.

The RAND study is a classic example of a piece of exploratory research being used as the definitive answer. It was, first of all, some of the first real research ever conducted on the investigative function. Although the RAND researchers had done precursory work in New York and Kansas City, the national survey was the first effort at using a quasi-experimental design (Eck 1996). There were shortcomings in identifying independent and dependent variables. The researchers simply looked for naturally occurring variation in investigative structure and workload, then compared what variation might exist with a *very questionable* dependent variable—agency reports on arrest and clearance rates. Both rates are subject to definitional ambiguity and manipulation. One would expect that a poorly run investigative unit would tend to inflate the numbers, while a well-run unit would be far more conservative in reporting arrests and clearances. To the extent that better-run investigative units would use more effective strategies, the use of conservative criteria for reporting arrest and clearance rates would conceal the efficacy of those efforts in any comparative analysis.

It is not that the RAND study was inherently flawed. Rather, we should not expect dramatic results from this type of research approach. At best, tentative conclusions might be reached, e.g., specialization in investigations appears to, or does not appear to, result in higher clearance rates for the specific crimes. It is grossly inappropriate to assert that investigative units are useless.

Further, the study overdoes the "clerk for the district attorney" issue. Moving a case from a standard of probable cause to a standard of proof beyond a reasonable doubt is not a trivial task, and it certainly should not be characterized as the work of a clerk. Moreover, the fact that relatively few offenders are identified from super-sleuth techniques does not negate the importance of skilled investigative follow-up. The deterrent effect of such an approach may be enormous.

John Eck's insightful analysis of the criminal investigations function stands in contrast to the overgeneralized conclusions often drawn from the RAND study (Eck 1983). Eck examined burglary and robbery investigations in St. Petersburg, Fla.; Dekalb County, Ga.; and Wichita, Kan. (Eck 1983). Eck concluded that detective effort made a difference—but only if focused on particular cases.

The point is that police efforts must be analyzed in terms of focus. If all investigative follow-up is aggregated, it is impossible to tease out effective strategies. However, when we sort cases, a different picture emerges. In particular, when we rule out the majority of cases for which investigative follow-up is largely a waste of time, then analyze only the very small subset for which it is potentially fruitful, a *very different* picture emerges. Detectives do make a difference, indeed a dramatic difference, with regard to those cases. Given the fact that very few offenders commit only one crime, it is easy to understand why, if a detective makes a difference in only 5 percent of the cases, that 5 percent may be critical. An offender committing only one crime every three weeks, will on average, be caught annually. A single "cleared by arrest" by a skilled investigator can prevent scores of crimes over a few years.

Conclusions From Our Research Legacy

Perhaps more than any other study, the 1993 Kansas City Gun Experiment demonstrates the very narrow effect of a particular police strategy. One might reasonably expect that with triple the number of patrol units in beat 144 conducting aggressive patrol in the evening, other crimes would drop as well. But while there was a very dramatic effect on the target—gun crimes—there was no measurable impact on other crimes. Police efforts targeted at particular offenders committing particular crimes produced results in Kansas City, as they did in Newport News and San Diego. And crackdowns conducted in situations previously lacking enforcement may produce results. But mere police presence does nothing. Further, diffuse strategies without a sharp focus have produced few results. Directed patrol in Pontiac and New Haven consisted of targeting various crimes committed by various offenders at various times of the day—and no definitive results materialized. The same held true for the Wilmington Split-Force Patrol Experiment. Likewise, research on the efficacy of investigations leads to precisely the same conclusion—it is focused police efforts that make a difference.

Among those who have been around since the 1960s, there is a universal fondness for pointing out to beginners that when we started out, all the books in the field could fit on one standard bookcase shelf. Indeed, the literature has greatly increased. But there has not been an explosion in controlled experiments designed to ascertain which police strategies produce the best results. In fact, there are still only a few controlled experiments in policing. And sadly, most of those were conducted 20 years ago during the golden era of the Police Foundation.

Controlled experiments are, of course, both complex and expensive. It is difficult to manipulate police field strategies. It is extraordinarily difficult to withdraw a service from a geographic area or clientele. It is a bit easier to differentially distribute new services, e.g., conduct saturation patrol in some beats but not in others. Even then, however, police managers face the dilemma of equity in distributing resources to the citizens they serve. If differential distribution might harm some citizens, ethical questions are obviously raised. Additionally, the situations for which excess resources are available for differential distribution, although not rare, are not common either. Beyond these difficulties, for a field experiment to occur, there must be a confluence of research expertise, a motivation to conduct the experiment, and a police administrator's willingness to take the risk involved. We can only hope that future years see more such experiments. First, however, we must be convinced that the police do make a difference.

References

Boydstun, J.E. 1975. *San Diego Field Interrogation: Final Report.* Washington, D.C.: Police Foundation.

Cordner, G.W. 1996. "Evaluating Tactical Patrol." In L.T. Hoover, ed., *Quantifying Quality in Policing.* Washington, D.C.: Police Executive Research Forum.

Cordner, G.W., and R.C. Trojanowicz. 1992. "Patrol." In G.W. Cordner and D.C. Hale, eds. *What Works in Policing?* Cincinnati: Anderson Publishing Co.

Eck, J.E. 1996. "Rethinking Detective Management." In L.T. Hoover, ed., *Quantifying Quality in Policing.* Washington, D.C.: Police Executive Research Forum.

Eck, J.E. 1983. *Solving Crimes: The Investigation of Burglary and Robbery.* Washington, D.C.: Police Executive Research Forum.

Eck, J.E., and W. Spelman. 1987. *Problem Solving: Problem-Oriented Policing in Newport News.* Washington, D.C.: Police Executive Research Forum.

Federal Bureau of Investigation. 1995. *Crime in the United States* (Uniform Crime Reports). Washington, D.C.: U.S. Government Printing Office.

Greenwood, P., and J. Petersilia. 1975. *The Criminal Investigation Process—Volume I: Summary and Policy Implications.* Santa Monica, Calif.: RAND Corp.

Hoover, L.T., and T. Caeti. 1994. "Crime-Specific Policing in Houston." *Texas Law Enforcement Management and Administrative Statistics (TELEMASP) Bulletin* series. Vol. 1, No. 9, December.

Kelling, G.L., T. Pate, D. Dieckman, and C.E. Brown. 1974. *The Kansas City Preventive Patrol Experiment: A Technical Report.* Washington, D.C.: Police Foundation.

Kenney, D.J. 1992. "Strategic Approaches." In L.T. Hoover, ed., *Police Management: Issues and Perspectives.* Washington, D.C.: Police Executive Research Forum.

Sherman, L.W., and R.A. Berk. 1984. *The Minneapolis Domestic Violence Experiment.* Washington, D.C.: Police Foundation.

Sherman, L.W. 1990. "Police Crackdowns: Initial and Residual Deterrence." In. M. Tonry and N. Morris, eds., *Crime and*

Justice: A Review of Research. Chicago: University of Chicago Press.
Sherman, L.W., J.W. Shaw, and D.P. Regan.   1995.   *The Kansas City Gun Experiment*. Washington, D.C.: National Institute of Justice.

Chapter 2

Tactical Patrol Evaluation

Gary W. Cordner
Dennis Jay Kenney

Preface

This chapter provides practical guidance for police personnel or others who are responsible for evaluating police tactical patrol. The reader who has a basic understanding of different forms of tactical patrol and at least a rudimentary knowledge of evaluation methods should be able to apply this information with little or no difficulty. Readers less well prepared, however, should be forewarned that they may need some additional help, either in understanding the full range of patrol tactics or in evaluating programs.

The first two sections provide general information on tactical patrol and on evaluation methods. Experienced and/or well-informed readers may find that they can skip these sections, although later sections do draw substantially on them.

The next four sections describe four different evaluation designs, illustrate their use in evaluating tactical patrol, and then provide step-by-step instructions. Readers who have the opportunity to choose which evaluation design they will use may want to read all four sections. Those readers whose choices are already limited or predetermined, though, can go right to the section or sections that apply to their situations.

A selected bibliography of materials on tactical patrol and on program evaluation is included for those readers who need more information.

The authors assume that the reader is already convinced of the desirability of evaluating tactical patrol programs. The field of policing, once chastised for its parochial views and its resistance to examination and critique, is now among the most inquiring of all "businesses," and one marked by a thirst for new ideas and better strategies. Evaluating what the police do, figuring out what works and what does not, is a crucial component of managing for results and a key element in improving the delivery of police services to individuals and communities (Hoover 1996). Evaluating programs is not a luxury or a frill in policing—it is necessary to improve efficiency and effectiveness (see Cordner, Gaines and Kappeler 1996).

Tactical Patrol

Doubts about the efficacy of routine preventive patrol began to increase in the 1970s among both police practitioners and researchers. Following the Kansas City Preventive Patrol Experiment (Kelling, Pate, Dieckman, and Brown 1974), which suggested that neither eliminating nor doubling patrol coverage had any significant effects on reported crime, fear, police responses, or citizen satisfaction, many administrators began seeking alternatives to their traditional reliance on random visibility and reactive handling of calls for service. More directed methods, targeting specific problems, became increasingly popular. Subsequent research and innovation have advanced the knowledge of what works in policing (see Cordner and Hale 1992). Those in the field are still a long way, though, from having authoritative knowledge about which specific tactics work best against which problems in which settings.

Background

As much as tactical patrol now seems intuitively logical and just plain common sense, its development out of the ashes of routine preventive patrol was aided immensely by research studies and accumulated police experience. For example, during a study of field interrogations (FIs) in San Diego in the 1970s, perhaps the first major test of tactical patrol, researchers found that suppressible crime increased significantly (by 39%) in areas where field interrogations were discontinued. Once the FIs were resumed, suppressible crime returned to approximately its previous level (Boydstun 1975). Quite importantly, this apparent FI effect was not simply a mask for an arrest effect, since arrests in the no-FI area actually increased by about 25 percent during the experimental period. In other words, the level of suppressible crime appeared to have been affected by the use or avoidance of field interrogations, independent of the number of arrests made in the area.

During the same time period, the Police Foundation tested the ability of crime analysis to support directed and traditional patrol approaches to criminal apprehension in Kansas City, Mo. (Pate, Bowers and Parks 1976). Two directed patrol programs were tested: Location-Oriented Patrol (LOP) and Perpetrator-Oriented Patrol (POP). As the names imply, the LOP strategy directed patrol officers to surveil *areas* with particularly high crime rates; POP officers, on the other hand, surveilled a selected group of suspected *offenders*. Both strategies were intended to increase arrests of suspects in the act of committing crimes, especially robberies and burglaries. A special Criminal Information Center (CIC) was created within the police department to develop and disseminate suspect information, intended to guide the efforts of both the special units and a selected group of regular patrol officers.

When the three groups (LOP, POP and regular patrol) were assessed, the evaluators concluded that the specialized units had out-performed the regular patrol officers on almost all comparisons. Results varied between LOP and POP, however. LOP officers were more efficient in terms of hours spent per arrest, they had a greater number of robbery arrests as a percentage of their arrest total, and they had more charges filed for prosecution per arrest. POP officers had a greater percentage of arrests resulting from officer-initiated activities, they arrested suspects with more extensive felony records, and they produced more information for CIC use and dissemination. POP officers also received fewer citizen complaints than their LOP counterparts. Considering all comparisons collectively, the Kansas City staff concluded that, in terms of apprehending suspects, the location-oriented strategy was slightly superior to the perpetrator-oriented strategy, and substantially better than traditional patrol. The staff also found that providing CIC information to the comparison group of regular officers significantly increased their arrest rates as well.

In the late 1970s, Pontiac, Mich., experimented with directed patrol as part of the federally funded Integrated Criminal Apprehension Program (Cordner 1981). Over a period of nearly 18 months, directed patrol responsibilities were shifted from all patrol personnel to a special directed patrol unit, and then back to all personnel. The study concluded that target crimes could be decreased through the use of directed patrol based on crime analysis. Interestingly, the most significant impact was achieved during the initial time period, when directed patrol assignments were widely distributed among all patrol officers. Overly large investments of time in limited areas, however, appeared to offer no additional benefits—perhaps because of the relatively limited number of "opportunities" in any particular target area for aggressive patrol efforts.

Calling them "crackdowns," Sherman (1990) noted that efforts to direct patrol resources to specific problems became quite widespread during the 1980s. Drunk driving, public drug markets, streetwalking prostitutes, and even illegal parking each became targets for various directed patrol responses in programs throughout the country. In the 1990s, drug problems have remained a popular target of directed patrol activity (see Weisburd and Green 1995), and, in addition, gun-related crime has been increasingly targeted (see Sherman, Shaw and Rogan 1995). Still, Sherman notes that some observers remain skeptical about whether these tactical applications of patrol have any real effects; they argue that lasting impacts, especially deterrence, have not yet been demonstrated.

Sherman goes on to point out that the debates about tactical patrol fail to make an important distinction among the different kinds of deterrent effects possible. Specifically, most planners fail to separate the *initial* deterrence that might be achieved once a tactical operation is undertaken from the possible *residual* deterrence that may remain following its completion. Additionally, the extent to which such impacts *decay* during or after the effort is seldom considered (Sherman 1990:2). Determining these differential effects, he argues, might suggest new ways of maximizing tactical patrol's effectiveness. An example might help to explain these varying forms of deterrence.

In the 1987 Minneapolis Repeat Call Address Policing (RECAP) Experiment, patrol officers were given directed assignments that called for problem solving at locations that had been identified as requiring frequent police services. The idea was to solve the problems generating the repeat calls, thereby reducing the volume of activity at those addresses. The officers involved in the project were formed into special teams. Each team participated in the repeat call analysis for its location, in the design of tactics for reducing the volume of calls, and then in the implementation of the tactics.

After six months, the RECAP officers had considerable successes to show—calls for service at their experimental addresses were reduced significantly. However, during the second six months, officers increasingly found their targets resistant to further improvement. In fact, by the fourth quarter of the project, all of the earlier results had disappeared.

To Sherman, the obvious conclusion was that an operational policy of short-term targeting might offer the best investment of police resources. Instead trying to maintain a tactical response over a long period of time, as many departments do, police might

> use their resources more effectively if crackdowns are seen as short-term efforts frequently shifted from area to area or problem to problem. By constantly changing crackdown targets, police may reduce crime more through residual deterrence than through initial deterrence. And by limiting the time period devoted to each target, police might also avoid wasting scarce resources on a decaying initial deterrent effect (Sherman 1990:3).

The Concept of Tactical Patrol

Obviously, any number of variations of tactical patrol are possible. Strategies focused on crime prevention might include directed assignments requiring officers to conduct security surveys, recommend housing repairs and self-protection steps, and encourage and work with citizen groups. Other programs focus more on crime deterrence. As suggested above, short-term tactics intended to raise the perception of risk might be most effective (and efficient).

Included might be saturation patrolling, field interrogations, increased traffic enforcement, and other "aggressive" patrol procedures causing increased or high visibility.   Still other strategies might concentrate on criminal apprehensions by using covert and stakeout activities designed not only to deter but also to catch offenders while they are committing crimes. Regardless, in each instance, virtually all tactical/directed patrol projects share four common characteristics (Warren, Forst and Estrella 1979):

1. They are proactive and aggressive.
2. Officers use noncommitted time to engage in purposeful activity.
3. Officers have specific instructions directing their activities.
4. These instructions ("directions") are based on thorough analyses of crime data.

Aside from the support it receives from recent research, tactical patrol is attractive to police managers for at least two additional reasons. One is its directed nature—seemingly the very opposite of random patrol, the approach so often criticized for not working. The other is that the strategy is neither officer- nor community-directed, but rather information- and management-directed. Traditionally, calls for service have dictated the use of a substantial portion of patrol resources, and the use of the rest of patrol officer time has been left to individual discretion. Tactical patrol strategies are a means for police managers to regain some control over their most significant resource, patrol officers' time and activities. Careful implementation and evaluation are essential, though, if tactical patrol's goals are to be reached and its potential benefits realized.

Implementing the Concept

As each agency designs its own tactical patrol system, managers have two basic models they can follow. First, and probably most common, is a *geographically focused* approach, which tries to increase police presence in a specific area. Much like the LOP strategy in Kansas City described earlier, this approach requires agencies to first identify through analysis the areas experiencing particular problems of police interest. Of course, these may include areas with crime or accident problems, with frequent demands for police services, with order-maintenance problems, or where fear is especially high. The areas chosen could be as small as a single address or as large as a park, a section of road or highway, several square blocks, or even a patrol beat or sector. Once assigned, the officers responsible for these areas—either routinely or as part of some special unit—then implement tactics selected to match the concerns identified.

With an *offense-* or *event-specific* approach, the agency seeks to change how it responds to some specific type of crime or incident, regardless of where it may be occurring. Examples might include domestic abuse, traffic violations or parking problems; officers are provided with pattern and trend data and instructions to make arrests, issue tickets or take other appropriate actions wherever the problem is encountered. Similarly, special units may be formed to help analyze a specific problem—say robbery or burglary. The unit's officers may then conduct tactical operations based on that analysis. Reacting to public alarm, the police in Savannah, Ga., for example, recently used this approach in response to a growing citywide problem of black-on-black crimes. Simultaneously, they implemented geographically focused efforts to address street robberies that analysis showed were occurring with regularity in the city's popular historic district.

An additional implementation question confronting the manager concerns whether tactical assignments should be given to routine or to specialized patrol units. In general, if the assigned tactic requires only short periods of dedicated time, it may be preferable to use regular patrol units. Field interrogations, vehicle checks, security surveys, and saturation patrols can usually be conducted by regular officers without serious disruptions to their ability to handle other calls for service. As the time needed to complete the directed activity increases, however, so does the desirability of developing specialized patrol capabilities. This would be a virtual necessity whenever the tactical assignment required an officer's full-time commitment, such as for covert surveillance, decoy operations and stakeouts. Fearing conflicts in communication and grumbling about elite units, some departments have preferred to create this capacity by relieving regular patrol officers for a single tour of duty on special assignment. Others, however, have chosen to establish specialized units with their own structure, training and deployment (Gay, Schell, and Schack 1977).

Beyond these basic options (geographic vs. offense focus, regular patrol vs. special unit) are a number of mundane but important implementation considerations. One concerns participation—it is vital that officers and supervisors who are expected to implement tactical patrol assignments be given every opportunity to participate in designing those assignments. Such involvement is likely to lead to better-designed tactics, and it will certainly lead to greater commitment to implementing them.

Another crucial consideration relates to information. It is utterly impossible to effectively design and target tactical patrols without accurate and up-to-date information on crimes, calls for service and other problems. Departments that lack solid crime analysis and operations analysis capabilities may need to consider upgrading their analytical capabilities as a prerequisite to implementing full-fledged tactical patrol systems.

Finally, implementing any program, including tactical patrol, requires that attention be paid to such basic management considerations as resources, communication, authority, responsibility, and accountability. Depending on the nature of the tactical patrol program, personnel reassignments may be necessary, new policies and procedures may be demanded, and training may be required. Personnel throughout the organization should be notified of the new program.   Systems should be put in place to ensure adequate supervision and reporting (forms for issuing and reporting directed patrol assignments can be found in appendixes A and B).   Assuming that tactical patrol is a good idea, attention to implementation helps guarantee that the idea becomes reality.

Evaluation

It is difficult, if not impossible, for a police department to know whether its use of tactical patrol is successful without a systematic evaluation.   Unless an evaluation is conducted, how will the department know whether the program was implemented as intended? What individual tactics were implemented?   Whether the program's goals were achieved? To what extent success or failure was the result of factors other than the tactical patrol project? To answer these questions, a two-stage approach to evaluation is recommended:

1. a *process evaluation* to capture the early development and actual implementation of the program and tactics, and
2. an *impact evaluation* designed to measure the program's effects and the extent of goal attainment.

Process Evaluation

An important aspect of any evaluation is documentation and analysis of program development and implementation. This *process evaluation* is directed at providing qualitative and quantitative measures of the program, its operation and its immediate outputs. Assessments are made regarding whether services are provided in the manner the program plan specifies, and whether expected program outputs are actually produced.   The process evaluation is also necessary for appropriate interpretation of impact evaluation data. Detailed knowledge about the intervention as it actually took place is invaluable for determining what worked and what did not.

A thorough process evaluation should address the following areas:

1. the environment within which the program is designed and implemented,
2. the process by which the program is designed and implemented,
3. the continuous measurement of the program's operation over time to ensure compliance and to document any changes that occur, and
4. the identification and description of intervening events that may affect implementation and program outcomes.

Each of these areas is discussed briefly below.

Description of the Program Environment

Before a program's effectiveness can be judged, one must understand the environment into which the program was introduced. Thus, a detailed description of the environment at the time of intervention is necessary in order to know what external and organizational factors were at work during the program period. Elements of such a description for a tactical patrol project should include

- demographics of the areas where the project is introduced;
- crime information for target areas, surrounding areas and any other areas involved in the evaluation;
- information about requests for services offered by the police, other city agencies and social service organizations emanating from the areas involved in the evaluation;
- descriptions of the activities of community groups, gangs and others that may be impacting the areas selected for study; and
- descriptions of the social history of the areas selected for intervention.

With such information, it becomes far easier to conclude, once a program's impact is determined, whether similar results might be expected in other neighborhoods or communities, or whether they are specific to the site being studied. If the environment is unique in some important way, then the results achieved in that setting may not necessarily be applicable elsewhere.

Description of the Program Process

The purpose of developing new technologies, ideas or programs is to help solve problems. But, as many have noted, the development of a "good idea" does not necessarily lead to a good program. Indeed, the critical stage—implementation—exists between (1) initiation and (2) program performance and outcome. Ideas must first translate into real activities, with resources, personnel and ideas being developed and committed to the effort. Only then can the program's true scope and nature be understood.

Further, if programs are to be replicated in other environments, a description of the implementation process is essential. As part of the process evaluation, project evaluators should observe the implementation process, using these observations to interpret and inform discussion concerning program effects later discovered. Among the elements for observation are

- the interactions among, and extent of participation by, the project's participants—officers, supervisors, research staff, and other support personnel;
- any training that officers, supervisors or support staff found necessary or were provided;
- the responsiveness of participants to the program itself and the process and steps of implementation; and
- the interactions among the project's participants and others in the organization who were not involved.

Description and Measurement of Program Operations

Rossi, Freeman and Wright (1979:132) explained the need to describe and measure program operations as they occur:

Monitoring the delivery of services to evaluate the actual implementation of a program is undertaken for a number of purposes. A large proportion of programs that fail to show impacts are really failures to deliver the interventions in ways specified. Actually, there are three potential failures: First, no treatment is delivered at all (or not enough); second, the wrong treatment is delivered; and third, the treatment is unstandardized, uncontrolled, or varies across target populations. In each instance, the need to monitor the actual delivery of services and identify faults and deficiencies is essential.

Efforts to "monitor service delivery" must be carried out in such a way that readers of the evaluation report will be convinced that sufficient valid evidence exists to describe the way the program worked, or failed to work. This description must include quantitative as well as qualitative data. Evidence of program implementation would include such elements as

- the extent of participation of officers, research staff and supervisors in identifying specific crime or incident problems;
- the number and nature of problems identified during the planning process;
- the extent of participation among officers, research staff and supervisors in identifying directed patrol tactics and operations;
- the number and nature of tactics identified and the process by which specific ones were selected for implementation;
- the feedback provided by officers for further analysis and by research staff for tactical adjustments; and

- the specific activities undertaken by officers in carrying out tactical patrol assignments.

Identification of Intervening Events

All evaluations, especially field experiments, operate in constantly changing environments. The result is that both evaluators and participants in a project must be concerned about the environment's impact on the outcome of their efforts. This has been referred to as "intervening variable analysis."

The purpose of intervening variable analysis is to try to understand external factors' impact on the program's outcome. Some of these effects can be controlled or eliminated using the techniques described in the section on impact evaluation. Others can be understood and interpreted, either intuitively or with expert judgments. In either case, those evaluating the program must understand that the intervening variables capable of affecting their program are complex, numerous and varied. For example, increases in gang activity in a project area should be noted and followed carefully since the potential to impact a geographically focused program is obvious. Similarly, increases in fines or mandated jail terms for drunk drivers could clearly change the outcome of a DWI crackdown. In either case, interpreting outcomes becomes much easier once these intervening variables are identified and understood.

Collecting Process Data

The process phase of the project's evaluation should begin as soon as the tactical patrol project gets under way (if not sooner, during the planning phase) and should continue until the tactical operations are completely in place. To complete the process study, two primary sources of data should be used.

The first includes official police, city and census data. What crime and call for service patterns exist throughout the city and in the areas where the program is to focus? Are trends identifiable and, if so, are geographic patterns present? Once an area has been selected for tactical patrol, the ethnic and economic conditions, residents' ages, and buildings' composition—residential or commercial, occupied or unoccupied—should be noted. Such data should be readily available and is essential if experimental areas are to be selected, program outcomes are to be generalized to other areas, and effective tactics are to be identified.

A second source of data should include observations of, and interviews with, program participants. The observations should begin with early developmental work and should continue throughout the evaluation. Focusing on major planning and tactical activities, observers should note participation and interactions at each project stage. Does the process appear to go smoothly, or are relations and communications difficult and strained? Do participants work together to identify a range of tactical options, or do the organization's hierarchy and traditional methods assert themselves? These observations should focus on process as well as content, with observers being careful to note the decisions and events that contribute to program planning and implementation.

To complement observational data, interviews with key participants that focus on process issues should be conducted. The reactions of officers, staff and supervisors to the program's development, the degree of participation, the tactics selected, and the difficulties in completing tactical assignments should all be noted and analyzed. Any problems that occur and the solutions attempted or suggested should be described. While the format for observations should probably remain open-ended so that observers are not limited in their focus, the protocol for interviews should be far more structured to ensure consistency and validity. Examples of process evaluation questions are included as Appendix C.

Impact Evaluation

In the following sections, four different evaluation designs are described, illustrations of their use in evaluating tactical patrol programs are presented, and then step-by-step instructions are provided. Each of the designs can produce very useful information about a patrol tactic's effectiveness, but the authoritativeness of that information is greater for some designs than for others. Designs that "track" effects over extended periods (*time series* designs) are generally superior to those that simply compare before and after periods (*pre-post* designs). *Comparison group* designs are superior to those that lack any basis for comparison. Designs that use true control groups (*experimental* designs) are better yet (see Chapter 4 for additional review of designs).

There is no reason why evaluations of tactical patrol should not employ, at a minimum, pre-post designs, and preferably, longer time series analysis and some kind of comparison or control groups. This is because data on the primary "pre" conditions of interest, reported crimes and arrests, are routinely gathered by police departments and are readily available. Even if the decision to evaluate a tactical patrol program is not made until after the program has started, it should be relatively easy to go back to the records and gather crime and arrest data for the period before the program started. Moreover, when a program targets a particular area, historical data can usually be gathered for both the targeted area and comparison areas.

Regardless of which evaluation designs are used to investigate tactical patrol's impact, a number of fundamental procedures should be followed. The most important of these are

1. careful specification of hypothesized effects,
2. identification of plausible unintended effects,
3. operationalized measures of effects,
4. determination of appropriate time periods,
5. monitoring of program implementation,
6. systematic collection of data,
7. analysis of data, and
8. replication.

Hypothesized Effects

Specification of *hypothesized effects* simply calls for a careful statement of the program's expected effects. In other words, if the program is correctly implemented, what should happen? The hypothesized effects are sometimes singular and direct, as in "saturation patrol will decrease street robberies." In other instances, there may be multiple expected effects, as in "saturation patrol will increase arrests, decrease street robberies and decrease citizen fear," or the expected effects may occur in stages, as in "saturation patrol will increase car stops and field interrogations, which will decrease street robberies." Regardless of the simplicity or complexity of the expected effects, though, it is important to think them through and spell them out early in the evaluation.

Unintended Effects

Thinking about hypothesized effects should lead naturally to thinking about *unintended effects*. Most programs have potential dangers or costs associated with them. These should be identified so that the evaluation can determine whether they occur. An example of an unintended effect might be "saturation patrol will increase car stops and field interrogations, which will negatively affect citizens' attitudes toward the police." Other examples might be "saturation patrol will simply displace street robberies to adjoining areas," or "saturation patrol will result in less activity per officer (less productivity) and more officer boredom because of the extreme concentration of officers in small areas."

Operationalization

Spelling out the program, its hypothesized effects and its plausible unintended effects pretty well identifies what will have to be measured in the evaluation. It is important, though, to explicitly *operationalize* these measures—to specify exactly what will be measured, and how. For example, it would certainly be necessary to define "street robberies" to ensure consistent, reliable measurement. It would be even more critical to carefully operationalize such conditions as "fear of crime" and "attitudes toward police," since they are such vague and multidimensional concepts.

Time Periods

Determining appropriate *time periods* is essential both to facilitate a meaningful evaluation and in terms of economy. Judgment must be used for such questions as "How long should the program be run in order to give it a fair opportunity to display its effects?" and "How far back in time should we go in collecting data to be sure that we have a good picture of things before the program's implementation?" Ideal time periods sometimes must be shortened for practical reasons, since data collection is costly and determinations of program success must sometimes be made sooner than evaluators would prefer.

Monitoring

Monitoring program implementation, which goes hand in hand with process evaluation, is required for several reasons. If difficulties are encountered in implementation, monitoring may provide the feedback that enables program managers to get things back on track. In situations where the program never is correctly implemented, evaluators cannot interpret results unless they are aware of what was, and was not, implemented. Monitoring in these situations may also lead to future improvements in program management that reduce such implementation failures.

Data Collection

The purpose of systematic *data collection* is simply to collect information on program implementation and on hypothesized and unintended effects. For tactical patrol, this typically involves such endeavors as gathering official records data on crimes and arrests and gathering officer activity information from dispatch records or individual activity reports. As with any kind of data collection, careful attention must be directed toward quality control, so that the information collected is as accurate as possible. If more than one person is involved in data collection, pains must be taken to ensure that everyone follows the same rules and definitions. Similarly, if data collection extends over a long period of time, it is important to ensure that the same rules and definitions are applied at the end as were used in the beginning.

A word about *sampling* is now in order. When evaluating tactical patrol, official records data on crimes, arrests and other activities are of principal concern, and sampling is not usually required. That is, the evaluation will generally be based on information about *all* the reported crimes, arrests, etc., in the target area and in any control or comparison areas during the appropriate time periods.

Occasionally, though, it may be necessary to measure such conditions as fear of crime or citizen satisfaction, in which case sampling of community residents probably will be required (unless the targeted area is so small that every resident can be surveyed). If sampling must be used, two considerations are paramount: (1) determining the size of the sample, and (2) choosing the sample in such a way that everyone in the population group has an equal chance of being selected. Since sampling will not usually be necessary when evaluating tactical patrol, the authors will not go into great detail on the subject in this chapter, but the reader is advised to seek additional information if sampling becomes an issue in an evaluation.

Data Analysis

Data analysis involves manipulating of collected data to derive results and conclusions. Data analysis related to program implementation should produce a description of the program-as-implemented. Analysis related to hypothesized and unintended effects should provide clear information on "what happened." If the research design was strong enough, analysis may be able to go beyond simply "what happened" and offer convincing explanations for "why it happened." In particular, the analysis should present evidence that helps determine whether the program had its hypothesized and/or unintended effects.

In some situations, it may be useful to determine whether differences in effects between target and control groups are "statistically significant." Statistical techniques such as t-tests and analysis of variance can be used to investigate whether observed differences are likely to have occurred merely by chance, or whether, instead, they are probably due to the program. Instructions on using these techniques can be found in any elementary statistics book. In most cases of tactical patrol evaluation, however, the statistical significance of a difference between target and control groups will be less important than its "substantive significance"—whether the program effect in the target area is large enough to really matter, and whether it represents enough benefit to outweigh the program's costs. These are practical judgments best left to police executives rather than to program evaluators or statisticians.

Replication

No matter how well an evaluation is conducted, no matter how strong the design, doubts about conclusions will linger at least until the study can be *replicated*. Replication is the surest hedge against the possibility that the documented effects of any particular program were a fluke, a chance occurrence, a lucky break, the result of unobserved intervening factors, limited strictly to one place, or limited to but one moment in time. Once a tactical patrol program has been found to have consistent effects in several applications, though, doubts can be allayed, and the strategy can be confidently deployed with predictable results.

Summary

Any evaluation of tactical patrol should include a process evaluation that documents the setting in which the program was implemented, the program's design and implementation (including design flaws and implementation problems), any variations in the program during the study, and any intervening events that must be considered when interpreting the results of the impact evaluation.

Four impact evaluation designs were briefly sketched in this section and are discussed, illustrated and described in detail in following sections: experimental, comparison group, time series, and simple pre-post designs. It should be emphasized that these four designs are not necessarily mutually exclusive—an experimental study can use extended time series data, for example. A few general principles should guide the choice of designs for evaluating the impact of tactical patrol programs:

1. Always use at least a pre-post design.
2. Use extended time series data (rather than just before/after data) whenever possible.
3. Use comparison or control groups whenever possible.
4. Use randomization to select program and control groups whenever possible.
5. Regardless of design, give careful attention to hypothesized and unintended effects, measurement, time periods, implementation monitoring, data collection, and data analysis.
6. Whenever possible, replicate.

Carefully conducted process and impact evaluations of tactical patrol can produce information of tremendous value for police administrators and, ultimately, for society. As we learn more about the effects of different patrol tactics on various problems in various settings, we will be able to make better decisions that lead to enhanced public safety and security.

Experimental Evaluation of Tactical Patrol

The distinguishing feature of an experimental design is *random assignment.* The use of an experimental design generally puts the evaluator in the best position, if an effect *is* observed, to argue that it is neither a chance effect nor a result of bias, but rather a true program effect. This is one of the basic aims of evaluation design—to be able to rule out as many alternative explanations as possible and to be able to attribute observed effects, if any, to the program itself.

The prospect of randomization may seem impractical or even dangerous in policing, but actually, it is sometimes quite feasible. In the Kansas City Preventive Patrol Experiment, randomization was used to decide which of the 15 patrol beats in the study got assigned to the proactive, control and reactive categories. In the Minneapolis Domestic Violence Experiment, random chance determined whether those who had allegedly committed misdemeanor spousal assaults were arrested, counseled or required to leave the premises.

Randomization makes one huge contribution to an evaluation—it ensures that mere chance determines who (or what neighborhood) receives the program and who, instead, serves as the control group. Without randomization, there is a greater likelihood that those who got the program were systematically different to begin with from those who did not get the program, or even worse, that those who got the program were in fact selected because they were likely to benefit from it. If this kind of *selection bias* is present at the outset, it becomes extremely difficult to distinguish later on between the program's true effects and the confounding effects introduced through the biased assignment of subjects to groups.

It is highly unlikely, of course, that we would ever really allocate tactical patrols purely on the basis of random chance. After all, tactical patrols are almost always meant to be *targeted* against a particular problem—random assignment would seem more in tune with random patrol than with tactical patrol. But there is a more rational approach to random assignment that makes sense and might sometimes be feasible. That approach is to select an overabundance of candidate problems for targeting, and then to randomly decide which ones actually get targeted and which ones serve as control groups.

For example, if a tactical patrol unit was to be assigned to work on a street robbery problem, we could first identify the two locations with the most serious problem, and then flip a coin to decide which one got the unit's attention. Similarly, if we had identified four areas with substantial rates of thefts from autos, we could randomly choose two to receive directed patrols and two to serve as control groups. Or, if we wanted to test the effects of different levels of field interrogation (FI) activity, we could select six beats and then randomly assign two each to no-FI, normal-FI and high-FI groups.

The practical, ethical and political issues involved in randomization must always be considered, but they are often manageable. The three examples cited above share several characteristics that make randomization supportable: (1) because of scarce resources, the "treatments" (tactical unit, directed patrol, high-FI) cannot be offered to everybody anyway; (2) those chosen to receive or not receive the treatments are equally deserving; (3) there is little or no authoritative evidence that "proves" that the treatments are beneficial (or harmful) to those who receive them; and (4) the information that could result from a randomized study would be of substantial value. Whenever these conditions are met, one should consider using randomization in the evaluation design.

Whenever randomization is used, though, it is wise to carefully monitor relevant indicators (such as reported crime) in treatment and control group areas. In this way, any unexpected harmful effects of the treatment or its absence can be detected quickly, enabling informed decisions to be made and averting any extended inequitable conditions caused by the evaluation design. On occasion, it may be necessary to call a halt to a study, even though the problem detected through monitoring (such as rapidly increasing crime in a control group area) may be caused by an external factor not connected to the program being evaluated. The truth is that field experiments are difficult to conduct, and they are sometimes contaminated by unforeseeable changes in the community.

An Illustration—Directed Patrol

Suppose we wanted to evaluate the effects of directed patrol, using an experimental design. For starters, we could pick two areas suffering from roughly the same problem, say, thefts from autos, at roughly the same rate. We could then flip a coin to decide which would get the directed patrol treatment (the DP area) and which would serve as the control group (the no-DP area). Our principal hypothesis would simply be that target thefts will decline in the DP area but not in the no-DP area. Two plausible unintended effects might be that target thefts will increase in areas surrounding the DP area (spatial displacement), or that other property crimes will increase in the DP area (displacement to other crimes).

The hypothesis and the plausible unintended effects point to several conditions that would need to be measured: target thefts in both DP and no-DP areas, target thefts in areas surrounding the DP area, and other property crimes in the study areas. These would need further definition. For example, "target thefts" should probably be defined as any thefts from autos or attempted thefts from autos. (The latter is often a judgment call between attempted theft and vandalism—it would be important to use consistent rules in making this judgment.) "Surrounding areas" would have to be defined in a way that made sense given the jurisdiction's particular geography. "Other property crimes" could be defined to include robberies, burglaries, thefts of autos, and all other thefts (with the possible exception of frauds and forgeries, if these were deemed unlikely to be taken up by those displaced from thefts from autos).

The determination of appropriate time periods is an important decision that should be based on information about the problem being addressed and the program being implemented. In this case, for purposes of discussion, we might determine that target thefts in the study areas had been at a high level for three weeks, and that two weeks of directed patrol in the DP area ought to be sufficient to affect the problem. Thus, we would decide on a three-week "before" period and a two-week "during" period; in addition, we might decide on a 10-week "after" period throughout which we would continue to measure target thefts and other property crimes to see whether the effects, if any, persisted after directed patrol was withdrawn.

Because of these unequal time periods, it would be important to compute and use daily or weekly *averages* of target thefts and of other property crimes for the before, during and after periods. Otherwise, we would almost certainly find fewer target thefts in the two-week "during" period than in the longer before and after periods, and we might be led to erroneous conclusions.

While directed patrol was being carried out in the DP area and not in the no-DP area, it would be necessary to monitor program implementation. Through some means, we would need to determine that directed patrols actually were being carried out in the DP area, and that no such directed patrols were being surreptitiously or accidentally applied in the no-DP area. This could be accomplished through various means, including supervision, formal reporting and review of dispatch center data.

The *amount* of directed patrol devoted to the project should be measured, if at all possible. Ultimately, questions will arise over how much directed patrol is enough to achieve an effect—three hours a day, one hour, every other day? Immediate outputs should also be measured, such as arrests, tickets, car stops, and FIs. This is important in determining whether directed patrol has a relatively diffuse effect achieved primarily through visibility, or a more specific effect accomplished via aggressive patrol tactics.

Data gathering in this illustration would not be particularly difficult or burdensome. Reported crime data on target thefts and other property crimes for the DP, no-DP and surrounding areas would be collected from routine departmental sources. Data on program implementation could also be collected from routine sources (such as officer activity sheets or communications logs) or from special directed-patrol assignment forms. Since emergencies often arise in policing and interfere with planned directed activities, it would be very important to document *actual* directed patrol efforts rather than planned efforts.

The principal form of analysis would be simple comparison of averages and percentage changes. Suppose the directed patrol experiment had the results shown in Table 1. One should immediately notice that only the DP area experienced a substantial decline in the target crime, thefts from autos, from the before period to the during period. The fact that the average weekly decline in target thefts in the during period was proportionately much greater in the DP area (−60%) than in the no-DP area (−14%) suggests that directed patrol caused the effect. The fact that total target thefts in the surrounding areas increased by only one per week in the during period discounts simple spatial displacement. The slight increases in other property crimes in the DP and surrounding areas does raise the possibility of displacement to other crimes, though—interviews of offenders would probably be required to determine whether this kind of displacement had really occurred or whether these changes were simply the result of other factors. The figures for the after periods suggest that directed patrol had a residual effect in the DP area long after the tactic had been withdrawn.

Table 1

Fictitious Directed Patrol Experiment

| | Weekly Averages | | | | | |
| | Thefts from Autos | | | Property Crime | | |
	Before	During	After	Before	During	After
DP Area	10	4	5	20	22	19
No-DP Area	14	12	12	28	26	29
Surrounding #1	3	4	5	15	18	12
Surrounding #2	0	1	1	7	10	12
Surrounding #3	4	3	3	12	10	8

The "numbers" do not always come out this clearly, of course—interpreting results and drawing conclusions are often more difficult than in this illustration, and frequently, the results are unavoidably inconclusive. With an experimental design, though, you put yourself in the best possible position to identify positive program effects if they are there.

Conducting an Experimental Evaluation

Outlined below are step-by-step instructions for conducting a basic experimental evaluation of a tactical patrol program. The instructions apply specifically to a tactical patrol program applied in one targeted area with a second area serving as a control. The same approach could be followed, with only modest adjustments, if multiple targeted areas and/or multiple control areas were to be used.

1. Carefully specify the form of tactical patrol (directed, saturation, etc.) to be used. Make any personnel assignments, develop any written guidelines, and provide any training necessary to implement the tactical patrol.
2. Begin the process evaluation by gathering information, making observations, and conducting interviews in order

to describe the program environment, program development, program operations, and intervening events.

3. Select two areas with the same kind and magnitude of problem that will be addressed by the tactical patrol. These two areas should be as similar as possible in other respects, as well.

4. Randomly choose one of the two areas to receive the tactical patrol program, and one to serve as control. This can be done by flipping a coin, rolling dice, picking a number out of a hat, or using any other random chance process.

5. Carefully specify the program-specific hypothesized effects of the tactical patrol in the targeted area. These should be stated as clearly and as simply as possible.

6. Also specify any important and plausible unintended effects of the program to be implemented. These should also be stated clearly and simply.

7. Develop and define operational measures of program implementation, hypothesized effects and unintended effects. Decide exactly what you are going to measure to describe the program-as-implemented and what happened as a result of the program.

8. Determine what time periods will be used. This may involve two time periods (before and after), three time periods (before, during and after), or more extended time series periods. Make sure the time periods are sufficiently long to give the tactical patrol program a chance to show its effects.

9. If any of the operational measures require baseline data collection before program implementation (such as surveys of citizens, surveys of officer attitudes, or observations of officer behavior), gather the baseline data.

10. Implement the tactical program in the targeted area.

11. Monitor the implementation of the program in the targeted area and the maintenance of normal conditions in the control area.

12. Begin data collection if this did not precede program implementation. If extreme conditions develop in the targeted or control areas, consider ending the experiment.

13. Continue data collection throughout the program implementation and any appropriate after periods.

14. Conduct data analysis. Describe the program-as-implemented and specify any changes in measures of hypothesized and unintended effects. Use averages, percentages, statistical comparisons, and graphical presentations as appropriate to show any changes. Consider whether changes can be attributed to the program and whether they are substantial enough for the program to be judged a success or failure.

15. Prepare any written reports required. At a minimum, make a permanent record of the experiment and its results. Consider sharing your findings with other police professionals.
16. Look for opportunities to replicate the program and its evaluation. Replications should include similar programs implemented in similar settings. Exact duplication is never possible, but replication does require a fair degree of similarity (otherwise, it's not a replication, it's a new study). Take advantage of any such opportunities, since replication is the key to developing confidence in evaluation findings.

Comparison Group Evaluation
of Tactical Patrol

The directed patrol experiment illustrated in the previous section included the use of surrounding areas to measure possible displacement effects—those surrounding areas exemplified one type of comparison group, selected solely on the basis of geographic proximity. Ideally, in a comparison group design (which does not have the benefit of a true control group), comparison groups can be found that are "comparable" in many other respects besides just proximity to the group receiving the treatment.

Suppose, in the thefts from autos illustration, randomization was not possible—instead, an area had already been selected to receive directed patrol. In that situation, it would make sense to seek out one or two other areas suffering from a similar problem. If such areas could be identified, they could serve as comparison groups. The more comparable the target and comparison areas, the more meaningful the eventual results. No matter how comparable the areas, however, two threats to validity that would be hard to dispel would be (1) the possibility that the target area was chosen because it was particularly amenable to directed patrol, or (2) that the problem in the area was about to decline naturally. Basically, without randomization, the various forms of *selection bias* are difficult to dismiss.

Nevertheless, in the absence of a randomized control group, a comparison group is better than nothing, and several comparison groups are often better than one (assuming they are all in fact comparable). Some highly respected police evaluation studies have used comparison group designs and produced worthwhile information.

An Illustration—Field Interrogations

Several years ago, a field interrogation study was conducted in San Diego using three patrol beats selected for their comparability. These beats were located in the same part of the city (although they were not adjacent), and they were deemed comparable on a host of crime and demographic measures.   For a nine-month period, the levels of field interrogation (FI) activity were manipulated: the *no-FI beat* had all FI activity eliminated, the *control beat* retained a "normal" level of FI activity (about 20 per month), and the *special FI beat* received extra FI activity (almost 50 per month).

In every respect except random assignment of these beats to control and treatment groups, the San Diego study adhered to the design characteristics outlined above. Hypothesized and unintended effects were carefully defined and measured, relevant time periods were specified, implementation was monitored, and data were systematically collected and analyzed.   The overall results are presented in Table 2.

Table 2

San Diego FI Study

Part I Suppressible Crimes
Monthly Averages

	Before	During	After
Control	40.9	42.9	38.6
Special FI	57.7	60.2	56.6
No-FI	63.1	83.2	63.2

As long as we can assume that the three beats really were comparable, the conclusions are inescapable that (1) eliminating FI activity for nine months in the no-FI area led to a substantial increase in Part I suppressible crimes, (2) resuming of FI activity in the no-FI area returned suppressible crime to its previous "normal" level, and (3) vastly increasing FI activity in the special FI area for nine months had little or no effect on suppressible crime.   But can we assume comparability?   The no-FI beat had over 50 percent more Part I suppressible crime to start with than the control beat—maybe crime increased when FIs were eliminated because it was a "rough" beat. Maybe if FIs had been eliminated from the quieter control beat instead, nobody would have noticed. Still, the no-FI beat's experience differed dramatically from the special FI beat's, despite the fact that these beats had similar levels of suppressible crime before the study began.   So something must have happened.   The question of comparability makes interpreting the results of the study more uncertain, yet using the comparison groups does strengthen our judgment that differing levels of FI activity had an effect on suppressible crime.

The principal unintended effect of concern in the San Diego study related to the possibility that increased FI activity would negatively affect police-community relations.   The evaluators measured the number of FI-related citizen complaints coming from the three beats, and found no differences among the beats nor any increases due to the additional FI activity in the special FI beat. They also conducted before and after community surveys in the three beats and found no negative effects on attitudes toward the police. Thus, they were able to rule out, in their case at least, the most worrisome of the plausible unintended effects of extensive use of field interrogations.

Conducting a Comparison Group Evaluation

Outlined below are step-by-step instructions for conducting a basic comparison group evaluation of a tactical patrol program. The instructions apply specifically to a tactical patrol program applied in an already targeted area, with a second area chosen subsequently to serve as a comparison group. The same approach could be followed, with only modest adjustments, if multiple targeted areas and/or multiple comparison areas were to be used.

1. Carefully specify the form of tactical patrol (directed, saturation, etc.) to be used. Make any personnel assignments, develop any written guidelines, and provide any training necessary to implement the tactical patrol.
2. Begin the process evaluation by gathering information, making observations and conducting interviews in order to describe the program environment, program development, program operations, and intervening events.
3. Identify as many comparison areas as possible with approximately the same kind and magnitude of problem as that to be addressed in the targeted area.
4. Carefully choose one comparison area that is most similar to the targeted area in other important respects, such as geography, demographics, etc.
5. Carefully specify the program-specific hypothesized effects of the tactical patrol in the targeted area. These should be stated as clearly and as simply as possible.
6. Also specify any important and plausible unintended effects of the program to be implemented. These should also be stated clearly and simply.
7. Develop and define operational measures of program implementation, hypothesized effects and unintended effects. Decide exactly what you are going to measure to describe the program-as-implemented and what happened as a result of the program.
8. Determine what time periods will be used. This may involve two time periods (before and after), three time periods (before, during and after), or more extended time series periods. Make sure the time periods are sufficiently

long to give the tactical patrol program a chance to show its effects.

9. If any of the operational measures require baseline data collection before program implementation (such as surveys of citizens, surveys of officer attitudes, or observations of officer behavior), gather the baseline data.

10. Implement the tactical program in the targeted area.

11. Monitor the implementation of the program in the targeted area and the maintenance of normal conditions in the comparison area.

12. Begin data collection if this did not precede program implementation. If extreme conditions develop in the targeted or comparison areas, consider ending the program or expanding it to the comparison area, as appropriate.

13. Continue data collection throughout the program implementation and any appropriate after periods.

14. Conduct data analysis. Describe the program-as-implemented and specify any changes in measures of hypothesized and unintended effects. Use averages, percentages, statistical comparisons, and graphical presentations as appropriate to show any changes. Consider whether changes can be attributed to the program and whether they are substantial enough for the program to be judged a success or failure.

15. Prepare any written reports required. At a minimum, make a permanent record of the evaluation and its results. Consider sharing your findings with other police professionals.

16. Look for opportunities to replicate the program and its evaluation. Replications should include similar programs implemented in similar settings. Exact duplication is never possible, but replication does require a fair degree of similarity (otherwise, it's not a replication, it's a new study). Take advantage of any such opportunities, since replication is the key to developing confidence in evaluation findings.

Time Series Evaluation of Tactical Patrol

Both the directed patrol (experimental evaluation) and field interrogation (comparison group evaluation) illustrations provided in the previous two sections relied on data representing three time periods—before, during and after. The use of three time periods is fairly typical, often quite satisfactory, and generally preferable to a simple pre-post design that uses only two time periods. In some situations, though, it makes sense to gather and analyze information representing a larger number of time periods. Using such a *time series* design is particularly helpful when the dependent variable (the condition the program hopes to affect) has trends or cycles in it. With time series data, one can attempt to identify such trends, and then determine whether the program interrupted the pattern of the dependent condition.

Time series designs are particularly feasible for evaluating tactical patrol programs because much of the data of interest (reported crimes, arrests, calls for service, etc.) should be routinely available for extended periods before program implementation. Police departments with good computer-aided dispatching (CAD) and automated records systems should be able to produce at least the previous year's worth of weekly or monthly data for a targeted area. Even departments restricted to manual systems should have the paper records to similarly recreate time series data for a targeted area.

Some conditions of interest for tactical patrol evaluation will not usually be susceptible to time series analysis, however. In the San Diego FI study, for example, it might have been interesting to look at repeated measurements of citizen satisfaction with the police department in the three study beats. Since such data are not routinely collected, though, they would not be available for months or years back in time. Two measurements (before and after) are generally all that is feasible for conditions such as citizen satisfaction that are not subjected to routine data collection.

A time series design could have been used in our directed patrol experiment discussed earlier. Instead of comparing *average* weekly target thefts in the before, during and after periods, one could have charted the *actual* number of target thefts by week. A graph of the 15-week period (three weeks before implementing directed patrol, two weeks during, and ten weeks after) would presumably have shown that target thefts dropped substantially when directed patrol was begun, and remained at a lower level throughout the after period. Similar graphs for the no-DP area and the three surrounding areas would probably have shown overall "flatter" lines throughout the 15-week period, although weekly fluctuations would certainly have been seen in all five areas (including the DP area). The graphs might also have revealed whether target thefts were already declining in the DP area when directed patrol was implemented, for example, or whether target thefts had begun to rise again in the DP area toward the end of the after period. These kinds of specific observations can be shrouded when data are averaged over long periods, but are sometimes quite apparent when time series analysis is used.

An Illustration—Field Interrogations

For another illustration, one can look at some time series data for the San Diego field interrogation (FI) study discussed earlier. Instead of presenting average monthly Part I suppressible crime data (as in Table 2), Figure 1 presents, month by month, the actual number of

Part I suppressible crimes for the 21-month study period (seven months before, nine months during, and five months after) in the no-FI, special FI and control beats.

San Diego FI Study

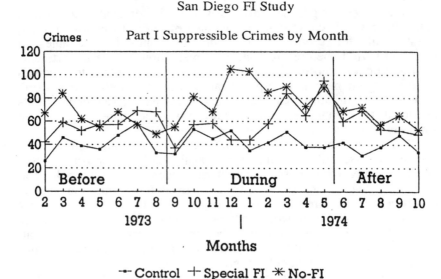

Figure 1

The figure clearly shows that the no-FI beat experienced a higher level of Part I suppressible crime in the during period, when FIs were eliminated, than in either the before or after periods. It would appear that it took two or three months without FIs for this effect to set in, after which suppressible crime stayed at a high level for six months, until FIs were resumed.

The special FI beat, in which the number of FIs was increased, had a more surprising experience. For the first six months of the during period, suppressible crime stayed at about the same levels despite the additional FI activity, or perhaps declined slightly. Crime in the special FI beat increased substantially in the last three months of the during period, however, to levels almost identical to those in the no-FI beat. Whether this rise in crime was caused by some external factors operating in the special FI beat, or by a diminishing return from the extra levels of FI activity in the beat, cannot be determined from the data.

The fact that the amount of monthly suppressible crime in the control beat was more consistent, as represented by a generally flatter line in Figure 1, lends further credence to the possibility that it was the elimination of FIs in the no-FI beat that caused that beat's increase in crime in the during period. When, four months into the during period, suppressible crime really jumped up in the no-FI beat in December 1973, and stayed very high in January 1974, crime levels stayed "normal" in both the control and special FI beats. Then, for the next five months, while suppressible crime stayed high in the no-FI beat, and crime in the special FI beat also increased, still the line for the control beat stayed quite flat.

Figure 2 shows another way of looking at the time series data for the no-FI beat. The line representing the number of Part I suppressible crimes per month in the beat is the same as in Figure 1. The two horizontal lines in the new figure represent what are sometimes termed "confidence intervals." Based on the average and standard deviation during the seven-month before period, these particular confidence intervals specify the range within which monthly suppressible crime would be expected to fall 90 percent of the time. The fact that six of the nine data points in the during period fell above the top line would not have been predicted and is unlikely to have occurred merely by chance. Also, note that all five data points in the after period fell within the 90 percent confidence interval.

San Diego FI Study

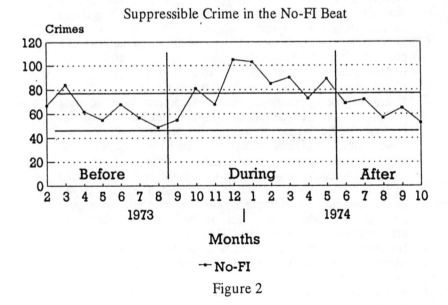

Figure 2

Conducting a Time Series Evaluation

Outlined below are step-by-step instructions for conducting a basic time series evaluation of a tactical patrol program. The instructions apply specifically to a situation in which there is no comparison or control group. The same approach could be followed, with only modest adjustments, if time series data were also available for one or more comparison or control groups.

1. Carefully specify the form of tactical patrol (directed, saturation, etc.) to be used. Make any personnel assignments, develop any written guidelines, and provide any training necessary to implement the tactical patrol.
2. Begin the process evaluation by gathering information, making observations and conducting interviews in order to describe the program environment, program development, program operations, and intervening events.
3. Carefully specify the program-specific hypothesized effects of the tactical patrol in the targeted area (which could be jurisdictionwide). These should be stated as clearly and as simply as possible.
4. Also specify any important and plausible unintended effects of the program to be implemented. These should also be stated clearly and simply.
5. Develop and define operational measures of program implementation, hypothesized effects and unintended effects. Decide exactly what you are going to measure to describe the program-as-implemented and what happened as a result of the program.
6. Determine what time periods will be used. Make sure the periods are sufficiently long to identify pre-implementation norms and trends and to give the tactical patrol program a chance to show its effects.
7. If any of the operational measures require baseline data collection before program implementation (such as surveys of citizens, surveys of officer attitudes, or observations of officer behavior), gather the baseline data. (Any such measures will not ordinarily be part of the main time series analysis, which will usually stretch back much further. However, analysis of unintended effects or of officer acceptance of the program may adhere to a pre-post design, while the main analysis of hypothesized effects follows a time series design.)
8. Implement the tactical program in the targeted area.
9. Monitor the implementation of the program in the targeted area.
10. Begin data collection if this did not precede program implementation. If extreme conditions develop in the targeted area, consider ending the program.
11. Continue data collection throughout the program implementation and any appropriate after periods.
12. Conduct data analysis. Describe the program-as-implemented and specify any changes in measures of hypothesized and unintended effects. Use averages,

percentages, statistical comparisons, and graphical presentations as appropriate to show any changes. Consider whether changes can be attributed to the program and whether they are substantial enough for the program to be judged a success or failure.

13. Prepare any written reports required. At a minimum, make a permanent record of the evaluation and its results. Consider sharing your findings with other police professionals.

14. Look for opportunities to replicate the program and its evaluation. Replications should include similar programs implemented in similar settings. Exact duplication is never possible, but replication does require a fair degree of similarity (otherwise, it's not a replication, it's a new study). Take advantage of any such opportunities, since replication is the key to developing confidence in evaluation findings.

Pre-Post Evaluation of Tactical Patrol

A simple pre-post design is one that has before and after measurements but no comparison or control groups. The pre-post measurements can indicate whether anything changed after the tactic or program was implemented, but the lack of a comparison or control group makes it much harder to know whether the program *caused* the change. If, in fact, the change happened everywhere, or at least in many other settings besides the program's, then the program probably did not cause it. But this would not be known in the absence of comparison or control groups, and hence a false claim of success would be likely. Similarly, if such a change occurred naturally and periodically in the program's setting, but no time series data were collected, a false causal interpretation would probably result.

When it is not possible to gather longer time series data or to use control/comparison groups, a simple pre-post design should be used, and it can yield valuable information. Moreover, a number of techniques can be used to make this design more powerful:

1. If the program or tactic can be subjected to pre-post testing several times (*replication*), any consistent patterns in the results will lend them more credence.

2. If the *timing* of the program or tactic can be arranged such that the probability of other factors causing any changes is minimized, one can more confidently interpret the results.

3. If different *levels* of the program or tactic can be tested, differential results can shed light on the program's or tactic's effects, if any.

An Illustration—Directed Patrol

A study of directed patrol in Pontiac, Mich., several years ago relied primarily on a pre-post design, without the benefit of control or comparison groups. Each week for 74 weeks, several geographically based directed patrol assignments were created. Data were collected on the number of target crimes in the target areas during the week preceding the assignment and during the week the directed patrols were implemented. The primary statistic of interest was the "weekly change in target crimes in target areas." This could be a positive or negative number—negative numbers would indicate the hoped-for decreases in target crimes.

The weekly changes were almost always negative, and averaged −7.6 crimes. The pre-post design showed that target crimes per week in target areas decreased once directed patrol was implemented. But did directed patrol *cause* the target crime decreases?

Two explanations were at least plausible. One was that perhaps crime was decreasing citywide throughout this period—the department's crime statistics refuted this possibility, though. Another explanation was that a phenomenon called "regression to the mean" had occurred. Any time one selects problems to target because they are at extreme levels, the possibility exists that they will begin to decline naturally, regardless of the program implemented. This is a recurring difficulty when evaluating any kind of targeted program such as tactical patrol; moreover, the better one is at choosing truly needy target areas, the greater the difficulty.

Two aspects of the Pontiac pre-post study help refute the likelihood that regression to the mean was responsible for the entire decline in target crimes. One is simply that so many pre-post comparisons were made (over 750 different directed patrol projects during the 74 weeks). It is not logical to think that each of these target areas, or even most of them, was selected at the precise time when its rate of target crimes was about to start dropping naturally. With all due respect to crime analysts, their powers of prognostication are not consistently that good.

In addition, three different *levels* of directed patrol were tested over the 74-week period (see Table 3). Initially, the department devoted about 3,500 minutes of patrol time per week to directed assignments; this jumped to 17,000 minutes per week during the middle period, and then dropped to 2,900 minutes per week. The amount of proactive work done during directed assignments (car stops, FIs, arrests) increased more or less proportionately from the first to the second period, but dropped off dramatically during the final period. The three levels of directed patrol implemented could thus be characterized as (1) moderate time and activity, (2) heavy time and activity, and (3) moderate time and low activity.

Table 3

Pontiac Directed Patrol Experiment

	Period 1	Period 2	Period 3
DP Minutes Per Week	3,467	17,045	2,895
Car Stops and FIs per Week	13.4	60.6	3.8
Arrests per Week	1.8	4.4	0.4
Weekly Change in Target Crimes in Target Areas	-9.2	-9.1	-3.5

Average weekly changes in target crimes in target areas were almost identical for the first two time periods, but were much smaller during the final period. This suggests two things: that the tremendous increase in directed patrol time and activity during the middle period had no additional effect over and above the baseline effect observed in period one; and that the substantial decrease in directed patrol activity in the last period reduced the tactic's effects.

If chance or regression to the mean were completely responsible for the decreases in target crimes in target areas, one would expect about the same magnitudes of decrease in all three periods. Instead, the finding of differential effects for different levels of directed patrol strongly implies that directed patrol did have some effect on target crimes in target areas—that the crime decreases that were measured did not occur merely by chance or solely due to regression to the mean.

Conducting a Pre-Post Evaluation

Outlined below are step-by-step instructions for conducting a basic pre-post evaluation of a tactical patrol program. The instructions apply specifically to a program applied in a targeted area (including jurisdictionwide), without benefit of a comparison or control group. The same approach could be followed, with only modest adjustments, if multiple targeted areas were to be used.

1. Carefully specify the form of tactical patrol (directed, saturation, etc.) to be used. Make any personnel assignments, develop any written guidelines, and provide any training necessary to implement the tactical patrol.
2. Begin the process evaluation by gathering information, making observations and conducting interviews in order to describe the program environment, program development, program operations, and intervening events.

3. Carefully specify the program-specific hypothesized effects of the tactical patrol in the targeted area. These should be stated as clearly and as simply as possible.
4. Also specify any important and plausible unintended effects of the program to be implemented. These should also be stated clearly and simply.
5. Develop and define operational measures of program implementation, hypothesized effects and unintended effects. Decide exactly what you are going to measure to describe the program-as-implemented and what happened as a result of the program.
6. Determine what time periods will be used. This may involve two periods (before and after) or three periods (before, during and after). Make sure the periods are sufficiently long to give the tactical patrol program a chance to show its effects.
7. If any of the operational measures require baseline data collection before program implementation (such as surveys of citizens, surveys of officer attitudes, or observations of officer behavior), gather the baseline data.
8. Implement the tactical program in the targeted area.
9. Monitor the implementation of the program in the targeted area.
10. Begin data collection if this did not precede program implementation. If extreme conditions develop in the targeted area, consider ending the program.
11. Continue data collection throughout the program implementation and any appropriate after periods.
12. Conduct data analysis. Describe the program-as-implemented and specify any changes in measures of hypothesized and unintended effects. Use averages, percentages, statistical comparisons, and graphical presentations as appropriate to show any changes. Consider whether changes can be attributed to the program and whether they are substantial enough for the program to be judged a success or failure.
13. Prepare any written reports required. At a minimum, make a permanent record of the evaluation and its results. Consider sharing your findings with other police professionals.
14. Look for opportunities to replicate the program and its evaluation. Replications should include similar programs implemented in similar settings. Exact duplication is never possible, but replication does require a fair degree of similarity (otherwise, it's not a replication, it's a new study). Take advantage of any such opportunities, since replication is the key to developing confidence in evaluation findings.

Selected Bibliography

Tactical Patrol

Bartch, F. 1978. "Integrating Patrol Assignments: Directed Patrol in Kansas City." In *Review of Patrol Operations Analysis: Selected Readings from ICAP Cities*. Washington, D.C.: U.S. Department of Justice.

Boydstun, J.E. 1975. *San Diego Field Interrogation: Final Report*. Washington, D.C.: Police Foundation.

Burrows, J., and H. Lewis. 1988. *Directing Patrol Work: A Study of Uniformed Policing*. Home Office Research Study No. 99. London: Her Majesty's Stationery Office.

Cawley, D.F., and H.J. Miron. 1977. *Managing Patrol Operations: Manual*. Washington, D.C.: Government Printing Office.

Cordner, G.W. 1981. "The Effects of Directed Patrol: A Natural Quasi-Experiment in Pontiac." In J.J. Fyfe, ed., *Contemporary Issues in Law Enforcement*. Beverly Hills, Calif.: Sage, pp. 37–58.

Cordner, G.W., and D.C. Hale, eds. 1992. *What Works in Policing?: Operations and Administration Examined*. Cincinnati: Anderson.

Cordner, G.W., L.K. Gaines, and V.E. Kappeler. 1996. *Police Operations: Analysis and Evaluation*. Cincinnati: Anderson.

Gay, W.G., T.H. Schell, and S. Schack. 1977. *Improving Patrol Productivity: Volume I—Routine Patrol*. Washington, D.C.: Government Printing Office.

Hoover, L.T. 1996. *Quantifying Quality in Policing*. Washington, D.C.: Police Executive Research Forum.

Kelling, G.L., T. Pate, D. Dieckman, and C.E. Brown. 1974. *The Kansas City Preventive Patrol Experiment: A Summary Report*. Washington, D.C.: Police Foundation.

Kenney, D.J., ed. 1989. *Police and Policing: Contemporary Issues*. New York: Praeger.

Krajick, K. 1978. "Does Patrol Prevent Crime?" *Police Magazine* (September):5–16.

Pate, T., R.A. Bowers, and R. Parks. 1976. *Three Approaches to Criminal Apprehension in Kansas City: An Evaluation Report*. Washington, D.C.: Police Foundation.

Schack, S., T.H. Schell, and W.G. Gay. 1977. *Improving Patrol Productivity: Volume II—Specialized Patrol*. Washington, D.C.: Government Printing Office.

Schnelle, J.F., R.E. Kirchner, J.D. Casey, P.H. Uselton, and M.P. McNees. 1977. "Patrol Evaluation Research: A Multiple-Baseline Analysis of Saturation Police Patrolling During Day and Night Hours." *Journal of Applied Behavior Analysis* 10 (Spring):33–39.

Sherman, L. 1986. "Policing Communities: What Works?" In A. Reiss and M. Tonry, eds., *Communities and Crime*. Chicago: University of Chicago Press, pp. 343-386.

_____. 1990. "Police Crackdowns: Initial and Residual Deterrence." In M. Tonry and N. Morris, eds., *Crime and Justice: A Review of Research*. Chicago: University of Chicago Press, pp. 1–48.

Sherman, L.W., J.W. Shaw, and D.P. Rogan. 1995. "The Kansas City Gun Experiment." *Research in Brief*. Washington, D.C.: National Institute of Justice.

Tien, J.M., J.W. Simon, and R.C. Larson. 1977. *An Alternative Approach in Police Patrol: The Wilmington Split-Force Experiment*. Cambridge, Mass.: Public Systems Evaluation.

Warren, J., M. Forst, and M. Estrella. 1979. "Directed Patrol: An Experiment That Worked." *The Police Chief* (July): 48, 49, 78.

Webb, K.W., B.J. Sowder, A.J. Andrews, M.R. Burt, and E.F. Davis. 1977. *National Evaluation Program: Specialized Patrol Projects*. Washington, D.C.: Government Printing Office.

Weisburd, D., and L. Green. 1995. "Policing Drug Hot Spots: The Jersey City Drug Market Analysis Experiment." *Justice Quarterly* 12,4 (December):711–735.

Wilson, J.Q., and B. Boland. 1979. *The Effect of the Police on Crime*. Washington, D.C.: Government Printing Office.

Program Evaluation

Campbell, D.T., and J.C. Stanley. 1963. *Experimental and Quasi-Experimental Designs for Research*. Chicago: Rand McNally.

Cook, T.D., and D.T. Campbell. 1976. "The Design and Conduct of Quasi-Experiments and True Experiments in Field Settings." In M. Dunnette, ed., *Handbook of Industrial and Organizational Psychology*. Chicago: Rand McNally.

_____. 1979. *Quasi-Experimentation: Design and Analysis Issues for Field Settings*. Chicago: Rand McNally.

Eck, J.E. 1984. *Using Research: A Primer for Law Enforcement Managers*. Washington, D.C.: Police Executive Research Forum.

Fitzgerald, J.D., and S.M. Cox. 1987. *Research Methods in Criminal Justice: An Introduction*. Chicago: Nelson-Hall.

Fitz-Gibbon, C.T., and L.L. Morris. 1987. *How to Design a Program Evaluation*. Newbury Park, Calif.: Sage.

_____. 1987. *How to Analyze Data*. Newbury Park, Calif.: Sage.

Hatry, H.P., R.E. Winnie, and D.M. Fisk. 1973. *Practical Program Evaluation for State and Local Government Officials*. Washington, D.C.: The Urban Institute.

Herman, J.L., L.L. Morris, and C.T. Fitz-Gibbon. 1987. *Evaluator's Handbook*. Newbury Park, Calif.: Sage.

King, J.A., L.L. Morris, and C.T. Fitz-Gibbon. 1987. *How to Assess Program Implementation*. Newbury Park, Calif.: Sage.

Maltz, M.D. 1972. *Evaluation of Crime Control Programs*. Washington, D.C.: Government Printing Office.

McCleary, R., and R.A. Hay, Jr. 1980. *Applied Time Series Analysis for the Social Sciences*. Beverly Hills, Calif.: Sage.

Maxfield, M.G., and E. Babbie. 1995. *Research Methods for Criminal Justice and Criminology*. Belmont, Calif.: Wadsworth.

McDowall, D., R. McCleary, E.E. Meidinger, and R.A. Hay, Jr. 1980. *Interrupted Time Series Analysis*. Quantitative Applications in the Social Sciences Series. Beverly Hills, Calif.: Sage.

Rossi, P., H. Freeman, and S. Wright. 1979. *Evaluation: A Systematic Approach*. Beverly Hills, Calif.: Sage.

Spector, P.E. 1981. *Research Designs*. Quantitative Applications in the Social Sciences Series. Beverly Hills, Calif.: Sage.

Vito, G.F., and E.J. Latessa. 1989. *Statistical Applications in Criminal Justice*. Newbury Park, Calif.: Sage.

Weiss, C.H. 1972. *Evaluation Research: Methods of Assessing Program Effectiveness*. Englewood Cliffs, N.J.: Prentice-Hall.

APPENDIX A

DIRECTED PATROL ASSIGNMENT SHEET

D Run #	Beat (s)	Date(s)	Shift(s)

Specific Location

Target Crime(s)	Time Period(s)

Suspect Information

Suspect Vehicle

M.O.

Suggested Tactics

Originator	Date

APPENDIX B

DIRECTED PATROL REPORT			
D Run #	**Beat(s)**	**Date(s)**	**Shift(s)**
Officer		**Time Period**	
Actions Taken			
Observations			
Suggestions			
Supervisor		**Date**	

Appendix C

PROCESS EVALUATION INTERVIEW	
Person Interviewed	Rank/Position

1. What is your involvement in the tactical patrol program?

2. How would you compare or contrast the tactical patrol program with traditional routine patrol?

3. What seem to be the priorities of the tactical patrol program? (Rank from 1 = highest priority to 4 = lowest priority.)

___reducing citizen fear of crime

___apprehending offenders

___preventing/deterring crimes

___improving community relations

4. Does the tactical patrol program have other goals or priorities? If yes, please explain.

Page 1

5. Exactly how does the tactical patrol program work?

6. What are the strengths, the good points, of the tactical patrol program?

7. What are the weaknesses, the bad points, of the tactical patrol program?

8. Given existing resources, what changes do you think should be made in the tactical patrol program?

9. Overall, how much do you think the tactical patrol program contributes to the police department's success in accomplishing its goals and objectives? (Check only one.)

( ) a great amount   ( ) a small amount
( ) a moderate amount   ( ) not at all

Page 2

10. What role do crime analysts play in the tactical patrol program?

11. What role do patrol officers play in the tactical patrol program?

12. Describe how target areas and target crimes are chosen in the tactical patrol program.

13. Describe how tactics are chosen.

14. Do you feel that you have meaningful input in the selection of targets and tactics?

( ) yes   ( ) no

15. Do you feel that other operations personnel have meaningful input in the selection of targets and tactics?

( ) yes   ( ) no

16. Once targets and tactics are chosen, is feedback from operations personnel solicited for making adjustments?

( ) yes   ( ) no

17. How would you rate the information provided by crime analysis? (Check one per row.)

	Excellent	Good	Fair	Poor
Timeliness	( )	( )	( )	( )
Accuracy	( )	( )	( )	( )
Presentation	( )	( )	( )	( )
Overall Usefulness	( )	( )	( )	( )

18. What suggestions do you have for improving the usefulness of crime analysis information for you in your job?

19. Overall, how would you rate the tactical patrol program in comparison to regular patrol? (Check one per row.)

	Strongly Agree	Agree	Disagree	Strongly Disagree
a. Tactical patrol is better than regular patrol at reducing citizen fear of crime.	( )	( )	( )	( )
b. Tactical patrol is better than regular patrol at apprehending offenders.	( )	( )	( )	( )
c. Tactical patrol is better than regular patrol at preventing/deterring crime.	( )	( )	( )	( )
d. Tactical patrol is better than regular patrol at improving community relations.	( )	( )	( )	( )

Interviewer   Date

Page 4

Chapter 3

Community Policing Evaluation

David L. Carter
Allen D. Sapp

Introduction

Evaluating community policing policies and practices poses some difficult problems. Community policing has been implemented in a wide variety of ways depending on the police department's vision, different communities' demands and characteristics, resource availability, and an array of other factors that contribute to the uniqueness of any given community-based initiative. Moreover, community policing is not a program or a uniform set of tasks. Rather, it is a *philosophy* of management and service delivery that makes the operationalization of an evaluation even more difficult. While certain practices may be transferred between departments, even those practices must be amended to meet the characteristics of specific jurisdictions.

A further problem is that community policing requires administrators, managers, supervisors, and officers to think about their responsibilities differently. Reactive and "incident-driven" policies are cleared away for implementation of proactive, innovative, "problem-driven" officer behaviors. As a result, evaluations cannot simply "count beans"—that is, merely tabulating the number of calls answered, response time, tickets written, reports written, and so forth will not accurately measure goal realization under the community policing philosophy.

Finally, there is a problem of unanimity. Community policing has different names around the country, as well as different ways of being implemented. Beyond the question of the types of activities (or tasks) community police officers perform, there is significant variation in allocation and deployment schemes—some departments use community policing departmentwide, while others experiment with the philosophy based on shift or location.

The reader must keep these issues in mind in developing a community policing model, as well as in evaluating it. To manage these issues, this model begins with the premise of definitions. Critical terms for both the development and implementation of community policing will be presented, as well as definitions for different steps in the evaluation. It is inherent in any research endeavor that *operational definitions* be used. These are consistent, measurable descriptions of phenomena that enhance the overall quality of program development and evaluation. It is in this spirit that the definitions are presented.

In the authors' opinions, simply providing a single model description of how to evaluate community policing will leave many questions remaining. Thus, this chapter addresses core issues related to both the development and evaluation of the community policing philosophy. Beyond descriptions of processes, the authors have appended some sample instruments to assist in an assessment.

Before effective evaluation can occur, one must first have a foundation against which measured criteria can be compared. This relates to the conceptual development of a community policing philosophy, as well as the specific operational activities that will be used.

Community Policing Defined

There are a number of definitions for community policing. For this model, community policing is defined as a philosophy, not a tactic. It is a proactive, decentralized approach to policing, designed to reduce crime, disorder and fear of crime, while also responding to the community's explicit needs and demands. Community policing views police responsibilities in the aggregate, examining consistent problems, determining underlying causes of the problems, and developing solutions to those problems (amended from Trojanowicz and Carter 1988, and Spelman and Eck 1987).

Among the fundamentally synonymous terms for community policing are problem-oriented policing (POP), community problem-oriented policing (CPOP), neighborhood-oriented policing (NOP), community-oriented policing and problem solving (COPPS), police area representatives (PAR), citizen-oriented patrol experiment (COPE), experimental policing (EP), neighborhood foot patrol, and community foot patrol. While there are some variations in these concepts' proffered definitions, for the purpose of this model, all these concepts are defined the same as community policing is above.

Operational Context for Evaluation

Of necessity, the evaluation of any policy or activity actually begins with the development of the policy. In this regard, it is essential that administrators and managers conceptualize how the community policing philosophy integrates with the police department's organizational existence. That is, the core values and implementation strategies of community policing policies must be clearly linked to the organization's purpose. The purpose can be viewed as having two elements: the department's *mission,* and the department's *goals.*

> *Mission*—The mission is the role the organization or unit fulfills—it specifies in general language *what* is intended to be accomplished.

It establishes the organization's *direction and responsibility,* which all other administrative activities are designed to fulfill. Thus, the administrative philosophy of policing and all organizational policies and functions should be guided toward fulfilling the mission.

It should be noted that mission goes beyond a statutory obligation. That is, statutes that empower police departments state that the police are responsible for law enforcement and crime repression— they generally do not stipulate any responsibilities for public order. However, city commissions, mayors or the public in general may require the police to fulfill additional responsibilities of providing public service, maintaining order and generally enhancing the quality of life in the community.

> *Goal*—The goal is the end to which all organizational activity is directed.

A goal is broad-based, yet *functionally* oriented. It must be *specific* enough for all department members to clearly understand it, it must be *measurable,* it must be reasonably *attainable* in the time period allotted it, and it must be *mission-related*—that is, accomplishing goals supports the department's mission. Since a department's mission will typically be comprehensive and incorporate diverse functions, multiple goals will typically be set. Goals will also likely vary between areas within a jurisdiction, and perhaps even between shifts.

In that the community environment will change over time, as will crime patterns and community problems, goal statements should be reviewed yearly and changed or revised to reflect current issues and trends.

> *Planning*—Planning anticipates situations, estimating organizational demands and resources needed to handle those situations, and initiating strategies to respond to them.

Particularly in community policing activities, planning is an ongoing responsibility of all organizational members. Middle managers and administrators are primarily responsible for *strategic* or long-range planning. This includes budget planning, facilities and equipment planning, and staff development. Planning projections should include multiple stages for up to 10 years. In these cases, information gained from program evaluations should be incorporated in the plans so appropriate changes can be made.

Community police officers and first-line supervisors are generally responsible for *tactical* planning. Tactical planning addresses problems, crime and quality-of-life issues affecting the community. The time frame for tactical plans is usually one year or less— accomplishing tactical planning objectives contributes to the department's overall goals. Once again, program evaluation assesses the tactics' efficiency and effectiveness.

Viewed in a different way, strategic plans could be viewed as *macro* plans that address the department's mission and goals. Tactical plans could be viewed as *micro* plans that are operationalized by units at the line level.

Evaluation and planning are interactive in that new plans (and, consequently, goals) depend on information gained from the department's evaluations. From a substantive perspective, planning issues can be classified based on

- organization and development issues,
- administrative issues, and
- operational issues.

Within this tripartite model, those responsible for planning should use the following questions as a checklist for program development:

1. *Organization and Development Issues*

   - How extensive will resource allocation to various programs be in comparison with that for the department as a whole?
   - Do the jurisdiction's crime patterns and service demands warrant specializations? If so, what types?
   - Regarding specializations, are the anticipated size, structure, goals, and responsibilities consistent with the crime and service demands?
   - How do community policing activities relate to other department activities?
   - Will changes be needed in the authority and responsibility for community policing activities?
   - How comprehensive will community policing activities be?
   - What growth patterns, if any, are expected in community policing activities, and what expertise will be needed to respond to growth?
   - What are the anticipated equipment needs, depending on changes in size, crimes, service demands, and community policing goals?

2. *Administrative Issues*

- What criteria and procedures will be used to target community policing activities and problems?
- What type of progress reports are expected, and when?
- What will be the relationship and extent of resource allocation and demonstrable results of community policing efforts?
- On what criteria will community policing goals be changed or revised?

3. *Operational Issues*

- How extensively will community policing activities permeate all departmental activities? Divisions? Shifts? Selected officers? Departmentwide?
- What will the performance measures be, and why?
  + Obviously difficult to assess—performance measures depend on department's and jurisdiction's goals, needs and unique characteristics.
  + Performance measures determine
    > whether goals are being met,
    > whether tasks and activities officers perform are *functionally* related to goals, and
    > whether tasks are cost-effective.
  + Performance measures, to have a true evaluative impact, must *not* be designed to weigh individual accountability, but *should* be designed to ensure that policy activities are responding to needs.
- How can ongoing, forward-looking goal preparation best be accomplished?
- Based on changing police service needs, are any unique staffing patterns emerging?
- Are new training programs needed or anticipated based on new and emerging officer responsibilities associated with community policing?
- Do changing responsibilities indicate the need for formal links with specialized agencies or groups ?
- How can community policing activities integrate with non-patrol activities?

Operationalizing Programs Within the Community Policing Framework

While community policing is a management and operations philosophy, a number of elements in most community policing initiatives are fairly consistent. Just as there should be evaluation of the total community policing initiative, there should be "micro-evaluations" for critical elements of the initiative. The following sections provide a summary discussion of those elements that can help guide a community policing evaluation.

Neighborhood Watch. Neighborhood Watch was not originally intended to establish a strong police-community alliance—it was viewed as a means to help prevent burglaries and increase the probability of apprehending criminals. The concept evolved to also include safe havens for children and to address other crime-related problems (such as vandalism) present in the neighborhood.

An obvious inherent element in Neighborhood Watch is to involve the community in crime deterrence and apprehension strategies. Organizing structured groups in neighborhoods not only increases the acquaintances among residents, but also provides a forum for the police to address the community on crime prevention techniques or other issues that may arise. Thus, it increases the quality of the relationship between the police and the community. Any assessment of Neighborhood Watch activities should be certain to include this additional benefit.

Crime Stoppers. Like Neighborhood Watch, Crime Stoppers was designed as a crime suppression and apprehension program, with no explicit intent to ally the police and the community. Crime Stoppers is a joint venture among citizens, the media and the police to identify and locate serious offenders (typically when there is a limited amount of evidence for investigators). Selected crimes are highlighted through descriptions and reenactments on television (or radio). Citizens may make anonymous calls to report information they have on the "focus crimes" or any other crime. They may receive a cash reward for information leading to an arrest and/or conviction.

It is difficult to say whether Crime Stoppers works, because it is very probabilistic: Someone must have information about a crime, *and* that crime must be chosen to be described on a Crime Stoppers program, *and* that person must see the program and recognize the crime, *and,* finally, that person must call the hotline. Despite these delimiting probabilities, Crime Stoppers has been surprisingly successful nationwide. This suggests that citizens are aware of crimes and are sufficiently concerned about them to both watch the program and provide information to the police.

One may infer that Crime Stoppers has served as an electronic means to develop stronger community relationships. While it lacks the traditional elements of face-to-face contact and individual "bonding" between officers and citizens, it nonetheless provides an avenue of understanding and involvement that can support other community alliance efforts.

Volunteers. For various reasons related to constrained resources, community relations and community activism, police departments began using volunteers to help with a wide range of organizational functions. At one end of the spectrum, volunteers were used as "reserve" or "auxiliary" officers to assist in law enforcement activities. Even these programs vary widely—some reserve officers are used simply for traffic control, while in Kansas City, Mo., and San Bernardino County, Calif., for example, reserve officers have full police powers and responsibilities. At the other end of the spectrum, volunteers do odd jobs at the department on an irregular or unscheduled basis.

Volunteers can be a valuable resource for a police department both because of the money saved in salaries and because of the expertise they can provide. For example, the American Association of Retired Persons (AARP) has a structured process for soliciting, screening and training volunteers to work with police departments. Retired accountants, psychologists, teachers, lawyers, and other professionals can provide a department with expertise that may not otherwise be available.

An obvious additional advantage of using volunteers is community alliance. Volunteers can provide a "citizen's perspective" of issues as well as serve as a sounding board for policies and practices. Ideally, they also serve as a community resource for police department matters.

Volunteer programs contribute to a police department's profile. Unfortunately, most organizations do not take complete advantage of the opportunities afforded through volunteers. Instead, there is a tendency to treat them as interlopers. This attitude will likely have a negative effect on the police-community relationship. Assessments should focus on how volunteers are used, as well as on their direct and indirect impact on the total police function.

Crime prevention. The sociologically based concept of crime prevention was generally a long-term approach aimed at young offenders. The hypothesis was that potential criminal behavior would initially manifest itself in youth. Juvenile delinquency was a precursor—an early warning system, perhaps—for adult criminality. Thus, to prevent future crime, one needed to identify young offenders and change their behavior. There are both theoretical and pragmatic limitations to this hypothesis. However, the basic premise appears to ring true. Unfortunately, because of legal, financial and practical restrictions, this hypothesis cannot be tested. Certainly, however, research in this vein contributed to greater thought about ways to *prevent* crime, not just apprehend offenders.

The 1970s saw a tremendous growth in the "physical crime prevention" movement. A very pragmatically oriented approach— sometimes known simply as "locks and bolts"—physical crime prevention initially relied on the premise that the more difficult it is for a thief to get access to and steal property, the less likely it is that he or she will commit the crime. The concept grew to include programs such as Operation Identification, wherein the premise was that a thief is less likely to steal property if he or she knows that the property is clearly marked and recorded, thereby making it more difficult to "fence." Variations of this theme grew in popularity among police departments.

From a theoretical perspective, this movement relied on a likely fallacious assumption: that the crime would be *prevented*. In fact, the likelihood is that the crime would still be committed, just not at the initially intended location: the phenomenon of *displacement*. Despite this theoretical concern, police departments embraced the concept, because as long as the community had been comprehensively canvassed with crime prevention surveys and "protections," displacement to another jurisdiction was fine. Indeed, most police administrators accept crime displacement as a legitimate goal.

Just as police departments embraced the concept, so did the public. The program seemed logical, and it provided physical evidence of behavior designed to reduce the probability of crime and, consequently, fear of crime. As with Neighborhood Watch, crime prevention programs helped police open doors to "law-abiding" citizens and perform a service they wanted. While physical crime prevention has many positive aspects, it lacks depth to deal with problems to any substantive degree. Instead, it provides a cushion on which concerns about victimization and fear of crime may rest.

From an evaluation perspective, a department obviously cannot measure prevented crime. Other variables can be measured, such as reductions in reported crime (which has a number of problems in itself), crime rate changes in adjacent areas or jurisdictions (which may indicate displacement), changes in levels of fear of crime, and changes in 911 calls or calls for service in the targeted areas.

Police-community relations. With its roots at the National Center for Police Community Relations at Michigan State University, in the 1950s, led by the late Louis Radelet, the police-community relations (PCR) movement tried to resolve the tension between law enforcement and citizens by opening lines of communication. While PCR was initially intended to develop a means to exchange information, it evolved to emphasize teaching officers about communications with the public, teaching the public about the challenges of police work, and developing empathy between law enforcement and the community.

The PCR movement was the first initiative to truly try to reach the community. The initial aim was to identify community leaders as a focal point for establishing a liaison with citizens. Positive relations between community leaders and the police, it was theorized, would "trickle down" (to borrow a Reaganomics term) to community members. At the outset, PCR was largely one-sided—its focus was predominantly on changing the community's view of the police and on making citizens more supportive and understanding of police actions (President's Commission 1967). By the 1970s, virtually every police department of any size had a police-community relations unit (or officer), and PCR courses had become a staple in law enforcement/criminal justice college curricula (Radelet and Carter 1994).

As the movement matured, the focus became somewhat more reciprocal. It was felt that police officers needed to learn more about the social-psychological dynamics affecting their relationship with the community. Moreover, all officers needed to practice PCR, not just those assigned to a PCR unit. As a result, police training was emphasized as a means to get all officers to be more communicative—sometimes civil—with the public. Particularly in the late 1970s, police departments also regularly incorporated crime prevention programs and Neighborhood Watch with the PCR unit. It was felt that this additional step would help the police and community communicate, as well as make an effort to reduce crime (Radelet and Carter 1994).

PCR was the first comprehensive effort to try to resolve the issues inherent in community alliance. The movement recognized that disequilibrium existed between the police and the community, and it developed programmatic strategies to address this dissonance. The goal of PCR was to establish an effective dialogue between citizens and law enforcement and, consequently, develop better support for the police, as well as enhance police accountability to the public.

Without question, PCR efforts were focused mainly on minority communities, for there is where the greatest disequilibrium existed between the police and citizens. The need for better relations with minorities became evident in the 1960s. With the force of the civil rights movement punctuated by civil disturbances and protest marches, it became evident that police practices had to change. The National Advisory Commission on Civil Disorders, the National Commission on the Causes and Prevention of Violence, and the President's Commission on Law Enforcement and Administration of Justice all cited problems in police-community relations—particularly excessive force, deprivation of constitutional rights, rudeness, insensitivity to minorities, and discriminatory practices. As a remedy to these and other strains in the police-community relationship, each commission recommended that police departments develop aggressive PCR programs.

The PCR concept is by no means dead, but it is being rethought. Police executives were concerned that PCR did not delve deep enough. Despite the intent, PCR appeared to have become a veneer for police inadequacies—a predominantly *reactive* method to deal with problems. PCR's proactive elements were limited and generally shallow.

Based on the evolving body of research on police practices and the increasingly apparent limitations of PCR programs, practitioners and theoreticians alike felt that the endemic issues of policing in general—not simply those related to community alliance—were not being effectively addressed. This is the framework from which the embryo of community policing was conceived.

A positive police-community relationship is obviously desired in community policing, although the locus and approach are different from the traditional PCR model's. That relationship must be redefined to include many of the issues discussed above, as well as such factors as respect and support for the police, numbers of complaints against officers, satisfaction with police service, and other quality indicators.

Collectively, evaluating these variables can provide important insights on the success of community policing vis-à-vis the police-community relationship.

The Political Dimension

Police involvement with the community in a new, proactive relationship is inherently a political dynamic.   The political elements of program development and evaluation should not be ignored.

Crime—and the need to prevent it—has consistently received substantial attention from politicians simply because it is of major concern to citizens.   Several explicit reasons come to mind when considering why crime is a political factor.

First, crime is an emotional issue that affects feelings of safety and security for oneself and one's family.   The political process feeds on emotion, as evidenced by political advertisements both for and against the "Brady Bill" handgun purchase waiting period.   A tug on the heartstrings has far more political clout than the weight of empirical evidence.

Second, crime will touch most people, either directly or indirectly, at some point in their lifetime.   Nearly every American will be a victim or know a victim; consequently, crime is something the public can relate to with near unanimity.   This comprehensive experience gives the politician a good frame of reference for communicating with his or her constituency.

Third, crime is one issue on which nearly all people can agree to some extent, regardless of political position, race, ethnicity, age, gender, or lifestyle—people do not want crime.   Democrat or Republican, black or white, young or old, man or woman, gay or straight: all agree that crime and violence must be controlled.   Consequently, it is politically safe to oppose crime and offer *reasonable* initiatives to control it.

Fourth, citizens are willing to make some sacrifices for protection against criminals. Fear of crime is pervasive, fueled by media reports, gossip and assumptions.   To abate this fear, many people are even willing to pay more taxes.   For example, the citizens of Flint, Mich., voted by a two-thirds majority to increase their taxes to support community policing (Kelling and Moore 1988).   In Texas, citizens voted to spend over $2 billion to build prisons, even though the state's financial status was lean. The point is that increased expenditures for crime control are relatively easier to justify than other government initiatives, because crime control efforts are not generally seen as a "pork barrel."   Spending money on issues of popular concern can be an important way to gain "political chips," as will be discussed later.

Finally, crime is visible and piques a morbid curiosity among people. News reports about murder and mayhem, television programs depicting "real crime," and nonfiction books on "true crime" are all evidence of this. As another illustration, people still go to rural Waco, Texas, where the Branch Davidian compound stood, just to see the sight of that calamity (and buy T-shirts).   Crime draws public fascination, particularly when the crime is senseless or an atrocity. Thus, crime makes great fodder for politicians to decry, examine, comment about, and act on.

While there is a common ground surrounding the concern for crime and the need to control it, there are also notable disagreements on the proper responses to it. For example, opinions vary widely on such questions as the following:

- Should police authority be increased to deal with crime?
- Should some legal rights be temporarily "suspended" in order to deal more effectively with criminals, notably drug dealers?
- What is the best way to prevent crime—educational programs, physical crime security, more police officers, stiffer prison sentences, youth diversion programs, the death penalty? All of the above? Some of the above? None of the above?
- Will crime be more effectively prevented (and will justice be more effectively served) if convicted criminals are punished or rehabilitated?
- Is punishment vs. rehabilitation a legal issue, professional issue or political issue?
- Should drugs be legalized to cut down on drug-related crime?
- Is crime a racial problem? A youth problem? An urban problem? A poverty problem? A media problem? A parental problem? A—fill in the blank—problem?

These questions present a number of controversial issues. Importantly, these questions—and the way they are answered—reflect political perspectives and beliefs far more than substantive knowledge and research. Several examples come to mind. Because violent crime has become a pervasive issue for the public, Congress and state legislatures have attempted to respond with a number of "get tough" measures to deal with the problem.

The label of "get tough" is important from a political perspective. Citizens are both tired and fearful of crime, consequently holding elected officials accountable for doing "something" (particularly as reflected in the November 1993 elections). With such explicit political sentiment, politicians recognize that some action must be taken, and that they cannot be viewed as being "soft" on crime or criminals. Consequently, opening youth boot camps, providing federal support for hiring up to 100,000 more community police officers, increasing the range of offenses for the death penalty, making life sentences mandatory for career criminals, increasing mandatory penalties for offenses involving firearms, and building more prisons have been among the common responses. Indeed, the creation of the Community-Oriented Policing Services (COPS) agency in the U.S. Office of Justice Programs in 1994 illustrates the political influence of crime in general and of community policing in particular. The political dynamic comes into play not because of actual knowledge about these measures' effectiveness, but because they lessen the political heat from the public.

Developing a new crime control strategy can be yet another political move. This is where community policing comes into play, and where the concept is jeopardized.

Increasingly, politicians are embracing community policing as the means to more effectively deal with crime and to provide better service to the public, with special concern for increasing the quality of life. In reality, there are probably few politicians who truly understand the philosophy. Despite this, they are providing their heartfelt support (in a political sense) for the concept because it addresses crime, strengthens the bond between the police and the community, and shows that community concerns are being addressed.

This is not meant to sound cynical or accusatory; rather, it is pragmatic. Most politicians realize they have an ethical responsibility to address public concerns. The fact that one's future is tied to this responsiveness is not inconsequential. It is, of course, the nature of the beast. Unfortunately, any new initiative—such as community policing—is also politically fragile, because if no "successes" can be shown, support will dwindle. Defining and measuring "success" is an inherent part of program evaluation, yet the political dynamics cannot be completely ignored.

Performance Evaluations

While not program evaluation, per se, a common issue that emerges in assessing community policing is performance appraisal. Because of this issue's prominence, the authors will address it in this discussion.

Wycoff and Oettmeir (1994), in addressing the need for personnel evaluation, identified six primary reasons for it:

- *Administration*. To help managers make decisions about promotion, demotion, reward, discipline, training needs, salary, job assignment, retention, and termination.
- *Guidance and counseling*. To help supervisors give feedback to subordinates and help them in career planning and preparation, and to improve employee motivation.
- *Research*. To validate selection and screening tests and training evaluations, as well as to assess the effectiveness of interventions designed to improve individual performance.

- *Socialization.* To convey expectations to personnel about both the content and the style of their performance, and to reinforce other means of organizational communication about the department's mission and values.
- *Documentation.* To record the types of problems and situations officers are addressing in their neighborhoods, and how they deal with them. This provides for data-based analysis of the resources and other managerial support needed to address problems, and allows officers the opportunity to have their efforts recognized.
- *System improvement.* To identify organizational conditions that may impede improved performance, and to solicit ideas for changing the conditions.

To fulfill these criteria, a system must be developed to validly and reliably measure individual activities. Unfortunately, this has been difficult to achieve. Police agencies seek a system that has the ease and objectivity of "bean counting," but also the substantive flexibility and ability to be reasonably subjective, as is found in qualitative or narrative evaluations.

Any policy that seeks effective performance evaluations must address several points:

- Who is to be evaluated?
  + Probationary officers
  + Patrol officers
  + Supervisors
  + Managers
  + Administrators
  + Nonsworn personnel
  + Volunteers
- How frequently will personnel be evaluated?
- Who will do the evaluations?
- What kind of training will evaluators need?
- What form will evaluations take (e.g., qualitative, quantitative, narrative, self-evaluation)?

Based on input the authors have received from various police managers seeking to evaluate community police officers, the following factors have consistently emerged:

- Does the officer have a clear sense of objectives?
  + Understands the department's mission and goals
  + Understands his or her role in achieving the department's goals
  + Has objectives he or she wants to accomplish in the job assignment
  + Has a sense of direction in work, rather than just "occupying space"

- Does the officer understand operational policies and procedures?
- What has the officer done for professional self-improvement (e.g., taken college courses; taken advantage of training opportunities; become famililar with research, current thought, issues, and trends in policing; applied diverse knowledge and research to his or her working environment)?
- What kind of feedback is received about the officer (e.g., commendations from the public and department, complaints from the public and department, informal feedback from peers)?
- What duties must the officer perform (e.g., write reports, identify and report problems, get involved with the community)?
- How does the officer perform his or her duties (e.g., competently, with understanding of the job, confidently, proactively, with professional pride)?

Expanding on the idea of performance assessment, the authors suggest that there be an opportunity for officers to evaluate "up the organization." That is, officers should be able to provide some input on supervisors' and managers' effectiveness. Inherently qualitative in nature, factors in this upward assessment may address the following:

- *Leadership*–Does the manager
  + set a good example?
  + motivate, using positive reinforcement?
  + take risks and experiment when appropriate?
- *Communication*–Does the manager
  + provide information critical to successful performance?
  + provide constructive criticism?
  + choose the right time to deliver messages?
  + sense others' mood and respond appropriately?
  + exhibit compassion and sensitivity?
- *Teamwork*–Does the manager
  + treat employees equally?
  + encourage group problem solving?
  + share credit with all team members?
  + hold effective team meetings?
- *Quality*–Does the manager
  + set a good example by constantly trying to improve?
  + provide training opportunities?
  + have a good sense of the customers and their needs?
- *Planning*–Does the manager
  + ask for help in planning?
  + set realistic, attainable goals?

+ follow through with the plan?
+ celebrate accomplishments?

While supervisors and managers may resist this form of evaluation, the organization will benefit from the practice. Each organization will need to refine specific procedures for the process to maximize its benefit and ensure that it is used equitably.

Police agencies should develop a broad range of flexible criteria that can accurately assess community police officers' performance. The criteria should be flexible to adjust to the officers' various duties. The criteria should also be evaluated subjectively. The process of developing a performance evaluation policy should also include a component for personnel to evaluate supervisors and managers (see Carter 1995a).

The Evaluation Structure

Evaluation has been defined in many ways—regardless of the definitions, it can be classified in two categories, depending on the general purpose:

Outcome evaluation—The process of determining the value or amount of success in achieving a predetermined goal by

- defining the goal in some qualitatively or quantitatively measurable terms,
- identifying the proper criteria (or variables) to be used in measuring success in attaining the goal,
- determining and explaining the degree of success, and
- recommending further program actions to attain the goal.

Process evaluation—The assessment of procedures used to attain goals under the following criteria:

- Do the procedures substantively contribute to the goal?
- Do the procedures effectively utilize resources?
- Are the procedures coordinated with other elements in the implementation process?
- Are staff members properly trained to execute the procedures?

More simply, each of these evaluations is characterized by the following questions:

- *Outcome evaluation:* Are the goals being accomplished?
- *Process evaluation*: Are the methods for accomplishing goals working with maximum utility?

Essentially, evaluation is a scientific process that involves making comparisons between "conditions."   These conditions may range from reported burglary rates to levels of fear of crime to levels of satisfaction with how courteous officers are when speaking to citizens. Regardless of the nature of the comparison, it must address some police department activities that support its goals as related to the mission.

When one says that evaluation is a "scientific" process, that means that it is logical, it is objective, and it has inherent procedures of quality control to try to ensure the accuracy of the information collected, analyzed and interpreted. These procedures are referred to as *research methods* or the evaluation's *methodology*. The type of methodology used will vary based on the nature of the program or activities being evaluated. Initially, this largely relates back to the idea of "comparisons"—the factors against which comparisons are made are typically built into the *development* of a program so that an effective *evaluation* can be made.   The comparisons made in law enforcement evaluations include the following:

- *"Real" vs. "expected" outcomes*—Serves as a means to assess the accuracy of projections and forecasts. It can be used to assess the accuracy of hypotheses, conclusions and recommendations. Actual or "real" results of a program or activity as determined by the evaluation are compared with the expected results developed in the planning and development phases.
- *"Before" vs. "after" status*—Examines whether specific activities have had an impact or contributed to a change in the goals or the phenomena peripheral to the goals. Measurements are taken before a new program is implemented, and again after a defined period of operation. Changes in the measured variables are attributed to the program's effects. (For example, one would measure burglary rates and citizens' perceptions of safety before a Neighborhood Watch was started, and then after the program had been in effect for a year. Changes, if any, in the burglary rates and/or the feelings of safety would be attributed to the Neighborhood Watch.)
- *Comparison of reactions to operations and administrative expectations*—Determines whether perceptions and quality (value) of community policing activities are consistent with expectations of administrative and operational consumers of the activities. Simply put, great ideas do not always work as planned—this comparison attempts to measure whether they do.
- *Contributory value*—Attempts to assess the degree to which the program activities contributed to goal attainment. A program may have some effect, but it may not necessarily be goal-related.   For example, a

community outreach program initiated by the police department may make citizens more aware of the public schools' or city recreation department's needs. While this may be viewed as a positive effect, it is not related to the police department's goals.

* *Quality control assessment*—Is an overall, broad-based assessment of the utility, accuracy, general value, and orientation of the community policing philosophy and its related programs. It may be learned that initial ideas and policies related to the philosophy are unrealistic for the department and/or community. As a result, "fine tuning" may be required to ensure that program and activity quality are reasonably attainable.
* *Processes and outputs*—Is an internal assessment of the correlation of expended efforts and procedures compared with the type and quality of output produced by the community policing activities.

The "Character" of Evaluation Methods

It was noted above that while sophisticated evaluation techniques should be used, they should be limited to conditions and times that require them. Supervisors or designated evaluators can use less rigorous methods for effective "evaluative sensing." When problems appear, then formalized evaluation may be warranted. For informal evaluation to work, it must be performed

* purposely,
* routinely,
* comprehensively, and
* critically.

Importantly, evaluation should be viewed as a positive, constructive activity to make the community policing policies more valuable to the organization—evaluation should *not* be viewed as "faultfinding".

At the heart of any evaluation is the identification and assessment (measurement) of relevant *variables*. In a formal evaluation, the variables must be critically selected from the particular activity being assessed. Informal evaluation can take a more generalized approach. To maintain an intuitive base of understanding about the philosophy, programs and activities to be evaluated, there are several types of variables and questions that may be asked during informal evaluations.

1. *Protocols of Officers' Tasks*
   * Are the proper or best activities being selected for the designated community policing needs?

- Are personnel properly trained to interpret and utilize the data being collected via the protocol used?
- Is the protocol fully within the agency's capability, or are resources and expertise being stretched?

2. *Information Processing*
   - Is information being adequately collected and assessed to evaluate the community policing goals?
   - Is the quality of information being adequately controlled and assessed?
   - Is too much raw, noncontributory (e.g., high-interest but low-utility, or simply "bean counting") information being introduced into the evaluative process?
   - Is information being effectively and logically categorized and indexed to evaluate all aspects of community policing?
   - Is too much or too little information being introduced into the evaluative process?

3. *Analysis*
   - Are the best and most appropriate analytic techniques being used for evaluative purposes?
   - Are logical conclusions being drawn?
   - How accurate are hypotheses and interpretations of collected data/information?
   - Is the analysis providing useful information for decision making?

4. *Reporting*
   - Are evaluation reports understandable?
   - Are they comprehensive?
   - Are they meeting their intended purpose?

5. *Dissemination*
   - Are the right people receiving the needed information (e.g., are community police officers and decision makers receiving the information needed to fulfill their responsibilities)?
   - Is the information being promptly disseminated?

6. *Personnel*
   - Are all staff members—e.g., community police officers, supervisors, evaluators—properly trained for their tasks?
   - Is the supervision of community police officers a style that is compatible with the proactive, innovative approach they must use?
   - Is officer expertise sufficiently diverse to meet the stated goals?

- Do personnel have effective relations and communications with other organizations that contribute to community policing activities?

The answers to these questions can pose significant challenges for successful program evaluation. The evaluation process is not simple: It requires *planning, expertise* and *thought*. Of these three, perhaps the most difficult is careful, logical, critical thought about the transition from a community policing philosophy to action—evaluation measures the dynamics of this transition.

Common Problems to Focus Evaluations

This section addresses some of the more common problems found in police operations as they relate to the evaluation process.

The department becomes too enmeshed in daily activities and has difficulty changing procedures to respond to fast-breaking or special needs.

Most police departments are bureaucratic, paramilitary organizations. As such, they rely heavily on uniform procedures, allowing limited discretion. Moreover, rigid accountability to the letter of procedures tends to take precedence over the spirit of procedures (embodied in the policy). Consequently, daily activities become routinized. Community policing requires greater flexibility, discretion and innovation. This *change* is difficult for personnel to accept. Human behavior is inherently dogmatic; thus, change is difficult. Yet, change is essential for community policing to suceed. Ideally, planning and leadership will promote change, and evaluation will measure it.

Little feedback, positive or negative, is given to the department's various units on the quality and value of community policing activities.

There is a tendency to keep evaluation results—particularly those that are intermediately collected in ongoing programs—among the administrative staff. Sometimes, supervisors in programs being evaluated do not receive the results. This information *must* be communicated to supervisors and line-level employees performing the community policing activities. This not only helps in "fine-tuning" activities to make them more workable, but it can also help in team building and enhancing the program participants' *esprit de corps*. Providing feedback is not only good for program development and implementation, but it is also good management.

Commonly used procedures for responding to calls for service and order-maintenance situations become institutionalized, allowing limited creativity.

More attention should be given to creative problem solving—it must, however, go beyond training and include good *leadership*.   There should be an ongoing awareness of the need for proactive efforts and innovation in dealing with all responsibilities.   When there is disagreement about the best alternative to use to deal with a problem or situation, personnel frequently *compromise* rather than present their various positions and supporting arguments to decision makers. Doing so would permit *informed leadership*, which, in turn, would contribute to more robust program development.

> *There must be ongoing communications between all department units—line and staff—to make community policing work most efficiently and effectively.*

Communications must be two-way—both horizontal and vertical.   Not only must leaders and line-level personnel communicate (and *listen*), but there must also be lateral communications between units.   For example, a community police officer may be trying to deal with an increase in "destruction of property" complaints in his or her assigned area.   The officer should be able to ask the department's crime analysts to conduct a special analysis of the complaints and receive a cooperative, rapid response.   If crime analysis personnel do not understand their role in community policing *and* the need to respond rapidly to such requests, then the potential effect of the officer's activities will be minimized.   *All* units must share information, thoughts and ideas as related to their responsibilities and the department's goals.   Evaluations should be designed to measure communications related to the program and activities in question.

> *Program evaluators must avoid "circularity" in facts—that is, not lose perspective and believe that earlier suggestions or assumptions are now fact.*

When there is significant investment in a philosophy and in activities that support that philosophy, there is an obvious desire to see one's beliefs confirmed.   Program evaluation is a way to objectively measure those beliefs.   Because of the desire for success and the reinforcement provided by continued discussion and consideration of the program activities, it is easy to confuse reinforced belief with scientific fact.   Thus, care must be taken to avoid this "circularity."

In sum, evaluation of community policing activities should ensure that activities and processes are

- *effective*—they accomplish what is intended; they contribute to goals;
- *efficient*—they are effective without waste or undue resource expenditures;
- *accurate*—they are valid and reliable;

- *timely*—they produce information within time frames that are useful for decision making; and
- *relevant*—they are all directly related to the department's mission and goal(s).

Because community policing requires substantially different personnel utilization, program evaluation is also critical for effective personnel allocation and deployment.

Allocation—The long-term assignment of personnel by function, geography and shift/duty tour, along with the commitment of required supporting resources to deal with crime and police service demands in the most efficient and effective way.

Deployment—The short-term assignment of personnel to address specific crime problems or police service demands.

Many departments, when initially adopting the community policing philosophy, will *deploy* officers to perform activities that support the philosophy. There is greater flexibility in experimental deployment, which leads to further program and policy development. When policies and practices have been tested and "fine-tuned," resources are *allocated* to fully operationalize the philosophy. In many ways, *allocation* can be viewed as a *strategic* activity, and *deployment* as a more *tactical* activity. In both cases, evaluation plays an important role in continued policy application.

Methodologies Used in Program Evaluation

In all cases, the first methodological issue is to decide *what information is wanted or needed in the evaluation*. The desired information must be clearly articulated so that the best method may be used to collect it.

Administrators and policy makers may sometimes simply say " I want to know about . . .," with no further delineation. In such cases, it is common that an idea is being explored, but that not enough is known to formulate specific questions. Evaluators and administrators must solidify the issues and formulate them into "researchable" questions.

Once it is determined *what information is wanted*, the methodology is selected based on a wide range of factors. In selecting the methodology, the evaluator must examine

- the variables that will yield the information desired, either
  + individually,
  + collectively (in the aggregate), or

+   interactively;
•   the ability to access and measure the variables;
•   the reliability of the variables; and
•   the validity of the information obtained.

Identifying and understanding variables are critical in the evaluation process.

Variable—Any characteristic on which individuals, groups, items, or incidents differ.

Examples of variables that may be measured in the evaluation of a community policing program include

•   types of community problems;
•   alternative solutions to the problems;
•   solutions that have been implemented;
•   quality of the relationship between the police and other departments and agencies;
•   fear of crime;
•   "signs of crime" in the community (the "Broken Windows" analogy);
•   citizen satisfaction with police;
•   employee job satisfaction;
•   degree of citizen involvement in program implementation and problem-solving activities;
•   complaints about police behavior (not the numbers of complaints, but the types of complaints);
•   responsiveness to citizen demands;
•   effectiveness of the management system;
•   efficiency of the management system;
•   crime patterns;
•   patterns in the flow and distribution of unlawful commodities; and
•   changes in demographics.

The reader will note that most of these variables are *qualitative*— that is, they are factors that are *described* rather than *counted*, per se. This is because community policing focuses on prevention, problem solving and resolution of issues, rather than documentation of activity. Moreover, community policing is concerned about the *quality of life* both in the community and in the police department. These factors simply cannot be quantified. The problem with qualitative information is that it is much more difficult to collect, analyze and base decisions on. Yet, qualitative dynamics are at the heart of community policing initiatives. This is not to say that quantitative data is never collected in community policing programs. Rather, it is a caveat of which one should be aware.

As a related point, one may asked, "Why should new data be collected if existing data may answer the questions at issue?" It is true that *new information* does not necessarily have to be collected to evaluate a program. Existing data can be used, but considered in light of the following points:

- How *available* are the data, and can they be obtained for research?
- How *valid* are the data (e.g., do the data measure what is wanted)?
- Do the data *reflect the universe* or a selected, nonrepresentative subset?
- How *reliable* are the data (e.g., would the same results be found time after time)?

If these questions can be answered to the satisfaction of the policy makers and research team, then there are distinct advantages of using existing data:

- It is *inexpensive.*
- It is more *rapidly available.*

In most cases, new data will need to be collected. Beyond the methodological issues involved, policy makers and researchers must also be concerned with

- maintaining data confidentiality,
- protecting human subjects,
- maintaining public service/safety obligations,
- getting the staff's cooperation, and
- avoiding the collection of too much data.

In addition, a *methodology* must be selected.

Methodology—A set of scientifically based procedures used to

- collect information from the variables,
- control the information collection for validity and reliability,
- analyze the information to describe the subject/target,
- analyze the information to make inferences about the subject/target,
- direct the interpretations of the analysis, and
- report the information.

There is an inherent difference between quantitative and qualitative methods. The essential difference is that quantitative methods collect and analyze information that can be "counted" or placed on a measurement scale that can be statistically analyzed.

Qualitative methods collect and analyze information given in narrative or rhetorical form and draw conclusions based on the cumulative interpreted meaning of that information. Thus, the nature of the methodology will depend on

- the *variables' characteristics* and/or
- *how* the information will be collected.

Methodologies and analytic procedures that can be used include

- survey research (both of citizens and of department members);
- case studies;
- qualitative descriptors based on interviews;
- expert analysis (such as the delphi technique);
- operations research (queuing theory, decision theory, modeling, simulation, gaming theory);
- experimental and quasi-experimental design;
- descriptive and inferential statistical analysis (including probability-based projections);
- econometric models;
- actuarial models;
- spatial analysis (location/geography and associated patterns of crimes, people, commodities); and
- temporal analysis ("time," e.g., monthly, weekly, daily, and hourly measures of incidents and changes in the targeted entity).

While many research methodologies are available, these are among the most useful for program evaluation. Obviously, many of these methods require specialized training to perform them properly. Others require less technical knowledge; personnel who have taken college courses on research methods may be able to conduct the research. However, it should be cautioned that most research is far more complex than many believe. For example, survey research requires expertise in item construction and analysis; case studies require careful analytic skills; interviewing requires controls in both questioning and inter-rater reliability. As a result, administrators must be aware of these concerns when making decisions based on research results. No methodology is "pure" or "conclusive"—they all require the evaluator's interpretation. Thus, the best-prepared evaluators will produce the best output.

Reporting the Results of a Program Evaluation

Once data have been collected in an evaluation, they must be put in a form that can be used for both administrative and operational purposes. The results from the evaluation can be used to make *administrative decisions* concerning program financing, personnel allocation and deployment, program continuance, and related issues. The information can also be used for *operational decisions* that reflect the specific activities, policies and approaches to be used in applying the community policing philosophy. Various evaluation report models can be used to meet different needs. Generally speaking, any evaluation report should have three component parts:

- *Descriptive*—The report describes the issues and processes that are subject to the analysis. The information and data are presented objectively.
- *Interpretative*—The evaluator interprets the data with respect to the issues or activities involved.
- *Available alternatives*—In light of the interpretations, the resources available, the community policing activities used, and the agency's capabilities/expertise, the evaluator recommends alternative actions and strategies for the future.

The general types of evaluation reports that may be written include the following:

- *Cost-effectiveness reports*—These show ratios of costs to results.
- *Comprehensive evaluations*—These show the correlation between program activities (i.e., independent variables) and the results of the activities (i.e., dependent variables).
- *Status and information reports for extra-departmental dissemination*—These are primarily prepared to inform non-law enforcement government administrators and legislators about community policing activities in general.

Caveats Regarding Program Evaluation

Despite sophisticated methodologies and analytic methods, program evaluations have limitations about which administrators should be aware. The results of evaluative efforts are only as good as

- the quality of raw data/information collected,
- the appropriateness of the methodology(ies) selected,
- the quality of all portions of the data collection process, and
- the quality of the analysis and data interpretation.

Program evaluation is not conclusive—it relies on samples of information and data that are generalized. As a result, it is always possible that the evaluation's findings are incorrect. While good research methods can significantly reduce this possibility, it nonetheless remains. Moreover, evaluations are also subjective, based on the experience of the evaluator(s) and decision maker(s), particularly when qualitative variables are measured (as is frequently the case in evaluating community policing). This subjectivity is both positive and negative. While on the one hand it permits the use of *experience* in the evaluation, it also introduces *emotion*, which can cloud objectivity.

Overall, program evaluation is *descriptive*, not *prescriptive*. That is, it can tell "what is" and "what may be." It can also provide *alternatives* for action. However, it cannot tell *what actions* to take. Decision making remains a human responsibility.

Evaluation is *program*-oriented, not *individually* oriented. That is, it examines aggregate issues—the cumulative effects of a program, policy or activity, not individual steps in the process.

Finally, program evaluation is a function that supports organizational goals—the evaluation's output is *not a goal in and of itself.*

A Final Note

Effective program evaluation largely depends on how well an initiative is developed. Thus, it is critical at the outset to establish a framework that will be the basis for operations, in order to have clear criteria to assess. The message, of course, is to comprehensively plan an initiative so that a meaningful evaluation can be performed.

There is no recipe for evaluating community policing, because the philosophy is conceived and implemented in widely varying ways. However, understanding the critical elements can provide a road map to assist in an assessment.

Program Evaluation Steps in a Nutshell

I. Program Development

A. Clearly and concisely state the following:

1. *Who* is involved in the program

- Officers
- Segments of the community
- "Target" criminal types
- Classes/groups of people who need a defined service
- Volunteers
- Representatives from other departments or agencies

2. *What* the program is intended to accomplish

- Goal(s)
- Objectives

3. *When* the program is to be implemented

- Time frames for planning and development
- Time line for employee, organizational, and resource preparation and allocation
- Dates for program initiation
- Dates for initial program monitoring review
- Dates for data gathering
- Time line for analysis and preparation of evaluation reports

4. *Where* implementation and evaluation will be made

- Unique community characteristics
- Unique geographic boundaries

5. *Why* the evaluation is proceeding (special evaluation requirements)

- Management decisions on effectiveness (with specific criteria delineated)
- Management decisions on efficiency
- Political issues/dynamics that influence the program
- Need for evaluation due to grants and/or experimental program funding

6. *How* the evaluation is proceeding

- Research methods being used
- Adherence to timetable
- Personnel responsible for program design, implementation and evaluation

B. Convert all applicable factors in the program into measurable variables.

C. Complete the following steps:

1. Select data-gathering methods.

2. Finalize and gain approvals for evaluation time frame.

3. Provide necessary training to program participants.

4. Set up the management structure and policies for the program.

II. Program Implementation

A. Put program policies into effect.

B. Have supervisors audit activities to ensure that

1. everyone is doing what they are supposed to, and

2. activities and duties are being performed correctly.

C. Begin data gathering (depending on research methods used).

D. Make program adjustments as necessary.

III. Evaluation

A. Complete data gathering.

B. Analyze data.

C. Write reports.

D. Disseminate results.

E. Have command staff review evaluation results in consultation with the research team.

1. Draw operational conclusions.

2. Discuss results, validity and reliability.

3. Discuss possible program amendments.

IV. Post-Evaluation Decisions

A. Is further data collection and analysis needed?

B. What strengths and weaknesses were found in the program?

C. How can the program be amended?

D. Should the program be dropped?

V. Evaluation Starts Over As Appropriate

References

Babbie, E. 1962. *Survey Research Methods.* 6th ed. Belmont, Calif.: Wadsworth Publishing Co.

Baltimore County Police, Field Operations Bureau. 1988. *Community Foot Patrol Officer Guidelines and Procedures.* Towson, Md.: Baltimore County Police Department.

Bohigian, H.E. 1971. *The Foundations and Mathematical Models of Operations Research With Extensions to the Criminal Justice System.* Doctoral dissertation in the School of Education, New York University.

Bureau of Justice Statistics. 1988. *Report to the Nation on Crime and Justice.* Washington, D.C.: U.S. Department of Justice.

Cahn, M., and J.M. Tien. 1980. *An Evaluation Report of an Alternative Approach in Police Response: The Wilmington Management of Demand Program.* Cambridge, Mass.: Public Systems Evaluation Inc.

Carter, D.L. 1989. *Research in Support of the Community Policing Concept.* Training document, FBI Academy, Quantico, Va.

_____. 1995a. *Keystone Human Resource Issues for Community Policing.* Paper presented at the NIJ/BJA Annual Conference on Criminal Justice Research and Evaluation, Washington, D.C.

_____. 1995b. "The Politics of Community Policing." *Public Administration Review* 191:6–26.

Carter, D.L., and A.D. Sapp. 1993. "A Comparative Analysis of Clauses in Police Collective Bargaining Agreements as Indicators of Change in Labor Relations." *American Journal of Police* 122:17–46.

Carter, D.L., A.D. Sapp, and D.W. Stephens. 1991. *Survey of Contemporary Police Issues: Critical Findings.* Washington, D.C.: Police Executive Research Forum.

Couper, D.C. 1991. *Quality Policing: The Madison Experience.* Washington, D.C.: Police Executive Research Forum.

Dolbeare, K.M., ed. 1975. *Public Policy Evaluation.* Beverly Hills, Calif.: Sage Publications.

Eck, J.E., and W. Spelman. 1987. *Problem-Solving: Problem-Oriented Policing in Newport News.* Washington, D.C.: Police Executive Research Forum.

Farmer, M. 1981. *Differential Police Response Strategies.* Washington, D.C.: Police Executive Research Forum.

Franklin, J.L., and J. Thrasher. 1976. *An Introduction to Program Evaluation.* New York: John Wiley and Sons.

Greene, J., and R. Worden. 1988. "Community-Based Policing and Foot Patrol: Issues of Theory and Evaluation." In J. Greene and S. Mastrofski, eds., *Community Policing: Rhetoric or Reality?* New York: Praeger Press.

Hartmann, F.X., L.P. Brown, and D.W. Stephens. 1989. *Community Policing: Would You Know It If You Saw It?* East Lansing, Mich.: National Center for Community Policing.

_____. 1976. *Program Analysis for State and Local Governments.* Washington, D.C.: Urban Institute Press.

Hatry, H.P., et al. 1981. *Practical Program Evaluation for State and Local Governments.* Washington, D.C.: Urban Institute Press.

Kansas City, Mo., Police Department. 1977. *Response Time Analysis: Executive Summary.* Kansas City: Board of Police Commissioners.

Katzer, J., et al. 1978. *Evaluating Information: A Guide for Users of Social Science Research.* Menlo Park, Calif.: Addison-Wesley Publishing Co.

Kelling, G.L., and Moore, M.H. 1988. "The Evolving Strategy of Policing." *Perspectives on Policing,* (4).

Kelling, G. 1981. *The Newark Foot Patrol Experiment.* Washington, D.C.: Police Foundation.

Kelling, G., et al. 1974. *The Kansas City Preventive Patrol Experiment: Technical Report.* Washington, D.C.: Police Foundation.

Kerlinger, F. 1973. *Foundations of Behavioral Research.* 2d ed. New York: Holt, Rinehart and Winston.

Larson, R.C., and M. Cahn. 1985. *Synthesizing and Extending the Results of Police Patrol Studies.* Washington, D.C.: National Institute of Justice.

Levine, M., and J.T. McEwen. 1985. *Patrol Deployment.* Washington, D.C.: National Institute of Justice.

McEwen, J.T., et al. 1969. *Evaluation of the Differential Police Response Field Test.* Washington, D.C.: National Institute of Justice.

Morris, L.L., and C. Fitz-Gibbon. 1978. *How to Deal With Goals and Objectives.* Beverly Hills, Calif.: Sage Publications.

Nagel, S.S., and M. Neef. 1975. *Operations Research Methods.* Beverly Hills, Calif.: Sage.

National Institute of Justice. 1991. *Evaluation Plan: 1991.* Washington, D.C.: U.S. Department of Justice.

President's Commission on Law Enforcement and Administration of Justice. 1967. *Task Force Report: The Police.* Washington, D.C.: U.S. Government Printing Office.

Radelet, L., and D.L. Carter. 1994. *The Police and the Community.* 5th ed. New York: Macmillan Publishing Co.

Skolnick, J., and D. Bailey. 1986. *The New Blue Line.* New York: The Free Press.

Spelman, W., and D. Brown. 1984. *Calling the Police: Citizen Reporting of Serious Crime.* Washington, D.C.: National Institute of Justice.

Spelman, W., and J. Eck. 1987 *Problem-Oriented Policing: The Newport News Experiment.* Washington, D.C.: Police Executive Research Forum.

Thierauf, R.J., and R.C. Klekamp. 1975. *Decision Making Through Operations Research.* 2d ed. New York: John Wiley and Sons.

Trojanowicz, R.C. 1990. "Community Policing Is Not Police-Community Relations." *FBI Law Enforcement Bulletin.* October:6–11.

Trojanowicz, R., and B. Bucqueroux. 1990. *Community Policing.* Cincinnati: Anderson Publishing Co.

Trojanowicz, R., and D.L. Carter. 1988. *The Philosophy and Role of Community Policing.* East Lansing, Mich.: National Center for Community Policing.

Weidman, D.R., et al. 1975. *Intensive Evaluation for Criminal Justice Planning Agencies.* Washington, D.C.: U.S. Department of Justice/Law Enforcement Assistance Administration.

Whitaker, G., et al. 1982. *Basic Issues in Police Performance.* Washington, D.C.: National Institute of Justice.

Whitmire, K., and L.P. Brown. Undated. *City of Houston Command Station/Neighborhood-Oriented Policing Overview.* Houston: Houston Police Department.

Wycoff, M.A., and T.N. Oettmeier. 1994. *Evaluating Police Officer Performance.* Washington, D.C.: National Institute of Justice.

Appendix A

Evaluation Ideas

The National Institute of Justice (NIJ) has established, as part of its research agenda, an evaluation plan that addresses approaches to program evaluations in NIJ-funded projects. Some of the points presented in the NIJ Evaluation Plan in general, as well as in its community policing evaluations in particular, may be insightful.

The following material is abstracted from National Institute of Justice. 1991. *Evaluation Plan: 1991.* Washington, D.C.: U.S. Department of Justice. Pp. 5–7.

Elements of an Evaluation Plan

No single method of evaluation is suited to all topics or goals. Thus, a comprehensive evaluation framework sets forth four types of research with methodologies of corresponding rigor and complexity.

- **Program assessments** answer the following: *What* are a program's salient features? Such assessments represent a critical analysis of both positive and negative attributes.
- **Impact evaluations** answer the following: *How* does a program affect crime? They are scientific studies of program operations and outcomes.
- **Intensive impact evaluations** answer the following: *Why* is a program effective? They are controlled experiments that may reveal specific causes and effects.
- **Evaluation reviews** answer the following: *What* did previous studies show, and what are the future directions?

Program assessments describe a program's strengths and weaknesses; they synthesize and measure the progress made in solving certain problems. They involve the critical examination of the elements of existing solutions and an assessment of their strengths and weaknesses. Extant data, field observations and available evaluation findings combine to inform expert judgment on the efficacy of various approaches and to develop recommendations for future programs in the topic area. In this way, program assessments are *descriptive* and *retrospective.*

Program assessments include

- assessment through extant data of recent attempts to solve the problem;
- isolation of key dimensions (e.g., effectiveness, fairness, cost control) of apparently successful programs;
- recommendations for program change and experimentation; and
- predicted impediments to implementing new solutions.

Impact evaluations describe how a program has impact; they are rigorous evaluations that provide compelling scientific evidence of program effectiveness and a thorough understanding of the processes critical to success. These evaluations typically occur in a later phase of development when goals can be specified clearly and program elements have evolved from lengthy experimentation.

Impact evaluations focus on *outcomes*. They usually examine similar programs at multiple sites and devote limited resources to understanding program structure and implementation. These evaluations develop broad descriptions of cross-site differences and experiences, discussing how sites compared.

Impact evaluations include

- sound scientific information on program effectiveness.;
- identification of mechanisms that link program activities to stated objectives;
- verified degrees of program implementation;
- assessment of program effectiveness in terms of multiple performance indexes;
- relationship of differences in site environments and implementation to differences in outcome;
- summary of findings across sites;
- identification of program development implications;
- rigorous design, with process and impact components;
- evidence on causal links between program activities and stated objectives; and
- findings extrapolated for national significance.

Field experiments, one way of conducting intensive impact evaluations, provide rigorous tests of new but promising solutions to important problems. Recent examples include NIJ programs on spouse abuse, market-based drug enforcement, and drug treatment with observed drug testing of participants. Field experiments are meant to provide solid empirical evidence of an approach's effectiveness, as well as guidance to practitioners on the structure of operational programs.

Field experiments include

- lengthy planning and design periods;
- involvement of the extended staff, the research community and the practitioner community in the design process;
- prior specification of all major research hypotheses;
- rigorous design and implementation plans;
- intensive collaboration between participating sites and evaluators in program implementation; and
- detailed reports on study methodology and findings.

Evaluation reviews examine topics where a number of evaluations are already complete but have never been synthesized for use by the criminal justice system. Evaluation reviews examine findings as objectively as possible, explain inconsistencies and suggest conclusions based on the evidence. Reviews generate original knowledge of program effectiveness or operations. They also distill and synthesize what has already been found in individual studies in an effort to form consensus.

Evaluation reviews include

- documented scope and extent of existing program activity and antecedent programs;
- assessment of the quality and credibility of prior research;
- identified limitations in existing evaluations, such as unique site circumstances or the scope of issues addressed;
- summary of knowledge of program practice and effectiveness; and
- recommendations for future research and program needs.

Communicating Evaluation Results

Evaluation is necessarily a time-consuming process, but the criminal justice community needs to know results as soon as they offer reliable direction for action.

Evaluation information must serve many needs. Legislators and governors want to know about successful policy initiatives. Justice system planners and managers want to understand the scope and level of effort required for innovative approaches. Practitioners and administrators want training in new approaches, as well as documentation that clearly explains how to adopt promising programs.

Sample Community Policing Program Goals, Objectives and Strategy (NIJ 1991:20–22)

Objectives

- Collect and analyze data on the implementation of innovative small-city and rural neighborhood-oriented policing projects and their elements.
- Collect and analyze data on the costs and value of innovative small-city and rural neighborhood-oriented policing projects and their elements.
- Prepare a comprehensive user-oriented report and executive summary of this evaluation for distribution to police departments, community groups and policy makers concerned with small-city and rural crime and drug abuse.

Program Strategy

Collect and analyze data on the implementation of innovative small-city and rural neighborhood-oriented policing projects and their elements.

To accomplish this objective, the grantee must collect data that will provide other jurisdictions with technical information to help them implement a similar neighborhood-oriented policing project. Special attention should be given to identifying the lessons learned at the various sites and the guidance those lessons can provide to other jurisdictions. The following questions suggest the kinds of information that will be useful:

- What was the neighborhood policing project's target population?
- When was the project initiated? What were the project goals and objectives and the project managers' expectations? What was the implementation plan and what problems were experienced in implementation? What lessons were learned? Were there unintended results?
- Was there an evaluation plan before the project was implemented? What was to be measured, and how were measurements made? What were the gauges of project success and failure? What gauges used for decision making were associated with project changes?
- Was there a management information system and/or a special information system associated with project implementation? How was the project to be organized into an effective and efficient operation?
- What was the context of the project in terms of geography, drug abuse and crime rate, police resources, community organizations, economic and social conditions, etc.?
- What kinds of police, community and joint police-community efforts constituted the project, and how did they operate?
- What were the project expenditures for police resources, community resources and other public agency resources? Were any funds from businesses or other private sources involved? What resources were accounted for by volunteers?
- How were the project resources organized in the community, the police department or other support agencies? What community organizations were involved? How were any organizational and personnel conflicts resolved?
- What were the attitudes of the police and the public and private sectors toward the project?

- What was the focus of project control and responsibility? What were the nature and extent of resource coordination and personnel interaction, of project monitoring and evaluation, of training provided for project personnel, and of management and organization skills?
- What technology was used for the project, and what was its cost?
- What other anti-drug or crime control efforts were made in the study setting in the past, and what were the results?
- How much did those results encourage or dampen support for the project? In addition, what other anti-drug or crime control strategies were operating in the study setting during the project (for example, police sweeps, citizen patrols, etc.)?

Collect and analyze data on the costs and value of innovative small-city and rural neighborhood-oriented policing projects and their elements.

To accomplish this objective, the grantee must collect data that provides management information for small-city and rural government officials and community leaders involved in funding decisions regarding community and police projects that relate to drug sales, drug abuse, drug-related crime, and all other crime.

The evaluation should distill the results of all projects to assess the effect of neighborhood-oriented policing on drugs and crime. Attention should be given to neighborhood-oriented policing's effects on community security as well as other quality-of-life issues. These issues include citizen mobilization and responsiveness to broader community problems, area economic viability, housing stability, neighborhood sense of order, and social problems such as alcohol abuse, truancy, etc. It should also be determined whether there is a general form of neighborhood-oriented policing that models the particularities of all projects.

The evaluation should also provide an assessment of neighborhood-oriented policing compared with other anti-drug and crime control strategies in small cities and rural areas. Widely accepted assessments of competing strategies should be used for this comparison. The assessment should focus on two separate comparisons involving (1) those factors relating to community safety and security, and (2) those broader factors relating to residents' quality of life. The evaluation should also compare the project's actual impacts with the expectations of the project managers and the initial community leaders and police personnel who conceived and planned the project.

A comprehensive user-oriented report and executive summary of this evaluation should be distributed to police departments, community groups and policy makers concerned with small-city and rural crime and drug abuse.

The report should include (1) a review and synthesis of the existing literature, (2) a description of each project evaluated, (3) a description of the evaluation design, (4) information on the costs and value of each project evaluated, (5) recommendations for program development, and (6) additional research needs. The executive summary should inform practitioners, policy makers and researchers of the project's results.

Appendix B

Conditions Under Which Controlled Experiments Are Most Likely to Be Appropriate

Abstracted from Hatry, H.P., et al. 1981. *Practical Program Evaluation for State and Local Governments*. Washington, D.C.: Urban Institute Press. P. 42.

1. There is likely to be a high degree of ambiguity as to whether the program caused the outcomes if some other evaluation design is used.

2. Some citizens can be given different services than others without significant danger or harm.

3. Some citizens can be given different services than others without violating moral or ethical standards.

4. There is substantial doubt about the program's effectiveness.

5. There are not enough resources to provide the program to all clients.

6. The risk in funding the program without a controlled experiment is likely to outweigh the cost of the experimentation because the program involves large costs and a lot of uncertainty.

7. The decision whether to implement the program can be postponed until an experiment is completed.

8. Experimental conditions can be maintained reasonably well during the experimental period.

9. The findings are likely to generally apply to a substantial proportion of the population of interest.

10. Sufficient staff and dollars are available to manage the experiment.

11. Client consent for participation in the experiment is not required or, if it is, can be obtained without invalidating the experiment.

12. The client's confidentiality and privacy can be adequately maintained.

Appendix C

Criteria for Selecting Issues for Program Evaluation

Abstracted from Hatry, H.P., et al. 1981. *Practical Program Evaluation for State and Local Governments.* Washington, D.C.: Urban Institute Press. Pp. 86–7.

Can the evaluation's results influence decisions about the program?

— Programs for which a decision regarding continuation, modification or termination should be made are obvious candidates.
— Poor candidates are those about which decision makers have strong preconceptions or for which there is considerable support by influential interest groups, if these circumstances make it very unlikely that the program would be altered. In some cases, however, the program may be so important to a community that government officials proceed with the evaluation and are prepared to seek changes, despite political risks.
— Can the evaluation be done in time to help decision makers? Evaluations completed after public officials commit to a decision are useless.
— Are sufficient data obtainable on important program effects? Program evaluations can never cover all effects, but before an evaluation is begun, it should be clear that it will be possible to gather meaningful data on significant aspects of the program.
— Can sufficient resources be obtained to meet the evaluation's time schedule and technical requirements?
— Is the program actually in place, and is it being implemented as originally planned? If not, an evaluation may not be appropriate.
— Has the program been stable enough for an evaluation to provide relevant information? A program that is constantly changing or about to change significantly is not a good candidate for evaluation.

Is the program significant enough to merit evaluation?

— Programs that involve a lot of government resources or that have important potential benefits or possible negative consequences for the public should be given higher priority. Thus, the evaluation's likely cost should be compared with the possible decreased cost or improved effectiveness that may result.

— Is program performance suspected of being marginal? If so, there may be opportunities to make major improvements or reduce costs. Relatively old programs that have not received an in-depth evaluation in a long time may fit this criterion.

— Is the program a new one whose potential benefits and costs are particularly uncertain? The program should be reviewed after operating long enough to show its effectiveness. This probably means a minimum of six months to one year of operation for most programs, though even these time periods are often too short for evaluating long-term effects. New programs are often more open to change because they have not yet gained a strong constituency.

— Programs that are candidates for expansion are particularly suitable for an evaluation.

Appendix D

Sample Research Instruments

The sample research instruments in this appendix are intended to serve as models. None of the instruments should be taken verbatim and used in either the department or community. Instead, they should be used as a foundation from which to borrow and amend questions to meet your jurisdiction's specific needs.

The two surveys from the National Center for Community Policing at Michigan State University—one for the community and one for the department—are examples of more complex survey instruments. They were used in a pretest/posttest time series study for the Aurora, Colo., Police Department.

The other instruments are obviously less formal and are useful for "feeling the pulse" in more informal evaluations.

The authors have amended all of the surveys so that they are more generic models.

This is an anonymous survey made for the Aurora Police Department. It is meant to determine Aurora citizens' concerns and views about their police department and how the police could best serve community needs. Because of the current economic situation— which affects all city services—the police chief wants to use police resources in a way that best serves the community's needs and desires. To do this, we must ask the community what it wants. *Your opinions are very important in this effort.*

The survey is being sent to a cross-section of the community. The National Center for Community Policing at Michigan State University will analyze the surveys. Your responses will remain completely confidential. Please return the survey in the enclosed envelope within the next week.

If you have any questions about this survey or project, feel free to call either 340-2207, Aurora Police Department, Community Services Bureau, or (toll free) 1-800-892-9051, Michigan State University, National Center for Community Policing, Dr. David Carter.

1. It is generally felt that patrolling police officers can discourage the following types of crimes. On which of the following would you like to see your police concentrate?

   How much *priority* should the police give to the following:

	Much Attention 1	2	Some Attention 3	4	Little Attention 5
Burglaries					[ ]
Property destruction					[ ]
Auto thefts					[ ]
Traffic law violations					[ ]
Robberies					[ ]
Prostitution					[ ]
Juvenile curfew violations					[ ]
Theft of car parts					[ ]
Loud parties					[ ]
Other (specify)_____					

2. Of the following crimes, which five do you think the police should make the most effort to solve? (Please check five items.)

Simple theft	[ ]
Assault and battery	[ ]
Credit card fraud	[ ]
Defrauding senior citizens	[ ]
Gambling	[ ]
Check forgery	[ ]
Auto theft	[ ]
Drug law violations	[ ]
Child neglect	[ ]

3. Which six of the following police services do you feel are most important?

Picking up found property	[ ]
Conducting home security checks for vacationers	[ ]
Helping people locked out of their cars	[ ]
Investigating of all vehicle accidents	[ ]
Conducting school truancy checks	[ ]
Conducting vehicle safety inspections	[ ]
Conducting security inspections of business buildings	[ ]
Teaching children pedestrian safety	[ ]
Checking on senior citizens	[ ]
Helping people locked out of their homes	[ ]
Helping stranded motorists	[ ]

4. If you observed a crime, which of the following would you do? (Check all that apply.)

Avoid involvement with the victim.   [   ]
Help the victim.   [   ]
Report suspicious activity.   [   ]
Avoid involvement with the police.   [   ]
Report the crime.   [   ]
Help the police.   [   ]
Testify in court.   [   ]

5. Keeping in mind that the *budget is limited,* please rank the importance of the following services (1 is the most important; 6 is the least important).

Motor vehicle patrols   [   ]
Foot patrols   [   ]
Crime investigations by detectives   [   ]
Crime prevention programs   [   ]
Police area representatives (PARs)   [   ]
Traffic enforcement   [   ]

6. For each of the following statements, check the degree of concern you have that the problem might happen in your neighborhood.

Very Concerned		Somewhat Concerned		Not Concerned
5	4	3	2	1

___Someone will try to rob or steal something from you.
___Someone will try to attack you while you are outside.
___Someone will try to break into your home.
___Someone will try to damage or steal your car.
___Someone will try to damage or vandalize your house or other property.
___Someone will try to sexually assault you while you are outside.

7. Indicate how often you walk/jog/ride a bicycle in your neighborhood by placing the most accurate number in each of the blanks.

Very Often		Occasionally		Never
5	4	3	2	1

___During the day
___In the evening
___Late at night

8. Do you participate in any community group or association?

   [   ] Yes—If yes, go to question 8a.
   [   ] No—If no, go to question 9.

8a. Check all the types of associations to which you belong:

   [   ] Neighborhood association
   [   ] Church
   [   ] Athletic group
   [   ] Civic group
   [   ] Community agency
   [   ] Other

9. Have you called the police to report a problem in the last two years?

   [   ] Yes—If yes, go to questions 9a–9d.
   [   ] No—If no, go to question 10.

9a. Circle the number that indicates how satisfied you were with how long it took the police to respond to your call.

Very Satisfied		Somewhat Satisfied		Not Satisfied
5	4	3	2	1

9b. How satisfied were you with how the police handled the problem?

Very Satisfied		Somewhat Satisfied		Not Satisfied
5	4	3	2	1

9c. Did the problem occur in your neighborhood?

   [   ] Yes
   [   ] No

9d. Were you the victim?

   [   ] Yes
   [   ] No

10. How important are the following problems in your neighborhood?

	Big Problem		Somewhat A Problem		Not A Problem
	5	4	3	2	1

___Appearance problems (for example, junk cars, trash, etc.)
___Parking/traffic
___Crime
___School-related problems
___Problems with neighbors
___Street/homeless people
___Noise
___Unsupervised juveniles
___Abandoned/run-down buildings
___Public intoxication
___Prostitution
___Drug use

11. How often do you do the following?

	Very Often		Occasionally		Never
	5	4	3	2	1

___Socialize in the neighborhood
___Worry about your children's safety
___Worry about other children's safety
___Enjoy entertainment/recreation

12. How serious a problem do you think crime is in your city compared with other large U.S. cities? (Circle a number.)

	Very Serious		About Average		Not Serious
	5	4	3	2	1

13. To what extent has fear of crime caused each of the following to change activities?

	To a Great Extent		To Some Extent		Not at All
	5	4	3	2	1

___You
___Others in your neighborhood
___People in general

14. Is your neighborhood dangerous enough that, during the last 12 months, you have considered moving?

[   ] Yes
[   ] No

15. In the United States as a whole, how do you think that personal safety is changing? (Circle a number.)

Increasing		Not Changing		Decreasing
5	4	3	2	1

16. How is safety in your neighborhood changing? (Circle a number.)

Increasing		Not Changing		Decreasing
5	4	3	2	1

17. In your neighborhood, how well do you think the police department performs its duties?

Very Well		Average		Very Poorly
5	4	3	2	1

___In general/overall
___Patrol officers
___Detectives

18. To what extent does your police department need improvement? (Circle one.)

To a Great Extent		To Some Extent		Not at All
5	4	3	2	1

19. How important is each of the following for improving your police department?

Very Important		Somewhat Important		Not Important
5	4	3	2	1

___Hiring more officers
___Having higher qualifications for new officers
___Improving officer training
___Responding to calls faster
___Improving relations with the community in general
___Improving relations with minority groups

20. How has local police performance changed in the past year? (Circle one.)

Improved		Stayed the Same		Worsened
5	4	3	2	1

21. To what extent do you think that police officers should do the following?

To a Great Extent		To Some Extent		Not at All
5	4	3	2	1

____Be accountable for professional behavior
____Concentrate major effort on crime prevention
____Be able to recognize neighborhood residents
____Teach residents to recognize and report suspicious activity
____Personally provide guidance to potential juvenile offenders
____Help residents increase their feelings of personal safety
____Work closely with schools and social agencies to deter crime
____Share problems and resources with community agencies
____Encourage more complete crime reporting by citizens

TO HELP OUR ANALYSIS, WE NEED TO KNOW SOMETHING ABOUT YOU.

22. How would you classify your work?

[   ] Professional (teacher, social worker, counselor, lawyer, etc.)
[   ] Clerical/technical
[   ] Blue-collar (factory worker, construction, laborer, etc.)
[   ] Homemaker
[   ] Currently unemployed
[   ] Retired
[   ] Other (part-time sales, small-business owner, etc.)

23. Do you work for the city government?

[   ] Yes
[   ] No

24. How long have you lived at your current address? _____years

25. Check one.

[   ] You own your home.
[   ] You rent.

26. How old are you? _____years

27. Check one.

[   ] Male
[   ] Female

28. What is your marital status?

[   ] Single
[   ] Married
[   ] Separated
[   ] Divorced
[   ] Widowed

29. How many children do you have (including those of whom you have guardianship)?

[   ] None   [   ] Three
[   ] One   [   ] Four
[   ] Two   [   ] Five or more

30. How many children live with you?

[   ] None   [   ] Three
[   ] One   [   ] Four
[   ] Two   [   ] Five or more

31. What is your education level?

[   ] Less than high school
[   ] High school diploma
[   ] Some college
[   ] Bachelor's degree
[   ] Graduate work

32. What is your racial/ethnic identity?

[   ] Asian
[   ] Black/African American
[   ] Caucasian/white
[   ] Hispanic
[   ] American Indian

PLEASE COMMENT ON ANY OF THE ISSUES ADDRESSED IN THIS SURVEY.

THANK YOU FOR YOUR COOPERATION.

Police Department
Officer/Employee Survey

This survey is to help in the planning and evaluation of the community policing program. Your responses will be completely confidential. All surveys will be retained by the National Center for Community Policing at Michigan State University.

1. What is your current assignment in the police department?

   [   ] Patrol
   [   ] Investigations
   [   ] Community police officer
   [   ] Sworn staff position (such as personnel, laboratory, etc.)
   [   ] Non-sworn/civilian
   [   ] Other

2. What is your rank?

   [   ] Patrol officer
   [   ] Sergeant
   [   ] Lieutenant
   [   ] Captain

3. What shift do you work?

   [   ] "Graveyard"
   [   ] Day
   [   ] Evening
   [   ] Swing

4. How long have you been employed by the police department? (Round your answer to the nearest whole year—use 00 for less than one year.)

   ___Years

5. How long have you worked in law enforcement all together? (Round your answer to the nearest whole year—use 00 for less than one year.)

   ___Years

6. After work, do you patronize businesses in your work area?

    [   ] None
    [   ] A few
    [   ] Many
    [   ] Your assignment does not have a defined "work area."

7. In a typical day, how much of your time is spent on each of the following activities? (Place an "X" in the blank if the activity does not apply to your work.)

Great Deal		Some		Very Little
5	4	3	2	1

    ___Patrolling, observing
    ___Checking out complaints
    ___Making security checks
    ___Enforcing traffic laws
    ___Conducting field interviews/investigations
    ___Initiating personal contact with citizens
    ___Initiating personal contact with businesses
    ___Counseling or referring families with juvenile problems
    ___Doing other follow-up on juvenile complaints
    ___Receiving complaints directly from citizens
    ___Counseling citizens on crime prevention
    ___Writing reports
    ___Appearing in court
    ___Investigating crimes
    ___Making contacts with other departments or agencies

8. If you had more time, what activity/ies would you engage in more often? (Place an "X" beside all that apply; if a statement does not apply to your current assignment, place "00" in the blank.)

    ___Patrolling, observing
    ___Checking out complaints
    ___Making security checks
    ___Enforcing traffic laws
    ___Conducting field interviews/investigations
    ___Initiating personal contact with citizens
    ___Initiating personal contact with businesses
    ___Counseling or referring families with juvenile problems
    ___Doing other follow-up on juvenile complaints
    ___Receiving complaints directly from citizens
    ___Counseling citizens on crime prevention
    ___Writing reports
    ___Appearing in court
    ___Investigating crimes
    ___Making contacts with other departments or agencies

PLEASE COMMENT ON ANY ASPECT OF THE SURVEY THUS FAR:

9. Which activity/ies would you do less often? (Place an "X" beside all that apply; if a statement does not apply to your current assignment, place "00" in the blank.)

___Patrolling, observing
___Checking out complaints
___Making security checks
___Enforcing traffic laws
___Conducting field interviews/investigations
___Initiating personal contact with citizens
___Initiating personal contact with businesses
___Counseling or referring families with juvenile problems
___Doing other follow-up on juvenile complaints
___Receiving complaints directly from citizens
___Counseling citizens on crime prevention
___Writing reports
___Appearing in court
___Investigating crimes
___Making contacts with other departments or agencies

10. When you think about your daily work activities, how important would you say each of the following kinds of training was in preparing you for your tasks?

Very Important		Somewhat Important		Not Important
5	4	3	2	1

___Recruit training academy for the department
___Police field training
___Specialized training programs (in-service training)
___College education
___Personal experience in police work
___Personal experience before entering police work
___Skills I picked up on my own

11. When you think about your daily work activities, how important would you say each of the following personal characteristics is in performing your tasks?

Very Important		Somewhat Important		Not Important
5	4	3	2	1

___Intelligence
___Efficiency
___Resourcefulness
___Courage
___Patience
___Good communications skills
___Flexibility
___Integrity
___Courtesy
___Friendliness
___Humanity

12. How adequate is the department's training in each of the following broad categories?

Very Adequate		Adequate		Not Adequate
5	4	3	2	1

___General police skills (e.g., firearms, driving, self-defense, report writing, etc.)
___Human relations skills (e.g., public relations, sensitivity, cooperation, etc.)
___Professional/career development (e.g., coping with stress, promotion, etc.)
___Other (specify)

13. Please rank the training areas in the order of their importance (1 = most important).

___General police skills (e.g., firearms, driving, self-defense, report writing, etc.)
___Human relations skills (e.g., public relations, sensitivity, cooperation, etc.)
___Professional/career development (e.g., coping with stress, promotion, etc.)
___Other (specify)

14. Please rank the training areas in which the police department does best (1 = most important).

___General police skills (e.g., firearms, driving, self-defense, report writing, etc.)
___Human relations skills (e.g., public relations, sensitivity, cooperation, etc.)
___Professional/career development (e.g., coping with stress, promotion, etc.)
___Other (specify)

**PATROL OFFICERS ONLY: ANSWER QUESTIONS 15–29.
NON-PATROL EMPLOYEES: GO TO QUESTION 30.**

15. In the patrol area assigned to you, how problematic are the following crimes?

Major Problem		Occasional Problem		Not A Problem
5	4	3	2	1

___Assault
___Sexual assault
___Burglary
___Theft (business or personal)
___Robbery
___Drug violations
___Vandalism
___Crimes against children
___Crimes against the elderly
___Crimes committed by juveniles
___Auto theft
___Community nuisances (e.g., trash, junk cars, transients, etc.)

16. In your patrol area, how safe do the residents feel doing the following:

Very Safe		Somewhat Safe		Not Safe
5	4	3	2	1

___Walking, jogging or riding a bicycle in the daytime
___Walking, jogging or riding a bicycle after dark
___Shopping in the neighborhood
___Participating in special neighborhood activities
___Participating in neighborhood sports
___Letting children play freely in the neighborhood

17. How would you evaluate residents' feelings of safety in your patrol area? (Check one.)

    [   ] Residents overestimate dangers.
    [   ] Residents' perceptions of danger are accurate.
    [   ] Residents underestimate dangers.

18. While working your assigned area, how safe do *you* feel doing the following?

Very Safe		Somewhat Safe		Not Safe
5	4	3	2	1

    ___Walking around the beat
    ___Entering buildings on the beat
    ___Answering complaints on the beat
    ___Helping victims on the beat
    ___Conducting field interviews on the beat

19. In your estimation, how do citizens' safety on your beat compare with the rest of the city? (Check one.)

    [   ] Safer here
    [   ] Same
    [   ] Less safe here

20. On your beat, how many of the people you see are familiar to you as being residents?

    [   ] None
    [   ] Fewer than one-third
    [   ] One-third to two-thirds
    [   ] More than two-thirds

21. Do residents "look out for one another" on your beat? (Circle one.)

Always		Often		Never
5	4	3	2	1

22. How active are the residents on your patrol beat with regard to the following?

Very Active		Somewhat Active		Not Active
5	4	3	2	1

    ___Reporting crime
    ___Helping victims
    ___Helping police
    ___Reporting suspicious activity
    ___Following police suggestions on safety

23. Is there a neighborhood association on your patrol beat?

[　] Yes, at least one—go to 23a.
[　] Yes, more than one—go to 23a.
[　] No—go to 24.
[　] Don't know—go to 24.

23a. If yes, to what extent does the association do the following:

To A Great Extent		To Some Extent		Not at All
5	4	3	2	1

___Help inform residents about crime prevention
___Cooperate with the police
___Support more complete crime reporting
___Encourage residents to report suspicious behavior
___Invite you to speak at their meetings
___Volunteer to help the police

24. To what extent does the work on your beat require you to contact the following?:

To A Great Extent		To Some Extent		Not at All
5	4	3	2	1

___Elementary schools
___Middle/junior high schools
___High schools
___Medical services
___Mental health services
___Programs for the elderly
___Drug or alcohol agencies
___Church groups
___Businesses
___Courts
___Youth organizations
___Other municipal agencies
___Other criminal justice agencies

25. How many contacts do you have with juveniles in an average week?

[　] One or less
[　] Two to five
[　] Six to 10
[　] 11 or more

26. What do you do if a resident complains to you about juvenile vandalism?

[   ] Acknowledge the complaint and monitor the area
[   ] Formally follow up on the complaint
[   ] Actively try to identify the juvenile
[   ] Refer the complaint to the juvenile/youth unit

27. Are there any community agencies you feel the department should work with more closely? (Check all that apply.)

[   ] Social services
[   ] Parks and recreation
[   ] Mental health
[   ] Youth services
[   ] Rape crisis center
[   ] Family violence organization
[   ] Substance abuse counseling organizations
[   ] Senior citizens organizations
[   ] Schools
[   ] Civic/service clubs
[   ] Salvation Army
[   ] Red Cross
[   ] Other (specify) _____

28. How long would you like to be assigned to a patrol beat?

[   ] Less than six months
[   ] Six to 12 months
[   ] One to three years
[   ] More than three years

29. Did you request the following?

a. Your current patrol assignment?

[   ] Yes
[   ] No

b. Your beat area?

[   ] Yes
[   ] No

c. Your shift?

[   ] Yes
[   ] No

**ALL EMPLOYEES: BEGIN ANSWERING QUESTIONS AGAIN,
STARTING WITH QUESTION 30.**

30. What do you plan to be your next career move?

[   ] Patrol work
[   ] Investigations
[   ] Staff assignment
[   ] Promotion
[   ] Leave the department for another law enforcement agency
[   ] Leave the department for a non-law enforcement career

31. How long do you expect to remain with the police department?
(Check the most appropriate response.)

[   ] Zero to five years
[   ] Five to 10 years
[   ] Ten to 20 years
[   ] More than 20 years
[   ] Only until retirement eligibility
[   ] As long as you can
[   ] Never thought about it

32. How does your current assignment affect your chances for a
desired career move?

[   ] Offers good chances
[   ] Offers average chances
[   ] Offers little chance
[   ] This is a dead-end job

33. To what extent do you encourage citizens to formally report
crime to the police? (Circle one.)

To A Great Extent		To Some Extent		Not at All
5	4	3	2	1

34. To what extent do you encourage citizens to formally report noncriminal matters to the police? (Circle one.)

To A Great Extent		To Some Extent		Not at All
5	4	3	2	1

**PLEASE COMMENT ON ANY ASPECT OF THE SURVEY
THUS FAR:**

35. Over the last few months, to what extent have you felt the following:

	To A Great Extent		To Some Extent		Not at All
	5	4	3	2	1

____You were doing an important job in the police department
____You were doing an important job on your patrol beat
____You were addressing true problems in your patrol beat
____You were using skills learned in police training
____You were improving police-community relations
____You were working as part of a police team
____You were cut off from main police activity
____You were having trouble being objective in your contact with people
____You were getting too closely involved with residents
____You were lacking other officers' support for your decisions
____You were lacking your supervisor's support for your decisions

36. To what extent do you agree that, ideally, police officers should do the following?

	To A Great Extent		To Some Extent		Not at All
	5	4	3	2	1

____Be accountable to other police officers for professional behavior
____Keep some distance between themselves and residents
____Maintain very close ties with other police officers
____Concentrate major efforts on crime prevention
____Be able to recognize area residents
____Try to teach residents to recognize and report suspicious activity
____Personally provide counseling/guidance to potential juvenile offenders
____Try to reassure residents by increasing their feelings of personal safety
____Coordinate closely with social service agencies to deter crime
____Coordinate closely with schools to deter crime
____Share problems and resources with community agencies
____Conduct community safety classes to help citizens
____Encourage more complete crime reporting by citizens
____Recognize victims' needs

37. How important is each of the following to you?

	Very Important 5	4	Somewhat Important 3	2	Not Important 1

____Maintaining order
____Enforcing the law
____Maintaining public acceptance of the police
____Helping crime victims
____Preventing crime
____Getting promoted
____Increasing personal skills
____Discussing problems with colleagues
____Moving to administrative work
____Avoiding trouble
____Helping fellow officers in follow-up investigations
____Staying on the street

38. How enthusiastic are you about your position in the police department today, compared with when you first entered the department?

[   ] More enthusiastic
[   ] About the same
[   ] Less enthusiastic

39. How do you view law enforcement as an occupation?

[   ] It is a profession.
[   ] It is a skilled trade.
[   ] It is just a job.

40. How important to you is the opinion of each of the following?

	Very Important 5	4	Somewhat Important 3	2	Not Important 1

____Acquaintances outside of the police department
____Colleagues in the department
____Residents in your city
____Residents in your patrol area
____The law enforcement community in general

41. If you could start all over, would you reenter police work?

    [   ] Definitely
    [   ] Probably
    [   ] Probably not
    [   ] Definitely not

BACKGROUND INFORMATION ON YOU WILL HELP US IN OUR ANALYSIS—ALL INFORMATION WILL BE CONFIDENTIAL AND WILL BE REPORTED ONLY IN THE AGGREGATE, NOT INDIVIDUALLY.

42. What is your age group?

    [   ] 20–25
    [   ] 26–30
    [   ] 31–35
    [   ] 36–40
    [   ] 41 or over

43. Check one.

    [   ] Male
    [   ] Female

44. What is your marital status?

    [   ] Single
    [   ] Married
    [   ] Divorced or separated
    [   ] Widowed

45. Enter the number.

    ___Number of children you have (including those of whom you
       have guardianship)
    ___Number of children living in your household

46. What is your racial/ethnic identity?

    [   ] Asian
    [   ] Black/African American
    [   ] Caucasian/white
    [   ] Hispanic
    [   ] American Indian

47. Enter the number of years of military experience you have.

    ___Years

48. What is your education level?

[   ] Less than high school
[   ] High school diploma
[   ] Some college
[   ] Bachelor's degree
[   ] Graduate work

49. In what type of area did you grow up?

[   ] Rural area
[   ] Small town
[   ] Suburb
[   ] City

PLEASE COMMENT ON ANY ASPECT OF THE TOPICS IN THIS SURVEY.

THANK YOU FOR YOUR COOPERATION.

Madison, Wis., Police Department
Customer Survey

The Madison Police Department would like to do a better job serving you and others. You have been selected to help us. Please take a few minutes of your time to fill out this questionnaire. If you wish to make additional comments, feel free to do so on the back of the questionnaire.

David C. Couper
Chief of Police

1. How many contacts have you had with the police department in the last 12 months?

    [   ] One
    [   ] Two
    [   ] Three or more

2. What was the nature of the contact(s)? (Check all that apply.)

    [   ] I called the department to report an incident.
    [   ] I was a victim of a crime.
    [   ] I witnessed an incident or crime.
    [   ] I was involved in a motor vehicle accident.
    [   ] I requested information from the department.
    [   ] I was arrested.
    [   ] I received a traffic ticket.
    [   ] Other (specify)

3. How would you rate us on each of the following? (Check the appropriate box for each item.)

	Excellent 5	Good 4	Average 3	Fair 2	Poor 1

    [   ] Concern
    [   ] Helpfulness
    [   ] Knowledge
    [   ] Quality of service
    [   ] Solving the problem
    [   ] Putting you at ease
    [   ] Professional conduct

4. How can we improve? (Please write your comments on the back.)

5. To help us analyze this survey, we need some information about you. All information is anonymous.

5a. Sex
    [   ] Male
    [   ] Female

5b. Race/Ethnic Identity
    [   ] White
    [   ] Black
    [   ] Hispanic
    [   ] Other

5c. Age Group
    [   ] Under 17 years
    [   ] 18 to 20 years
    [   ] 21 to 24 years
    [   ] 25 to 39 years
    [   ] 40 or over

5d. Family Income
    [   ] Under $5,000
    [   ] $5,001 to $13,000
    [   ] $13,001 to $20,000
    [   ] $20,001 to $35,000
    [   ] $35,001 or over

5e. Where do you live?
    [   ] In the city of Madison
    [   ] Other

**THANK YOU FOR TAKING THE TIME TO FILL OUT THIS
SURVEY.**

National Crime Prevention Council
Police Service Planning Questionnaire for Citizens

1. In general, would you say that in the last year your neighborhood has become a better place to live, a worse place to live, or has stayed about the same?

   [   ] Better
   [   ] Worse
   [   ] Same

2. The following are neighborhood problems people often mention. Please rate how problematic each is in your neighborhood.

	Big Problem 1	Somewhat A Problem 2	Little Problem 3	Don't Know 4

   ___Shopping facilities
   ___Crime
   ___Schools
   ___Noise
   ___Trash
   ___Traffic
   ___Kinds of residents
   ___Abandoned/rundown buildings
   ___Vandalism/graffiti
   ___Unsupervised kids

3. To what extent do you agree or disagree with this statement: "There is little that my neighbors and I can do to solve problems in this neighborhood."

   [   ] Strongly agree
   [   ] Agree
   [   ] Disagree
   [   ] Strongly disagree

4. What kinds of community groups are you active in? (Check all that apply.)

   [   ] Church
   [   ] Fraternal
   [   ] Service club
   [   ] Social club
   [   ] Political
   [   ] School
   [   ] Block/neighborhood association
   [   ] Sports
   [   ] Youth programs

5. How do you feel about going out for meetings at night?

Walking . . .

[   ] Very safe
[   ] Pretty safe
[   ] Somewhat unsafe
[   ] Very unsafe
[   ] Don't go

Driving . . .

[   ] Very safe
[   ] Pretty safe
[   ] Somewhat unsafe
[   ] Very unsafe
[   ] Don't go

6. How often do you and your neighbors get together . . .

. . . for social events?

[   ] Often
[   ] Sometimes
[   ] Occasionally
[   ] Rarely/never

. . . for community-needs discussions/meetings?

[   ] Often
[   ] Sometimes
[   ] Occasionally
[   ] Rarely/never

Here are some contrasting ways to describe your neighborhood.
Please pick the alternative that is closest to how you feel:

7. [   ] My neighborhood is a real home.
        OR
   [   ] My neighborhood is just a place to live.

8. [   ] People help each other.
        OR
   [   ] People go their own way.

9. [   ] It is easy to tell a stranger from a resident.
        OR
   [   ] It is hard to tell who's a stranger.

10. If you really wanted to get something done for the neighborhood, whom would you ask for help—and why?

11. How many people in your neighborhood can you ask for a small favor (such as giving you a ride to the store if they are already going there, or picking up your mail while you are away)?

    ___People

12. How do you find out about neighborhood news? (Check all that apply.)

    [   ] School newsletters/announcements
    [   ] Television
    [   ] Metropolitan newspaper
    [   ] Community/neighborhood newspaper
    [   ] Radio
    [   ] Neighbors call you or chat
    [   ] Family/friends
    [   ] Self (your own observations)
    [   ] Other (specify)

PLEASE FEEL FREE TO COMMENT ON ANY ISSUES RAISED IN THIS SURVEY.

National Crime Prevention Council
Neighborhood Check-Up Survey
For Citizens

1. In general, would you say that in the last year your neighborhood has become a better place to live, a worse place to live, or has stayed about the same?

    [　] Better
    [　] Worse
    [　] Same

2. In general, do you think this area will be better, worse, or about the same a year from now?

    [　] Better
    [　] Worse
    [　] Same

3. Please rate each of the following statements:

	Mostly True 1	Mostly False 2	Don't Know 3

    ___If I were sick, I could count on a neighbor to run an errand for me.
    ___If I have to be away from home a day or two, I know a neighbor who will watch my place.
    ___There is very little my neighbors and I can do to change things around here.
    ___Crime in my neighborhood is more of a problem than in other nearby areas.
    ___If I had to borrow $25 in a real emergency, I could turn to someone in this neighborhood (not family).
    ___My neighbors and I don't talk about community problems and how to solve them.

4. Have you heard of community group meetings to discuss local problems?

    [　] Yes—go to 4a.
    [　] Vaguely recall some—go to 4a.
    [　] Not at all—go to 5.

4a. If yes or vaguely recall some, did you ever attend a meeting?

    [　] Yes
    [　] No

5. The following are neighborhood problems people often mention. Please rate how problematic each is compared to a year ago.

	Big Problem 1	Somewhat A Problem 2	Little Problem 3	Don't Know 4

___Shopping facilities
___Crime
___Schools
___Noise
___Trash
___Traffic
___Kinds of residents
___Abandoned/rundown buildings
___Vandalism/graffiti
___Unsupervised kids

PLEASE FEEL FREE TO COMMENT ON ANY ISSUES RAISED IN THIS SURVEY.

National Crime Prevention Council
Crime Victims

1. In the past year have *you* been the victim of any crime?

   [   ] Yes
   [   ] No
   [   ] Unsure

2. If yes, did you report the incident to the police?

   [   ] Yes
   [   ] No

3. How safe at night do you feel being outside in your neighborhood?

   [   ] Very safe
   [   ] Somewhat safe
   [   ] Somewhat unsafe
   [   ] Very unsafe

4. In the last year, do you feel that crime has increased, decreased, or stayed about the same?

   [   ] Increased
   [   ] Decreased
   [   ] Stayed about the same

5. For each of the following statements, check the degree of concern you have that the problem might happen in your neighborhood?

	Very Concerned 1	Somewhat Concerned 2	Not Concerned 3

   ____Someone will try to rob or steal something from you.
   ____Someone will try to attack you while you are outside.
   ____Someone will try to break into your home.
   ____Someone will try to damage or steal your car.
   ____Someone will try to damage or vandalize your house or other property.
   ____Someone will try to sexually assault you while you are outside.

PLEASE FEEL FREE TO COMMENT ON ANY ISSUES RAISED IN THIS SURVEY.

National Crime Prevention Council
Crime Prevention Programs

1. Have you heard of _____ (name of local program)?

    [   ] Yes—go to 1a.
    [   ] No—go to 2.
    [   ] Don't recall—go to 2.

    1a. If yes, have you attended a program meeting or activity?

    [   ] Yes
    [   ] No
    [   ] Don't recall

2. Please answer the following statements about crime prevention activities in the past year.

	Yes	No	Previously Done So	Don't Recall
	1	2	3	4

    ___You had a security system installed in your home or you upgraded door and window locks.
    ___You had better outdoor lighting installed.
    ___You used a timer to turn indoor lights on and off.
    ___You marked valuables with an identification number.
    ___You watched a neighbor's house while he or she was away.
    ___You reported suspicious neighborhood activity to the police.
    ___You served as an officer in a neighborhood or business watch program.
    ___You participated in a community cleanup or other improvement.
    ___You helped someone who was victimized.
    ___You participated in a community program to help protect children.

PLEASE FEEL FREE TO COMMENT ON ANY ISSUES RAISED IN THIS SURVEY.

Chapter 4

Proactive Investigations Evaluation

Clifford L. Karchmer
John E. Eck

Proactive Investigations

The complex mix of crime problems the police are expected to control continues to increase. One important consequence is that police are expected to take the initiative and seek out both offenders and offenses. In sharp contrast to the traditional police strategy of waiting for people to report offenses, police are increasingly going undercover as victims or criminal entrepreneurs to snare certain kinds of offenders. Where the traditional mode of victim- and informant-initiated response is known as *reactive*, the alternative of police-initiated investigation is the reverse: *proactive*. As the following discussion notes, this term is short on thoughtful definition and long on diverse and uncritical local interpretation.

Issues of integrity and responsiveness have dramatically increased the professionalism with which proactive investigations have been conducted. Ironically, there has been lagging attention to the question of defining this response mode in an evolving enforcement environment, and to the more important question of whether proactive enforcement is having the desired impact on targeted crimes. This chapter explores both issues and closes by offering some operational questions that departments can ask to assess the impact of various proactive strategies.

The issue of determining the effect of proactive strategies falls squarely in the broad category of evaluation. However, both the departmental needs for short-term feedback (to adjust strategies) and the availability of data for use in rigorous evaluations force the authors to qualify what is reasonable to expect. Therefore, this chapter will focus on gathering readily available data and analyzing it in an objective framework. In the following pages, issues of definition and research design will be discussed in tandem with available and accessible information—much of it broadly termed *intelligence*—that can be used to determine the effect of specific enforcement strategies.

Looking Critically at Proactive Policing

Enforcement agencies increasingly rely on proactive strategies to target crimes that are *predictable* in some way. This predictability is usually reflected in some attribute(s) that police can exploit to obtain intelligence or other (e.g., crime analysis) information in order to intervene independent of a complaining victim or other citizen. The character of proactive strategies is determined by the particular crime problem's salient attributes and the operational context in which the police have defined them—e.g., according to the *market organization* of activities (e.g., fencing, hijacking); the *geographic organization* of locations (e.g., decoys, stakeout squads); and—perhaps most important—the *criminal organization* of offenders (e.g., drug trafficking, gang violence).

The last time the reader probably heard mention of the term *proactive* was in a recommendation that the department be more so. The problems for which the proactive mode is the ready solution vary considerably, from drug trafficking, stolen car rings and gang violence, to burglary and robbery. Although the concept has rarely been subjected to the kind of rigorous analysis that it will be in this chapter, it describes police-initiated actions where officers serve as the complainants in the absence of readily available victims. In its most commonly used sense, proactive enforcement is the preferred intervention against so-called victimless crimes, where citizens who seek illegal goods or services help create a market that would go uninterrupted, were the police not determined to gather information on such wrongdoing and serve as the formal complainant.

There is nothing inherently effective or ineffective, good or bad, right or wrong, about proactive enforcement. Simply put, it is a strategy born of necessity, where in order to uncover violations, police seek them out and assume the role normally occupied by the citizen-victim. One might think this active search for violations is a less-than-ideal response. But usually, it is the only feasible response that police can mount against crime problems with unknown dimensions but known political volatility.

The markets, transactions and customers involved in profit-motivated crime are necessarily secret. The task confronting police in trying to act against narcotic, vice and other crimes is to attack the markets and servicing organizations by identifying and acting against *offenders*—often approaching their activities piecemeal, arresting them one by one. Thus, the police attack them at their most visible levels, even though they may work in large organizations.

Although structured information-gathering processes, such as intelligence collection and analysis, serve other strategy development processes well, police agency commitment to such drawn-out formal processes is more the exception than the rule. As a consequence, police have difficulty moving from understanding the complexity of a problem to taking carefully developed and effective actions against it. Although police may appreciate the interdependence of the organizers, managers, manufacturers, wholesalers, and retailers of illegal goods and services, it is difficult to translate that understanding into strategies. All too often, the rigorous demands of gathering complete information about basically hidden crimes makes asking the broader questions about market size, structure and leadership a luxury the police cannot afford. Simply put, police may feel that they do not have the resources—time, staffing and equipment—to pay for the information and analysis that help to shape strategies.

Even if the police have close to perfect knowledge about the dynamics of a local cocaine market, do they have the staffing and other resources to eliminate both the market and the criminal leaders who serve it? Probably not. Consequently, some of the most important questions—regarding market size, who is involved in the market, and how the market and offenders are organized—are never asked. But if they are not asked, how can police hope to measure the impact of their undercover and other investigative techniques against the problem?

The problem of large illegal marketplaces and how to measure their dimensions does not absolve police of the responsibility to account for the resources they expend in this area, or to discontinue enforcement operations that are having no effect. Quite the contrary, the void that has developed around the understanding of profit-motivated crime has been filled with hastily conceived, well-intended, but potentially misleading measures—numbers of arrests, volume of contraband seized, numbers of "kingpins" caught and sent to prison. Because it is difficult for police to measure the impact of a raid or long-term enforcement campaign against an illegal market, the typical response is to proclaim results, and occasionally, to declare victory. Having no benchmark against which to measure such claims, the frightened public often accepts them without question. This chapter is about analyzing those claims in an objective, constructive way, so that police can be directed toward more effective strategies and use the results of such analyses to build their credibility with citizens.

In sum, the purpose of using the proactive mode of policing is to combat a crime problem about which there are no complainants, or there are so few that police actions based on them would leave the problem virtually untouched. In discussing proactive enforcement, it is important to address two central concerns that have become perennial issues in this field: *selectivity* and *impact*. Ironically, very little is known about these issues, and using proactive strategies to influence them may not go the full distance in solving the problem. Therefore, the discussion moves to the central problem of definition— actually, operational definition—so that the reader may understand proactive enforcement well enough to evaluate its results.

Moving From Definition to Evaluation

For reasons noted above, police executives have paid limited attention to maximizing proactive enforcement's effectiveness in their departments. The most distinguishing factor about proactive enforcement is that police initiate action, serving as the complainant. As noted, police serve as the complainant because the crimes in question leave too few unhappy customers to complain, or victims do not realize they have been victimized, such as in some frauds. If they do realize they have been victimized, they are often too embarrassed to report the offense. In other cases, e.g., extortion, victims may fear retaliation and be too scared to complain. These factors all contribute to a problem: the inability to measure the magnitude of the crimes.

A closer look at what police mean by the term *proactive enforcement* reveals some common factors present in most operational contexts. The most important is the "iceberg" quality of crime problems that become subjects of proactive efforts. This means that such vital dimensions of a problem as its incidence, level of organization and service delivery structure are, at best, only partially known and thus subject to wide disagreement. Therefore, one of the first accurate statements that can be made about proactive enforcement is that police truly know little about the crime problems that end up as subjects of it. Obviously, it is difficult to measure the impact of proactive efforts when the size of the problem remains unknown.

What *proactive* means depends on the context in which it is used. Within police agencies, the exact meaning may depend on the type of crime problem that happens to be under consideration and for which proactive enforcement is thought appropriate. For example, an agency may be under a general charge to develop a proactive response, otherwise undefined, against an influx of new gangs. In another context, possibly in the same department but at another time, the term's meaning may be much more specific, for example, using decoy officers to identify and arrest a serial rapist plaguing a small area. The point here is that lack of a standard definition of the term, coupled with colloquial meanings that shift from one context to another, make its use in an analytic framework somewhat difficult.

In an effort to understand how police "operationalize" the term—i.e., connect their special meanings to particular enforcement situations—the discussion turns to the kinds of crime problems that have become subjects of proactive enforcement.

Parameters of Proactive Law Enforcement

Although very few field studies have addressed proactive enforcement, a number of researchers have written on the general topic of proactive policing, especially from the viewpoint of how frustrating it can be to try to measure the impact of police responses

to selected problems (see Reiss and Bordua 1967; Skolnick 1966).
The bulk of literature is found on the topic of enforcement responses
that address a variety of consensual and sophisticated crimes (see, e.g.,
Goldstein 1977; Sherman 1974; and Reuter 1983, 1989). In spite of
researchers' calls to evaluate the alternative responses they
recommend, there have been surprisingly few efforts to implement
those responses.

The literature on proactive enforcement began to develop around
the time of the President's Crime Commission, which was created in
1965 and lasted until publication of its set of landmark reports in
1967. Some of the interest in proactive enforcement (e.g., Skolnick
1966) appeared to stem from the same concerns for propriety and
effectiveness that gave rise to the need for a presidential commission.
The real proliferation in literature followed by a few years the creation
of the Law Enforcement Assistance Administration (LEAA), with its
early and ongoing investment in organized crime, drug enforcement
and other so-called "sophisticated crime" demonstration projects.
However, that literature was largely prescriptive—certainly in keeping
with the LEAA mission to identify and subsidize alternative courses of
action.

The literature reached its apex in LEAA's later years, when all the
money channeled into the enforcement of sophisticated crime raised
the legitimate question of whether that enforcement had much of an
impact. Those concerns produced some provocative experimental
designs (see, for example, Overly and Schell 1972), as well as
interesting sections in otherwise prescriptive enforcement manuals (see
Walsh 1976; Karchmer, Walsh and Greenfield 1980; and Edelhertz et
al. 1977), but virtually no evaluations, unfortunately. It is unclear
whether this was due to the lack of data to complement the generally
lofty evaluation designs, or simply the lack of attention that LEAA
paid to this issue when it was fighting a losing battle for its survival.
As a result, the literature on proactive policing is limited to a fairly
narrow prescriptive treatment of the design and implementation of
proactive responses to particular crime problems—and not whether
the responses are either well-suited to those problems or susceptible to
routine measurement.

Building on Existing Research

The above discussion identified some problems in prior efforts to
address the measurement of proactive enforcement responses. To put
that discussion in perspective and use it as a foundation to frame some
reasonable evaluations, it is important to note that the bulk of the
writing on proactive enforcement has focused on the *retail* provision
of such goods and services as gambling, sex, liquor, and drugs. This
may well be the result of the ease with which researchers found they
could compare visible police responses in observable street situations

with public pressures for police to "do more" about illicit marketing of such goods and services.

The police incentive to enforce laws dealing with such behavior often stems from concern for media or political criticism of the *openness* of the illicit trade. Therefore, most proactive enforcement efforts try to force the *retailers* to ply their trade or sell their wares other than in plain view, or to give the impression that the police are sincerely trying to "control" such activities. In short, most forms of proactive vice enforcement are concerned primarily with street-level retailers and characteristics—such as customer access, harassment of visitors and open visibility—that police actions can readily influence.

Less frequent are critical analyses of the economic foundations, internal dynamics and management structures of criminal organizations. Rather, the results of those studies have been published as prescriptive manuals focusing on strategies to attack the "behind the scenes" offenders who manage such activities as drug trafficking, white-collar and organized crime, and other sophisticated crime operations (e.g., "fencing" and arson-for-profit).

The term *organized criminal* applies broadly to the criminal entrepreneurs who organize and manage illicit enterprises, and who are removed spatially or organizationally from street-level commerce. Targets of proactive police enforcement efforts aimed at organized crime include managers of gambling, loan sharking and drug distribution, and others whose levels of stealth and organization have placed them under the rubric of organized crime: e.g., receivers of stolen goods (fences) and public officials whose integrity is tested through Abscam-like sting operations.

In terms of the public threat and overall enforcement problems posed by a criminal enterprise, the degree of a group's organization is not as important as the presence of managerial entrepreneurs and individuals who serve in support capacities to them. That is, whether the criminals are organized in a complex hierarchy with many fixed roles and responsibilities is not as important as the functions that various criminals perform and their level of sophistication both in performing the functions and evading police detection.   Critical support personnel include tipsters, touts and brokers, who create networks that range from very small to very large and that nurture and sustain the illicit organizations. Entrepreneurs and support personnel should be of primary concern to law enforcement, because the former are preoccupied with breaking into new markets, and the latter shield criminal enterprises from a variety of hazards, such as police, competitors and thieves. Accordingly, enforcement strategies should be developed around the probable existence, and entrenchment, of these specialists. Perhaps ironically, proactive strategies that target illegal operations in this comprehensive way are the exception, rather than the rule.

Police either seem unconcerned that their output measures address the activities of entrepreneurs and support specialists, or are simply unable to think up responsive measures. To appreciate why this is the case, it is necessary to examine the peculiarities of the traditional system for measuring police activities against such criminals.

Proactive Strategies That Address Less-Organized Crime Problems

At this point, it may be helpful to explain the organizational dimension of enforcement problems for which proactive strategies are deemed appropriate. The preceding discussion and examples have focused on illegality that is organized to some degree—illicit markets of one form or another—which attracts police attention because of its degree of organization and leadership structure. There are other crime problems that are not necessarily characterized by high degrees of organization—or, for that matter, any noticeable degree of organization—and   for   which   proactive   interventions   are   a recommended response.

Robbery and burglary are two traditional crime problems with dimensions that have shown some susceptibility under either experimental or demonstration program conditions (Schack et al. 1977).   A number of other police efforts have targeted career criminals, termed so according to criteria such as prior arrest records (Pate et al. 1976).   Special police units, such as repeat offender squads, target robbers and burglars according to a variety of criteria, including locations where such offenders hang out or that fit a profile of favored crime sites (Bowers and McCullough 1982; Martin 1985). They also conduct surveillance and investigation of key support personnel—such as fences—who help create the market that the offenders feed (Bowers and McCullough 1982; Walsh 1977).

The point is that police may initiate enforcement action in a number of ways that satisfy the working definition of proactive enforcement.   One popular way is for police to serve as decoys— potential victims—in high-crime areas (Halper and Ku 1975). Another is for police to work undercover as fences seeking out new clients. Although the market for stolen goods may be specialized and highly structured in many communities, here the focus is not on the degree of organization, but rather, on the removal of as many thieves as possible from that marketplace. However, it should be noted that the popularity of the "sting" approach is not without its critics, who argue that police may unwittingly be alerting thieves to be more cautious and not stray from well-known fences (Walsh 1976, 1977). According to that argument, it should be much more productive to target fences than thieves.

In designing and evaluating proactive strategies, it is important to keep in mind that although many proactive street crime operations target offenders who work in some type of organizational network, the loose clusters of offenders often are "organizations" in name only. Frequently, their organizational affiliation lasts for the venture or score only, although some offenders may soon work together in the next caper.   The challenge to those designing better proactive strategies is to determine whether the intervention will have an impact on the targeted crime problem—whether organized or unorganized—all the while considering the level of organization as perhaps one of several central variables.

The Need for Realistic Impact Measures

There has been a lot of discussion of the value of clearance rates and arrest quotas as measures of police output (Skolnick 1966; Wilson 1968).   This concern has more recently been defined as one of productivity, where maximizing outputs is stressed, with inputs remaining roughly constant (Heaphy and Wolfle 1975).   Assessments of patrol productivity include measures such as average departmentwide response time to calls for service.   Programs to increase detectives' productivity focus on adopting screening criteria to choose cases that conform to a formula of "solvability factors" (Eck 1983).

Several innovative projects have been implemented that are designed to increase the productivity of a patrol or detective function. For example, patrol sector configurations have been redesigned, and workload has been shifted by reallocating officers to peak periods according to an objective hierarchy of public safety objectives (Larson 1972).   In more and more departments, the general detective function has been redefined so that patrol officers and detectives work together as teams, thus lessening competition between the two branches (Bloch 1976).   In both cases cited above, staffing and equipment inputs remained constant or were increased only slightly, while output improved substantially.   In both cases, information technology was at the heart of the demonstration effort.   It was developed to the point where its application enabled administrators to reallocate staff and equipment more efficiently, and with quantifiable results.

Productivity concerns about proactive enforcement must be addressed in a special way.   Because the actual volume of illicit consensual transactions is unknown, data on police productivity cannot be contrasted against a set of known or even assumed incidents.   Arrest quotas for both specialized units and individual officers are set so that the aggregate number of arrests can be publicized to document police concern for a problem, such as prostitution, and increases over time in those statistics can be taken as a measure of increased police resolve to address the problem. However, while arrest rates can serve as reliable indicators of reactive patrol and detective productivity, arrests made as part of proactive investigations of unreported offenses cannot.   Since the size of the crime problems cannot be measured independent of police actions (i.e., enforcement), the number of arrests can be increased at will, limited only by the resources available.   Doubling the number of investigators enforcing prostitution laws, for example, may double arrests but still have no impact on the size of the problem. Under these conditions, police managers often set arrest quotas. But achieving or exceeding the arbitrarily set quota is not evidence of greater effectiveness, but only of greater activity. Indeed, if doubling the activity still has no impact on the problem, this is tantamount to doubling the waste of resources.

Improving the productivity of proactive enforcement directed at the street and managerial levels of criminal enterprise is difficult. Again, it requires a separate analysis of the factors that govern productivity in this mode of enforcement. The problem is the ineffectiveness of arrest as a means to reduce vice activity and corruption.

To understand this productivity concern, it should be noted that the actual objective of vice control is not the stated objective of eradication, but rather, of regulation. This may be viewed as a corollary to the statement that "the role of the police is not enforcement of the law but the regulation of criminal activities" (Whyte 1955). Realistically, police concern is not so much with the *existence* of illegal transactions among consenting parties, but rather, with the *visibility* of such transactions. Arrests serve to let criminals know that the police expect them to conduct their business outside of public view, and to let the public know that the police are making a good-faith effort to reduce vice. The realistic police administrator realizes that an effective proactive strategy against vice is one that forces criminals to provide services and contraband discreetly. There is little indication that street-level proactive efforts are concerned with reducing entrepreneurship or profitability. Therefore, at best, the arrests made to meet quotas have a symbolic effect on people's perception of the problem, rather than an instrumental impact on it.

The low productivity of street-level proactive enforcement has also been attributed to corruption. Presumably, police who have been compromised care little about the public or private availability of vice services. Although corruption is an extremely serious problem with respect to proactive enforcement, it may be so not so much because it reduces police capabilities to control vice, but because it causes other serious problems. These include creation of an alternative and illegitimate incentive system, lowered morale among honest officers, and a perception of overall reduced effectiveness to perform the entire range of police functions (Burnham 1976; Goldstein 1977). It is widely believed that corruption related to proactive enforcement is endemic, given the bureaucratic need to resolve conflicting demands for prohibition and tolerance, and further, that such corruption is an expected cost of trying to control uncontrollable behavior by invoking impractical laws (Rubinstein 1973; Skolnick 1966). So long as arrests are ineffective for controlling criminal behavior, police will be open to bribes to refrain from using a sanction that is of marginal value to them anyway.

A closer look at police effectiveness suggests that corruption is not necessarily the only culprit in granting criminals a virtual license to operate. Far more prevalent—and arguably, just as serious—is the police practice of granting a degree of *de facto* immunity to criminal informants. What this means is that the police agree not to interfere in the activity of the drug dealer or burglar who "cooperates" with them by turning in higher-level operators (or perhaps competitors). In this case, the police capacity to sanction that criminal is not neutralized by a bribe, but rather, by a system of trading information for immunity from arrest or other police interference. Arguably, the result is close to the same: that criminal stands to become a greater menace to the community because the police protect his activities. Clearly, any departmental effort to upgrade the impact of proactive enforcement through evaluation must analyze how police "pay" for the information they receive, and whether they are paying too high a price.

Research Issues in Studying Illegal Operations

As a rule, criminal enterprises are organized much like legitimate ones. After all, the objectives of thieves, gamblers and most other economically motivated criminals are to control the "inputs" (labor, raw materials) that combine to produce their illegal good or service; to minimize environmental risks that threaten their profits; and to maximize profits. The issue of risks—at least for criminals—is a complex matter because, in the underworld, there are probably more risks overall, as well as certain risks (such as arrest and imprisonment) that threaten to liquidate the illegal activity much more quickly than market forces or regulatory intervention would with a legitimate business.

To stabilize their illicit operations, criminals take a variety of precautions to control or minimize risks. Because the risks in the underworld are more varied, and potentially lethal, there are possibly more offsetting activities to address them. Some of the more common ones include selling a portion of the risk to others (e.g., a gambling layoff system); sharing the risk with others (e.g., joint ventures with other organizations); preventing police interference (e.g., paying bribes); encouraging victims to remain silent (e.g., by hiring extortionists); or controlling competition (e.g., buying franchises or entering into cartel arrangements).

Those who perform support functions for criminal enterprises are valuable because they can contribute to maximizing profits. However, they are often needed to ensure basic survival in risky illegal marketplaces. For example, no bookmaker could long survive without selling part of the risk on heavily bet events to a "layoff" operation, lest his capital be depleted by one major or several sustained losses. Narcotics dealers have different kinds of risks (e.g., breaches of contract for which they obtain the services of someone who enforces, or threatens to enforce contracts), or they face loss of their proceeds and, eventually, their market share. Unfortunately, most enforcement strategies rarely take into account the vital role of support systems. There are some exceptions, such as the corruptor in gambling and narcotics investigations, and the fence in theft investigations.

To summarize, many factors contribute to the low sustained impact of proactive enforcement. A direct way of phrasing the problem is to note that *most* proactive strategies to combat illicit enterprises (whether organized or unorganized) are not based on an understanding of the economic, organizational and other dynamics of the illicit marketplaces the criminals serve, or of the roles that key support systems play. Once again, the example of drug enforcement may be helpful here. Traditional productivity measures have included arrests of large numbers of retail dealers and amounts of drugs removed from traffic through confiscation, together with their (often inflated) street retail value. Good-faith efforts to identify more accurate indicators have included noting changes in the purity of drugs confiscated as some measure of their harmfulness.

As pressures have increased over time to move beyond retailers to the wholesalers who supply them, productivity measures have likewise been subject to change. Beginning in the early 1970s, police strategies were revised by focusing on so-called "mid-level" dealers—a broad designation that seems to apply to any trafficker in a local distribution system above the rank of street-level retailer. Yet most drug distribution networks contain several wholesale levels, leaving unclear the precise role or value of any one "mid-level" dealer (Karchmer 1990). What is clear from recent research is the relative ease of replacing any one dealer, wholesaler or otherwise, with another waiting in the wings (Reuter 1989).

For police to develop more effective problem-specific proactive strategies, it is critical that a core focus on activities, locations and offenders drive the evaluation effort, whose principal purpose should be to identify approaches that work. Only in this way can the police identify why certain tactics work, and under what specific conditions, so that they can do more of what works and less of what does not.

Evaluating Proactive Enforcement Tactics

As discussed above, proactive enforcement tactics can be valuable policing tools for addressing specific crime problems and community harms. Evaluations of these tactics are needed, however, to determine if this potential can be converted into reality. Proactive enforcement tactics can also be quite controversial. Critics often claim that these tactics impinge on civil rights and due process and have dubious crime suppression value. Advocates assert the opposite. Evaluations of the tactics can assist police officials in such debates. Evaluations can demonstrate the tactic's crime-control utility and provide evidence that they are applied fairly. For example, the Minneapolis Police Department was faced with conflicting demands from members of its African American communities. Many residents demanded increased enforcement against street drug dealing. As part of an attempt to address these needs, the police department launched a number of street drug stings to curtail street purchases by users in these neighborhoods. Others in the community claimed that the police unfairly targeted black neighborhoods for such enforcement, while ignoring similar behavior in other areas. The police replied that they used the stings in areas where street dealing and buying were known. But to test this hypothesis, the department purposely conducted several similar stings in other areas where they had no evidence of street drug dealing. The results showed that undercover officers posing as dealers were unable to attract any customers in those areas. The department used the results to successfully fend off a court challenge to the sting operations.

But even if the fairness and propriety of proactive tactics are not being challenged, police leaders know that these tactics use resources and that the expenditure of these resources must be justified. Evaluations of proactive enforcement tactics can show how effective some tactics are, suggest improvements that might be made, and reveal tactics that are not effective.

What Is an Evaluation?

An evaluation is a systematic attempt to determine if a specific intervention caused a change in a social problem. Evaluations are used throughout government to determine the utility of programs and recommend changes. They are used in health care, housing, transportation, education, and many other fields, in addition to criminal justice and policing. In the police field, they have been used to look at the effectiveness of neighborhood watch programs, career criminal programs, random preventive patrol, foot patrol, spouse abuse intervention policies, and a host of other programs. The authors will discuss evaluations in the context of proactive investigations but many of the basic concepts are the same, regardless of the type of program being evaluated.

Evaluations can be divided into two parts: an impact evaluation and a process evaluation. The impact evaluation is designed to determine whether a proactive investigation has caused a decline in the problem. The process evaluation is designed to show how an intervention was implemented. As an example, a unit is established to investigate illegal gun trafficking, with the goal of reducing gun violence among street drug dealers and gang members. A process evaluation would seek to determine whether the unit was established, whether its members were properly trained, and whether it performed the activities it was designed to perform. Process evaluation measures might include the number of illegal gun possession arrests made, the number of guns confiscated from gun traffickers, or the conviction rates for arrested gun traffickers.

An impact evaluation would be concerned with the availability of guns to gang members and street dealers, the use of guns to commit crimes, and the level of harm created by illegal gun possession. Impact evaluation measures might include the number and types of guns found at dealing locations after a raid, the number of gun-related fatalities and injuries, the street price of guns, or the number of citizen telephone reports of gun shots.

Under ideal circumstances, the process evaluation demonstrates that the intervention was implemented as planned, and the impact evaluation shows that the intervention had the desired impact. Using the example above, the process evaluation shows that many arrests of gun traffickers were made and a great many guns seized. The impact evaluation shows that gun-related deaths and injuries have declined, and fewer guns are showing up in the possession of gang members and street dealers.

But there are three other possibilities. First, the intervention could be implemented as planned, but have no impact on the problem (or make the problem worse). For example, the gun unit could make many arrests and confiscate many guns, but gun-related deaths and injuries remain constant, and gang members and street dealers still are armed as before the intervention. Second, the intervention could be implemented in a way other than was planned (or not implemented at all), and have the desired impact on the problem. For example, the unit made a small number of arrests and confiscated few guns, but gun-related deaths and injuries declined. Third, the intervention could be implemented in a way other than was planned, and have no impact on the problem. For example, the unit made few arrests and confiscations, and gun-related deaths and injuries continued as before. These possibilities are shown in Figure 1.

The results in the first column are unambiguous—the intervention was implemented, and it worked or did not work. In either case, something was learned from trying the intervention. Results from the second column are more difficult to interpret. If the desired impact was achieved, but the plans were not followed, then adjustments in the plans will be needed if the success is to be replicated in the future. Drawing again on the gun unit example, it may be that the few arrests made were of key traffickers, and this severely disrupted the gun-trafficking network. In this case, the unit manager may want to shift from a focus on many arrests to a focus on a few arrests of important individuals. If the desired results were not achieved, and the intervention was not implemented as planned, it is difficult to determine whether the poor results were due to failure to implement the plan as specified, or whether the same poor results would have been achieved even if the plans were followed. Not only will the police department not know if the intervention works, but it will also be difficult to learn what does not work.

Process Evaluation Shows . . .

Intervention as Planned

Impact Evaluation Shows . . .		Intervention as Planned	
		YES	NO
Desired Impact	YES	Intervention works. No changes in basic intervention needed.	Something works. Look for alternatives to plans that may have led to success.
	NO	Intervention does not work. Try something else.	Did not learn anything. Start over.

Figure 1

Possible Evaluation Results

Process evaluations are critical for understanding impact evaluation results. However, because process evaluations are similar to activities police routinely perform to scrutinize ongoing programs, the authors will focus on impact evaluation techniques. Of particular importance will be gathering the data needed to demonstrate that the intervention caused a decline in the target problem.

Cause and Evaluations

Impact evaluations are designed to demonstrate a causal link. For example, if a surveillance team and decoy vehicles are used to combat auto thefts from a parking lot, then the impact evaluation of this intervention will seek to determine (1) whether auto thefts declined, and (2) whether this decline can be attributed to the proactive tactics used. These two goals are analogous to the process of making an on-scene arrest: the officer must first determine that a crime was committed, and then determine that the person at the scene committed the crime. If the officer decides that no crime was committed, then he or she cannot arrest the suspicious person picked up at the scene. Similarly, if the evaluator determines that there was no decline in the problem, then there is no point in determining what caused the decline. If the officer finds that a crime was committed, then he or she can investigate whether the suspect was the offender. Similarly, if the evaluator finds a decline in the problem, then he or she needs to determine whether the intervention caused the decline, or whether something else was responsible.

Three elements are required to demonstrate that an intervention has caused a decline in a problem:

1. **Correlation**—the intervention and the results must vary together, i.e., when the intervention is strong, the problem must be weak, and when the intervention is weak, the problem must be strong;
2. **Temporal order**—the intervention must precede the results; and
3. **Nonspuriousness**—the results cannot be fully explained by other causes.

Each of these elements will be discussed in greater detail.

Correlation. Imagine an upsurge in business burglaries. To curtail these, a department initiates a property fencing sting operation specializing in the goods most commonly stolen during such burglaries. The sting operation is conducted for six months, and then closed down. Forty-three people are arrested and charged with business burglaries as a result of this effort. The number of business burglaries declines following the arrests. This is an example of a correlation between an intervention and the level of a problem: sting arrests are associated with low levels of burglaries, and the absence of arrests is associated with high levels of burglaries. This is a necessary condition for demonstrating that proactive investigations caused a decline in business burglaries, but it is not a sufficient condition.

To see why this is a necessary condition, consider the alternative scenario. The sting operation is run for six months. But following the arrests, business burglaries continue at about the same level. In this scenario, one can find no correlation between the intervention and the results. Clearly, absent such a correlation, one cannot claim that the intervention had any effect. So a correlation between the intervention and the results is necessary. To see why, by itself, a correlation is insufficient evidence to claim an intervention caused the observed results, one must look at the other two elements.

Temporal order. Temporal order is the most obvious requirement for attributing causality: cause follows effect. If the business burglaries declined before the sting arrests, then the evaluator could not make any claim that the intervention caused the decline. But in the first scenario above, temporal order is not in dispute: declines in business burglaries followed the intervention (see Figure 2). Note, however, that the sting was prompted by an increase in business burglaries, so based on temporal order alone, we could claim either that increases in arrests caused a decrease in business burglaries, or that increases in business burglaries caused an increase in proactive enforcement. Though temporal order is a necessary condition for attributing cause, it is insufficient by itself or in combination with correlation. A third element is required.

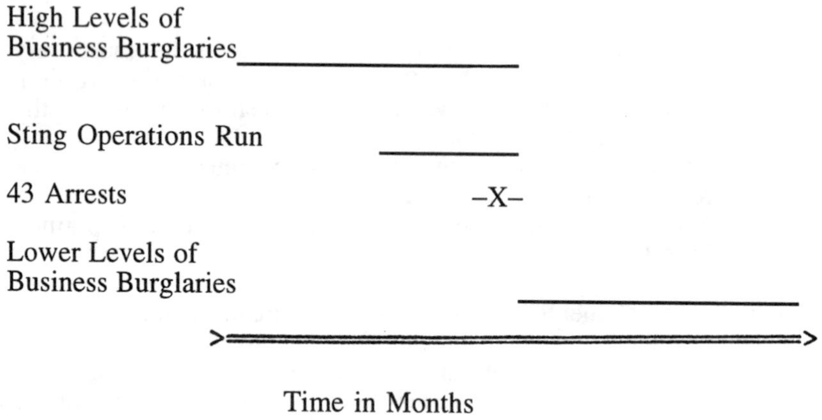

High Levels of
Business Burglaries_____

Sting Operations Run   _____

43 Arrests   –X–

Lower Levels of
Business Burglaries   _____

                        >══════════════════════════>

Time in Months

Figure 2

Temporal Order of Events in Burglary Sting Example

Nonspuriousness. Nonspuriousness simply means that some other unaccounted-for third factor is not causing both the intervention and the change in the problem. The intervention may be correlated with the observed outcome, and the intervention may precede the outcome, but one more element is needed to be able to confidently claim that the intervention caused the outcome. Let's go back to the business burglaries and elaborate on the story to show how what appears to be a straightforward example of intervention causing the result could be something else entirely.

As business burglaries increase, two things happen: the police begin planning a proactive intervention, and businesses become increasingly security-conscious. Business owners also put pressure on the police to intervene, and this speeds up the implementation of the proactive investigation. Now there are two rival hypotheses about the decline in burglaries. The first hypothesis claims that the police intervention caused the decline. Under this hypothesis, the police intervention's effect on the business burglaries is direct and nonspurious. The second hypothesis claims that the businesses' actions reduced the number of available targets for attack—thus causing the decline in burglaries—and simultaneously caused the police to act. But according to the second hypothesis, police actions did not cause the decline in burglaries, so the police intervention's effect on the business burglaries is spurious: a third factor (business actions) causes both the proactive investigation and the decrease in burglaries. Note that both hypotheses are consistent with the available evidence.

Spuriousness can be illustrated using path diagrams. In Figure 3, the arrow linking the police intervention to the burglary level represents the direct causal process of the first hypothesis: the sting arrests cause the decrease in burglaries. Business security measures are not linked to either the intervention or the burglaries in this diagram, thus showing that they are not causally linked to the intervention or results.

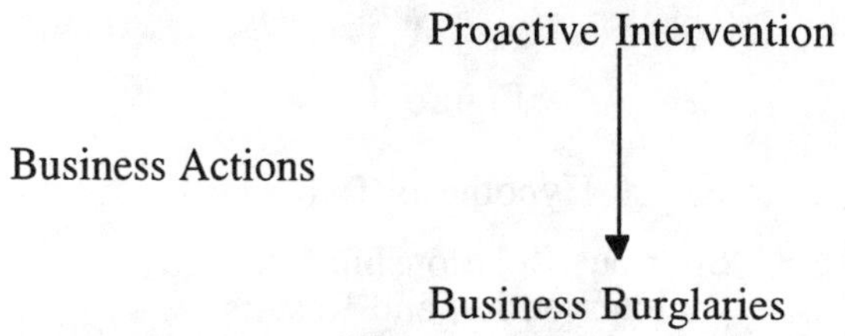

Proactive Intervention

Business Actions

Business Burglaries

Figure 3

Hypothesis One

Nonspurious Relationship Between
Intervention and Results

Figure 4 illustrates the spurious relationship between the intervention and burglaries claimed by the second hypothesis: businesses called upon the police to act and caused the drop in burglaries with crime prevention actions. Since the burglaries and intervention have a common cause (business actions), they are correlated, even though they are not causally linked. Further, the intervention may precede the decline (temporal order), but only because business actions cause both the intervention and the decline. If the evaluator can find evidence to support the first hypothesis and rule out the second hypothesis, then he or she will have better evidence that the intervention caused the decline in the burglaries. If the evaluator cannot rule out the second hypothesis, then he or she will have to admit to the possibility of something other than the intervention causing the decline.

These are not the only two hypotheses possible, given the facts about this example. It is possible that the decline in business burglaries is partially spurious and partially a direct cause of the intervention. If this is the case, then the evaluator can state that the intervention was effective, but that it was not fully responsible for the decline.

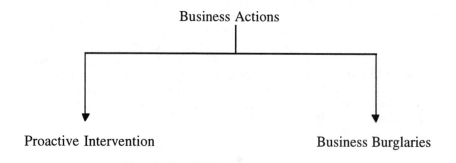

Figure 4

Hypothesis Two

Spurious Relationship Between
Intervention and Results

In summary, to conclusively demonstrate that an intervention has caused the observed decline in a problem, the evaluator must show evidence of three things: (1) that a correlation exists between the intervention and the results, (2) that the intervention preceded the results, and (3) that the relationship between the intervention and the results is nonspurious.

Evidence demonstrating that any one of these elements is false is sufficient to justify a claim that the intervention had no impact. Often, however, evaluators can demonstrate only that one or two of these elements are true, and cannot find evidence regarding the truth or falsity of the other element(s). Usually, evidence justifying the claim of nonspuriousness is absent, and sometimes temporal order cannot be fully demonstrated. In these cases, there is insufficient evidence to be fully confident that the intervention caused the observed results. In other words, the evidence available is consistent with the intervention having the desired impact, but it is not conclusive.

The evaluation designs described below have been developed to reveal correlations between the intervention and the level of the problem, establish the temporal order of events, and rule out some of the most common spurious relationships. Some of these designs are better at achieving these three objectives than others. But it is also true that in most situations, the evaluation designs that are the best at conclusively demonstrating a causal link between the intervention and the results can be more expensive and administratively more difficult, and they sometimes raise more ethical questions than evaluation designs that yield less conclusive results.

Evaluating Evaluations

What are the characteristics of an evaluation design that will provide evidence of a correlation, temporal order and nonspuriousness?

First, the design must allow some variation in the intervention. That is, the evaluator must be able to observe situations in which the intervention is in place and in which the intervention is absent. One approach is for the evaluator to compare the situations in which the intervention took place with those in which it was not used. Or the evaluator can look at changes in a problem from before an intervention to after the intervention. Without such variation in the intervention, the presence of a correlation cannot be established.

Second, the design should allow the evaluator to clearly determine when the intervention occurred and when changes in the problem occurred. To establish temporal order, the changes in the problem must occur after the intervention. A design that does not reveal the temporal order of the intervention and the results will not provide conclusive evidence of a causal link. The standard method for ensuring that temporal order can be established is for the evaluator to control the timing of the intervention and who will get the intervention. If the intervention is not controlled by the evaluator, but is instead allowed to be applied at unspecified times to unspecified people or places, then it is impossible to conclusively establish temporal order.

Third, the design should rule out all other possible causes of the change in the problem other than the intervention. Since it is seldom possible to rule out all other causes, the design should rule out the most likely competing explanations (hypotheses) for the change. If the design cannot even do this, then a causal link cannot be established. The standard method for ruling out all other explanations is randomization of assignment. Randomization ensures that the people or places that receive the treatment (experimentals) are like the people or places that do not receive the treatment (controls). This means that before the intervention, the controls and experimentals are the same, but after the treatment they are different, and this difference can be attributed only to the intervention. In the absence of randomization, it is possible to select experimental and control groups that are similar, or almost the same. This means that any differences between the control group and the experimental group that existed before the intervention may be the cause of the changes noted after the intervention. The greater the differences between the experimental and control groups before the intervention, the more difficult it is to establish nonspuriousness.

In summary, the ideal evaluation design for establishing a causal link between a proactive investigation intervention and changes in a problem will have

- large variation between people and places receiving the intervention and those not receiving the intervention,
- explicit designation of who or what receives the intervention, and
- randomized assignment of people or places to experimental and control groups.

In general, the smaller the variation in the intervention, or the less control the evaluator exerts over who or what receives the intervention, or the greater the differences between the experimental and control groups before the intervention, the less certain the evaluator can be about causality.

There are three types of evaluation designs useful for determining interventions' impacts on problems. The first is a randomized experiment. This is the strongest design available for assessing the causal relationship between the intervention and the observed results. A randomized experiment best achieves the three criteria listed above. However, this design can be difficult to administer and can create ethical concerns under some circumstances. The second design is a quasi-experiment. It usually is most helpful at establishing a correlation and temporal order, but it can be weak in ruling out spurious relationships. Quasi-experiments are easier to administer than randomized experiments and create fewer ethical problems. The third design is a passive statistical design. It is best at establishing a correlation, but it may have problems demonstrating temporal order, and it is weakest at establishing nonspuriousness. Passive statistical designs have the fewest administrative problems and virtually no ethical problems.

All three of these designs are useful for evaluating proactive investigation programs and tactics when quantitative (numerical) data are available. In the absence of quantitative data, it is possible to use a descriptive approach, or case study design, to evaluate the intervention. Unfortunately, it is very difficult to establish any of the three elements of causality with a case study design because variation in the intervention is hard to document, control over the intervention is seldom achieved, and randomization is not used.

Experimental Designs

The basic form of an experimental design is as follows. An intervention is selected for testing on a target group of people or places. The target group is randomly divided into two groups: an experimental group that receives the intervention, and a control group that does not. Measurements of the problem are taken before and after the intervention for the people or places in the experimental and control groups. A change in the problem in the experimental group is then compared with a change in the problem in the control group. The difference in these changes is attributable to the intervention.

Because the target group is randomly assigned, before the intervention, the two group's members are statistically equivalent. Therefore, after the intervention, any significant differences between the two groups can have been caused only by the intervention.

Figure 5 illustrates the basic randomized experimental design. The R indicates that assignment to the experimental and control groups was random. The experimental and control groups' members are measured (M) for the problem before and after an intervention (I), but the experimental group's members receive the intervention.

```
           M   I   M
       R
           M       M
```

Figure 5

Basic Randomized Experimental Design

An example of a randomized experiment on drug enforcement. One target of proactive investigations is retail drug dealing. Police learn about dealing locations from informant tips and citizen complaints. They then start an investigation to determine if drug dealing is taking place. A standard technique is to make a controlled purchase of drugs at the location. Once narcotics officers collect sufficient evidence, they seek a warrant to arrest the dealers and search the premises for additional evidence. They then raid the location, make arrests and secure additional evidence. Some agencies follow up on raids by contacting landlords and requesting that they do more to prevent drug dealing on their property. A randomized experiment is a useful method for evaluating the effectiveness of landlord contacts, and the San Diego Police Department has conducted such an experiment (Eck and Wartell 1997). The following example is loosely based on that study.

After drug enforcement at a rental property, each place is assigned a number and then randomly assigned to one of the two treatment groups. Department records of reported serious crimes and citizen drug complaints for the place are compared for periods before and after the treatments.

Figure 6 diagrams the experimental design for this example. Since the department routinely collects the before intervention data, the evaluator can look at crime and drug complaint information before the assignment decision and the intervention.

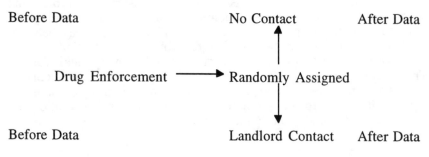

Figure 6

Randomized Experimental Design for
Evaluating Landlord Contacts After Drug Enforcement

An example of a randomized experiment on career criminal investigations. Another example of the use of a randomized experimental design for proactive investigation evaluation comes from a Rand Corp. study of the Phoenix Police Department's repeat offender program (ROP) (Abrahamse et al. 1991). The evaluators wanted to determine if proactive investigations of repeat offenders increased the chances an offender would be convicted and receive a longer sentence. When an ROP investigator identified a person who met the program eligibility criteria, the person was assigned a code number. The Rand Corp. evaluator then randomly assigned that offender to the control or experimental group. Control group members were not assigned to an ROP investigator (though this did not preclude officers in other units from arresting the offenders and taking the cases to the prosecutor). Experimental group members were identified as repeat offenders to police department personnel (to increase the chances of arrest), and, if arrested, ROP unit investigators sought additional evidence (to increase the chances of a prosecution and conviction) and conducted an extensive background check (to increase the chances of a long prison sentence).

Control and experimental offenders were compared to determine if experimental offenders were arrested more, prosecuted more, convicted more, incarcerated more, and sentenced to longer terms than control offenders. The results showed that the ROP unit's targeting and investigations significantly increased arrest chances (from 88.2% for controls to 93.3% for experimentals), increased the likelihood of a prison sentence (from 67.8% to 79.4%), and increased the length of sentences (from an average of 73 months to an average of 91 months) (Abrahamse et al. 1991). An illustration of this design is shown in Figure 7.

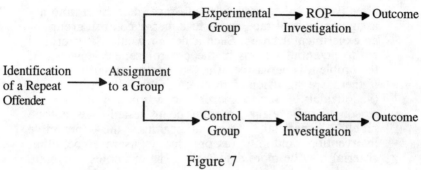

Figure 7

Randomized Experimental Design for Evaluating ROP Unit

When randomized experiments are appropriate. Randomized experiments on proactive investigations are suitable for situations with the following four characteristics.

- There are many subjects for experimentation—in the two example designs, the evaluators had many subjects to assign to experimental and control groups. In the first example, the evaluators assigned addresses. In the second example, the evaluators assigned people. Often, one does not have a lot of subjects. For example, if an intervention's effect on crime in city parks was to be assessed and there were only five suitable parks, then an experiment would not be feasible.
- There are repeated interventions of the same type—in both the examples, the same intervention was used on the experimental subjects. This condition cannot be achieved for every type of proactive investigation. For example, a proactive investigation of political corruption would most likely be undertaken once.
- Each intervention is a discrete action in a short period—evaluating the impacts of an organized crime unit may be difficult using a randomized experiment, since intervention is likely to take place over a long period and may change as evidence is uncovered.
- Ethical concerns are absent or can be allayed—a randomized experiment necessitates depriving some people of the intervention and imposing the intervention on others. If the intervention is likely to confer benefits (e.g., improve safety) or impose sanctions (e.g., arrest), then randomization will confer benefits or impose sanction without regard to need or just desserts. In some cases, this allocation cannot be defended on ethical grounds. For example, one would not want to test the

effectiveness of a proactive anti-rape unit by randomly assigning several rape series to either a control group or an experimental group. Such a design would deny critical aid to potential victims in the control series. However, if the problem is pervasive, if it is not extraordinarily serious, if there are insufficient resources to handle it normally (i.e., denial of service occurs anyway), and if there is reason to believe the program being tested may not be highly beneficial, then allocating the proactive intervention randomly (as opposed to using some other criteria) may be more defensible. The examples above are ethically feasible largely because the police departments have insufficient resources to address all drug locations at once or handle all career criminals simultaneously. In such situations, resource constraints force police officials to make decisions that confer benefits or impose sanctions, and a random process can make this allocation more equitable.

In the absence of any one of these characteristics, an alternative design is required.

Quasi-Experimental Designs

Randomization of people or places receiving the proactive investigation ensures that the nonspuriousness criterion can be met. If randomization is not used, the evaluation findings may be spurious. So giving up randomization brings with it a potentially high cost. Nevertheless, randomized experiments are often inappropriate or difficult to use. For this reason, alternative designs are useful. The best alternative to a randomized design is a quasi-experiment. A well-crafted quasi-experiment provides variation (it has a group that receives the intervention and a group that does not), so correlation can be determined. It also permits the evaluator to determine if the intervention preceded the effect, so temporal order can be ensured. However, because the control and experimental groups cannot be made equivalent, the evaluator cannot be assured that the results are nonspurious. This does not mean that the results are definitely invalid, but only that it is impossible to be sure how valid they are: the results may exactly reflect reality, or they may be totally misleading. There are many types of quasi-experiments (see Campbell and Stanley 1963, for clear descriptions of some of them), but the two used most are the nonequivalent control group design and the interrupted time series design (Cook and Campbell 1979). Both can be easily applied to the evaluation of proactive investigations.

Nonequivalent control group design. Figure 8 depicts the basic nonequivalent control group design. Note that the difference between the randomized design shown in Figure 5 and this design is the absence of randomization. This means that the group receiving the intervention (I) is different from the group not receiving it. If these differences are irrelevant for the intervention's success, then the results of a nonequivalent control group evaluation will be equivalent to those of a randomized evaluation. But if these differences affect the intervention's success, then the evaluation's results cannot be attributed solely to the intervention, and it may be the case that the intervention had nothing to do with the results. Further, a finding of no intervention effect may be invalid if the group differences act to mask effects. Obviously, this design's utility critically depends on making the two groups similar enough to rule out the most likely alternative explanations for the results.

M   I   M

M   M

Figure 8

Basic Nonequivalent Control Group Design

The basic procedure is to select an area (e.g., a neighborhood) or a group of people (e.g., a drug-dealing network) for an intervention, and select a similar area (e.g., a neighborhood with similar demographic characteristics) or group (e.g., another drug-dealing network) that will not receive the intervention. Measurements of the problem in question are taken before and after the intervention for both the control and the experimental areas or groups. A change in the problem for the experimental group is then compared with the change in the problem for the control group. The difference in these changes is assumed to be attributable to the intervention. This assumption's validity depends on the persuasiveness of the argument that any differences between the experimentals and the controls do not affect the outcome.

Langworthy (1989) reports an example of the use of a nonequivalent control group design to evaluate a proactive investigation. He reviews the evaluations of sting operations, including a study by Raub (1984) of a sting operation in two Illinois counties. Property crime rates in the counties before, during and after the operations were compared with property crime rates in adjacent counties not involved in the stings for the same periods. The evaluator found that stings did not increase property crimes in the sting counties (relative to the control counties) during the operations, but neither did they reduce crimes in the sting counties (relative to the control counties) after the operations were stopped and the suspects were arrested.

Interrupted time series design. With an interrupted time series design, a group or area serves as its own control. That is, repeated measures of the problem are taken before the intervention in order to account for any preexisting trends or cycles. Then repeated measures of the problem are taken after the intervention. This design is depicted in Figure 9.

M   M   M   M   M   M   M   I M   M   M   M   M   M   M

Figure 9

Basic Interrupted Time Series Design

Langworthy (1989) evaluated an auto theft sting operation in Birmingham, Ala. He compared the trends and fluctuations in auto thefts for 92 pre-sting days with those for 136 days during the sting operation and for 138 days after the operation was closed down with the arrests of suspects. Note that the property sting has two intervention points: when the storefront opens for business and starts buying stolen property, and when the storefront is shut down and the suspects are arrested. By using statistical software that accounts for trends and cycles, Langworthy showed that while the program was in progress, auto thefts increased somewhat, and once it was terminated, there was no decline in auto thefts.

The validity of the conclusions resulting from interrupted time series designs depends on the evaluator's ability to demonstrate that preexisting trends or cycles did not cause the results. If the problem was declining before the intervention, then further reductions in the problem cannot be readily attributed to the intervention. In the example above, Langworthy (1989) could rule out the influence of trends and cycles using some very sophisticated statistical software.

Just as important, and less obvious, is another confounding factor. Often, several things change at once. If the intervention occurs at the same time that other changes occur that affect the problem, then the intervention may not be the cause of the decline in the problem. This type of confounding can be ruled out by using a control group, since the problem should peak in both the experiment and the control group, and any decline in the experimental group not found in the control group can be attributed to the intervention. So a combination of an interrupted time series design and a nonequivalent control group design can yield a very powerful evaluation. This combination is shown in Figure 10.

M M M M M M M I M M M M M M M

M M M M M M M   M M M M M M M

Figure 10

Mixed Design

Time series designs require data that have been collected the same way for many periods before and after the intervention. Reported crime data, calls for service data and other routinely collected police or other agency records are very useful for this purpose. Citizen surveys or other special data collection initiatives cannot be used with time series studies. They are much more appropriate for nonequivalent control group designs.

Quasi-experiments can provide useful alternatives to randomized experiments. While they cannot ensure nonspuriousness (like randomized designs), they can often provide convincing evidence of nonspuriousness. Unfortunately, there are many situations in which even quasi-experiments are difficult or impossible to use. It may not be possible to specify a control area or population, for example. Or the evaluator may be called in to look at the program after it has been implemented. Or time series data may not be available. In these and other cases, the evaluator will have to turn to yet another alternative design.

Passive Statistical Designs

Just as one sacrifices assurance of nonspuriousness when one moves from a randomized experiment to a quasi-experiment, one also sacrifices something when one moves to a passive statistical design. In this case, assurances of both nonspuriousness and temporal order are given up. This does not mean that arguments about causality cannot be made, but it does mean that with passive statistical designs, it will be more difficult to make strong claims than with randomized or quasi-experimental designs.

Take a situation in which a police chief wants to know how effective the department's gang suppression unit is at making neighborhoods safe. The evaluator is asked to make this assessment after the unit has been operating for two years in 10 target neighborhoods, and, as a consequence, the evaluator has no control over the treatment or where it is being applied. The only thing the evaluator can do is analyze existing records of the unit's past activities and crime rates for the neighborhoods. Since the unit's presence in the 10 neighborhoods varies, the evaluator looks at the unit's enforcement activities (i.e., arrests and field interrogations) and reports of shootings during the 24 months. The evaluator analyzes 240 neighborhood-months and finds a positive correlation between the unit's activities in a neighborhood and the numbers of shootings. In other words, in an average neighborhood during an average month, if there was more gang enforcement, then there were more shootings.

How should these results be interpreted? Maybe the gang unit destabilizes gangs, disrupting established social patterns, and thus creates violence. But does the unit's activities cause an increase in shootings? A genuine positive correlation has been demonstrated, so the first criterion for causality has been met. But have the other two criteria been met? The answer is no for both: neither temporal order nor nonspuriousness has been demonstrated. Since the unit is likely to make more arrests and field interrogations in a neighborhood when there are more shootings, it may be that the temporal order is reversed—gang shootings cause unit activity. It could also be that a third factor is causing both gang shootings and anti-gang activities. For example, increased drug sales may spark gang shootings to threaten citizens.

To account for these two rival hypotheses, the evaluator correlates the gang unit arrests in a month with the shootings in the following month, and statistically controls for citizen reports of drug dealing. The evaluator finds a negative relationship between arrests and shootings in the following month, even after accounting for citizen reports. Based on this analysis, the evaluator claims that the unit does suppress gang shootings.

The basic process for conducting a passive statistical design is to collect data on three types of indicators.

The first type of indicator measures the level of the problem. In the example above, reports of shootings are such an indicator. Often, these indicators come from reported crime statistics, but victimization surveys and other data sources can also be used. In an evaluation context, these indicators are often called *dependent variables,* because the level of the problem depends on the level of other indicators.

The second type of indicator measures the level of the intervention. This type of variable is often called an *independent variable,* but to distinguish it from another type of independent variable, the authors will call it a *policy variable.* In the above example, the gang unit's arrests and field interrogations are policy variables. The purpose of the evaluation is to determine if the policy variable caused the change in the dependent variable. Measures of the level of the intervention usually come from project performance statistics: numbers of arrests, numbers of hours of staffing, numbers of warrants served, and so forth.

The third type of indicator is also an independent variable and serves as a proxy for having a control group. The authors will call these variables *control variables.* These indicators measure other possible influences on the level of the problem and are used to help reduce the chance of a spurious relationship. If the evaluator finds that even when control variables are accounted for, the policy variable is highly correlated with the dependent variable, then the program is likely to have caused the decline in the problem. In the gang unit example, citizen reports of drug dealing are independent control variables and are used to eliminate the rival hypothesis that citizen calls cause both the shootings and the intervention. For each rival hypothesis, a control variable should be introduced. Since there are an infinite number of possible influences on the problem, and only a small number of control variables can be used, the evaluator cannot be absolutely sure that the intervention caused the effect. The evaluator can rule out only the most obvious contenders.

Passive statistical designs can be developed using contingency tables and a variety of statistical measures. They are most frequently used when the evaluator is called in to examine a program after it has been implemented (so a control group cannot be established), and before-after information is unavailable. Because of their inherent weaknesses, passive statistical designs should be avoided for evaluation purposes, unless there is no other alternative.

Case Study Designs

Case study designs are the weakest designs available. They cannot ensure a correlation, temporal order or nonspuriousness and, as a result, are virtually useless for demonstrating causality. In a case study, the evaluator documents the existence of the intervention, how it operated, staffing levels and procedures, and difficulties faced. Often, the evaluator solicits participants' and others' opinions. He or she may collect some effectiveness data—perhaps on the level of the problem before and after the intervention—but the total absence of a control group or compensatory statistical analysis makes causal inferences impossible. Case study designs are useful for program documentation and for suggesting results that may be attributable to the program.

It is critical, however, to remember that some proactive investigations may not be evaluated in any other way. If the target of the investigation is highly secretive, or the link between multiple targets is complex, then a design stronger than a case study may not be possible and, even if possible, is very likely to show no impact, even if an impact occurred. Proactive investigations of heads of large and geographically diverse organized crime groups, for example, are probably best evaluated through case studies.

Overview

This section described three criteria for establishing a causal link between an intervention and a program outcome. These three criteria are correlation, temporal order and nonspuriousness. Four types of evaluation designs were then reviewed in terms of these three criteria. Two of these designs, randomized experiments and quasi-experiments, are clearly preferable for evaluating proactive investigations because they can meet all or most of these criteria. Passive statistical designs are inherently weak but can be useful if the first two designs cannot be used.   Case study designs can be used only to determine if the program operated in the way it was designed to; they cannot demonstrate if the program had the desired impact.   Case studies can be useful supplements to randomized experiments, quasi-experiments or passive statistical designs.

Evaluation Measures

One of the most difficult aspects of evaluating a proactive investigation is finding adequate measures of the problem.   This is especially the case if the problem involves consensual crimes (e.g., prostitution, criminal receiving, gun trafficking, or drug dealing) that are hidden from the view of the police or the public.   If no one records changes in the problem, then it is difficult to know whether proactive strategies are having an effect.   For example, a series of proactive investigations of high-level drug traffickers may result in the arrest and successful prosecution of major kingpins, but it is difficult to know whether this makes it more difficult for dealers to get drugs and whether users who are unable to buy drugs commit fewer crimes.   Or, for example, does stepped-up enforcement against street prostitution decrease the spread of AIDS and other diseases in a neighborhood?

If one first starts with a problem that the proactive investigation is meant to reduce, then a decline in the problem is the goal one is trying to achieve.   The question is, how can you measure the problem?   There are as many possible measures as one can imagine. However, there are a few common measures that can be useful, either singly or in combination.

Requests for Service

Police departments receive thousands of requests for service. These requests usually indicate that there is a problem, and that the problem is of sufficient magnitude that someone wants something done about it.   The following types of requests should be considered in measuring effectiveness.

Calls for service.   Recently, repeat call analysis has shown that a few locations generate a disproportionate number of calls. These "hot spots" are potential problems (Sherman, Gartin and Buerger 1989).   Analyzing calls for service before and after a proactive investigation of places can be useful in measuring effectiveness.

Crime calls.   Changes in reported crime can be used to gauge the effectiveness of a proactive policing strategy.   For example, in an undercover investigation of a criminal receiver ring, reports of thefts (especially thefts of goods the ring likes to buy) will be a useful measure of the investigation's impact.

Other special requests. Some police agencies have a variety of mechanisms for the public to request services or report problems. For example, San Diego Police Department ministations provide citizen request forms for people to report on problems. If some of the requests are due to the problem being investigated, changes in the number and type of requests may indicate how effective the investigation is.

Data From Other Agencies

Though data from police sources are the most readily available, other data sources can also provide useful information for evaluating proactive investigations. The utility of any particular data source will depend on its accessibility and how well the data describe the problem. The data sources listed below are examples of only some of the types that could be used. The list is not exhaustive.

Health. Health information can be particularly useful for describing aspects of consensual crime problems—drug abuse and prostitution, in particular. Drug overdose data can be gleaned from hospital records, for example. Fluctuations in drug-related health data can be used to gauge the effectiveness of proactive drug investigations.

Taxes. Taxes are sometimes a measure of economic vitality. For example, sales taxes are proportional to businesses' revenues. Changes in sales taxes can be used to show how proactive investigations improved public safety in a shopping area, inducing more people to patronize the stores.

Permits. Like taxes, permit applications are sometimes useful for measuring economic activity. Requests for building permits, business permits, and so forth can be used to measure improvements in area economic activity, which may be attributable to improved public safety due to proactive investigations.

Observations

Official records, as discussed above, can be very useful, but some circumstances require special observations. Two types of observations are described below.

Physical environment. Careful documentation of the physical environment can be used to show proactive investigation's effects. For example, examination of litter in a drug-dealing area before an undercover operation may reveal a lot of drug-related debris. After the investigation, no such material may be present. Similarly, a proactive investigation of gangs may be evaluated, in part, by a decline in gang-related graffiti. Or, a surveillance of a parking area with a lot of auto break-ins may be evaluated by examining the frequency with which broken auto glass is found in the lot before and after the intervention.

Activities. Sometimes it is possible to directly observe, or obtain records describing, people's activities. Changes in activities can be used to show the effectiveness of some proactive investigations. For example, systematic observation of who uses an area can be used to determine the effectiveness of a proactive investigation of prostitution in and around a park. The absence of prostitutes and their customers may increase the legitimate use of the park, so one might expect to see more children and parents in the park after the crackdown. Or, for example, customer counters used by businesses can be used to document greater community patronization of local stores following a proactive investigation of neighborhood gangs.

Surveys

Surveys of the public are often useful for gathering effectiveness data, especially if the proactive investigation is meant to change people's perceptions. For example, one goal of proactive investigation of violent crimes may be to reduce community members' fear. This is especially true when the same person or group—a serial rapist or a gang, for example—commits the crimes in a specific area. Since fear of crime is a mental state, a survey of the public is needed to determine if mental states have changed. Surveys can be complex and expensive, so it is worth considering behavioral changes that are barometers of perceptions (above, we discussed two examples of such barometers: greater park use by families, and increased shopping). However, substitutes for surveys are not always available.

Photos and Videos

Nonquantitative demonstrations of effectiveness must also be considered. Systematic photos or videos of an area before and after a proactive investigation can provide valuable documentation of how the area has changed. Though they cannot show that the problem increased or decreased by x percent, their impact may be even greater than quantitative measures. Photos and videos should be taken at the same places and times both before and after the intervention so as to control for normal daily and weekly cycles (e.g., commuting, school hours, sporting events, etc.).

Conclusions

There is a large variety of measures one can use to evaluate the effectiveness of proactive investigations. Though the most common measures come from data sources within the police department, there are many other sources that can indicate changes in the target problem that may be attributable to the proactive treatment. The selection of measures will depend on several considerations:

1. The problems being addressed—for example, neighborhood drug problems will require different measures than a citywide auto theft problem—as well as other considerations.
2. The design being used—for example, a time series design will require data available for many points in time, before and after the intervention, while a nonequivalent control group design will require before and after data for two or more areas or groups.
3. The availability of data—for example, crime statistics usually are easy to obtain, but survey data or tax information may be very expensive or inaccessible.
4. The appeal of the measures—for example, police department personnel may want to see statistical data, and photos will not be convincing. But for presentations before elected officials, before and after photos may be more dramatic.

Unanticipated Consequences

Proactive investigations seek to change the behavior of offenders and potential offenders by deterring them from further criminal activity or removing them from the community. However, offenders may not always change their behaviors in the manner desired, offenders may start committing different crimes, or new offenders may replace those who have been incapacitated by prison sentences. Such changes may make the problem worse or shift the problem to other victims. If such changes are expected, and the proactive investigation and evaluation take them into account, then they pose no direct threat to the integrity of the evaluation. This section describes several common unanticipated consequences of proactive investigations, ones of which evaluators should be aware.

Displacement

Displacement of crime from one location to another or from one group to another is a concern whenever focused police activity is applied. If proactive investigations are used in one neighborhood, then it is feared that offenders will move to another neighborhood. If one set of criminal opportunities is blocked, it is feared that offenders will take advantage of other opportunities. Though there are a great many stories about displacement, the scientific evidence for its existence is scanty. In fact, a recent review of the research on this topic revealed no study demonstrating that displacement made things worse, and very few studies have found that displacement offset all gains (Barr and Pease 1990; Gabor 1990; Eck 1993). When displacement was found (and many of the studies found no such evidence), the net effect of the crime reduction effort was a reduction in crime. That is, adding displaced crime to the reduced crime in the target area still showed an overall reduction in crime.

Though research indicates that displacement is not an omnipresent threat, it can occur, and evaluators should design their evaluations to look for evidence of it. Five forms of displacement may be considered. Not every form will be a potential threat to every proactive investigation, and the forms the evaluator should consider will depend on the type of investigation and the target problem. The forms of displacement are as follows:

Temporal—offenders change the time when they commit crimes (for example, from days to nights);

Spatial—offenders switch from targets in one location to targets in another location (for example, a drug dealer stops selling in one neighborhood and starts selling in an adjacent one);

Target—offenders switch from one type of target to another (for example, a burglar switches from apartment units to single-family detached homes);

Method—offenders change the way they attack targets (for example, a street robber stops using a knife and starts using a gun); and,

Crime type—offenders switch from one form of crime to another (for example, from burglary to check fraud).

Diffusion of Benefits

Just as evaluators should look for possible displacement effects, they should also look for the opposite effect, the diffusion of crime reduction to areas and people not the subject of the intervention (Clarke and Weisburd 1994). For example, an undercover operation is conducted against drug distributors in an apartment complex. The evaluation finds that crime at the location declined (relative to a control apartment complex several miles away). Additionally, crime declined in the two square blocks surrounding the complex. In this example, the benefits of the operation extended beyond the targeted apartments. Evidence for diffusion of benefits is weaker than evidence against displacement, largely because few people have looked for it. Nevertheless, this possibility cannot be rejected on empirical or theoretical grounds. In fact, there are good theoretical reasons to believe diffusion of benefits might be common.

Care must be taken that the control areas or people are not influenced by diffusion. If crime reduction diffuses from the target places or people to the controls, then a comparison of the target and controls will show less difference than would be the case if the controls were not contaminated. Thus, diffusion can make a successful effort look less effective. With a separate control, evaluators can more accurately estimate program effects.

Replacement

If an offender is arrested and imprisoned, he cannot continue committing crimes in the community. So incapacitating offenders is one method of reducing crime. Proactive investigations often have incapacitation as their goal, and this is especially true of operations against career criminals, mid- and upper-level drug dealers, criminal gangs, and organized crime participants. However, the gains from incapacitation can be offset if new offenders replace those who have been removed from the street. It is unclear how much replacement is a concern when the targets of proactive investigations are unorganized offenders acting alone, but it is clearly a concern when dealing with organized offending. If the targeted offenders operate within a peer group, then the free members of the group may simply recruit a new member (Reiss 1988). Jankowski (1991) studied street gangs in Boston, New York and Los Angeles over a 10-year period and could find no example of a gang disappearing because the leader was imprisoned. Therefore, if the proactive investigation is targeting offender groups and following an incapacitation strategy, the evaluator should try to document replacement.

Accelerated Criminal Activity

As described in an earlier example, a common criticism of property sting operations is that they "create crime" by either inducing active offenders to become more active or inducing non-offenders to begin offending (Langworthy 1989). Proactive investigations that offer an attractive target in the hopes that offenders will reveal themselves run a risk of accelerating criminal activity (Marx 1988). Evaluators of such proactive investigations should look for evidence of this unanticipated consequence.

Increased Violence

Reuter (1992) suggests another unanticipated consequence of proactive investigations, particularly those designed to break up street drug dealing. If dealers have reached an agreement as to who will deal where, when, and to whom, then disruptions of this arrangement can lead to increased violence as dealers jockey for market position. One type of disruption is aggressive enforcement. Changing a problem from one of much drug dealing and little violence to one of less dealing but more violence may not be a net gain, especially for uninvolved community members who get caught between the criminal combatants. Since little systematic research has been done in this area, it is unclear when and where this unanticipated consequence should be a concern. Nevertheless, evaluators should collect information that could reveal any increased violence due to disruption of preexisting arrangements among offender groups.

Other Harms

This short list of unanticipated consequences does not exhaust the possibilities. Other unanticipated consequences can occur, but many of these may be specific to the type of proactive investigation being undertaken, the community setting within which it operates, and other situational factors. Though it will be impossible for an evaluator to take all possible unanticipated consequences into account, the evaluator should be cognizant of those that are most likely to occur. Even if a particular consequence is highly unlikely, it may be worth looking for it simply to allay public concerns. For example, it may be better to look for displacement and not find it, but be able to answer elected officials' questions about it, than to collect no data on the subject and be left without any evidence to refute charges of it.

Selected Bibliography

Abrahamse, A.F., P.A. Ebener, P.W. Greenwood, and T.E. Kosin. 1991. "An Experimental Evaluation of the Phoenix Repeat Offender Program." *Justice Quarterly* 8(2):141–168.

Barr, R., and K. Pease. 1990. "Crime Placement, Displacement and Deflection." In M. Tonry and N. Morris, eds., *Crime and Justice: A Review of Research*. Vol. 12. Chicago: University of Chicago Press.

Bloch, P. 1976. *Managing Investigations: The Rochester System*. Washington, D.C.: Police Foundation.

Bowers, R., and J. McCullough. 1982. *Assessing the Sting: An Evaluation of the LEAA Property Crime Program.* Washington, D.C.: University City Science Center.

Burnham, D. 1976. *The Role of the Media in Controlling Corruption.* New York: John Jay Press.

Campbell, D.T., and J.C. Stanley. 1963. *Experimental and Quasi-Experimental Designs for Research.* Chicago: Rand McNally.

Clarke, R.V., and D. Weisburd. 1994. "Diffusion of Crime Control Benefits: Observations on the Reverse of Displacement." In R.V. Clarke, ed., *Crime Prevention Studies.* Vol. 2. Monsey, N.Y.: Willow Tree Press.

Cook, T.D., and D.T. Campbell. 1979. *Quasi-Experimentation: Design and Analysis Issues for Field Settings.* Chicago: Rand McNally.

Dintino, J., and F. Martens. 1979. "The Intelligence Process: A Tool for Criminal Justice Administrators." *Police Chief* (February).

Eck, J.E. 1983. *Solving Crimes: The Investigation of Burglary and Robbery.* Washington, D.C.: Police Executive Research Forum.

———. 1993. "The Threat of Crime Displacement." *Criminal Justice Abstracts* 25:527–46.

Eck, J.E., and J. Wartell. 1983. *Reducing Crime and Drug Dealing by Improving Place Management: A Randomized Experiment.* San Diego: San Diego Police Department.

Edelhertz, H., E. Stotland, M. Walsh, and M. Weinberg. 1977. *The Investigation of White-Collar Crime.* Washington, D.C.: Law Enforcement Assistance Administration.

Gabor, T. 1990. "Crime Prevention and Situational Crime Prevention: Toward the Development of Some Principles." *Canadian Journal of Criminology* 32(1):41–74.

Gardiner, J.A. 1970. *The Politics of Corruption.* New York: Russell Sage.

Goldstein, H. 1977. *Policing a Free Society.* Cambridge, Mass.: Ballinger.

Greenberg, P., J. Petersilia, and J. Chaiken. 1975. *The Criminal Investigation Process.* Santa Monica, Calif.: Rand Corp.

Halper, A., and R. Ku. 1975. *New York Police Department Street Crime Unit: An Exemplary Project.* Washington, D.C.: National Institute of Law Enforcement and Criminal Justice.

Heaphy, J., and J. Wolfle, eds. 1975. *Readings on Productivity in Policing.* Washington, D.C.: Police Foundation.

Jankowski, M.S. 1991. *Islands in the Street: Gangs and American Urban Society.* Berkeley, Calif.: University of California Press.

Karchmer, C. 1970. "Productivity Problems in Organized Crime Enforcement." *Police Chief* (September).

———. 1990. *Strategies for Combating Narcotics Wholesalers.* Washington, D.C.: Police Executive Research Forum.

Karchmer, C., and J. Eck. 1991. "Local Drug Control." In *Local Government Police Management* (3rd ed.). Washington, D.C.: International City Management Association.

Karchmer, C., M. Walsh, and J. Greenfield. 1980. *Strategies for Combating Arson-for-Profit Schemes: Volume I.* Washington, D.C.: U.S. Government Printing Office.

Klockars, C. 1974. *The Professional Fence.* New York: Free Press.

Langworthy, R. 1989. "Do Stings Control Crime? An Evaluation of a Police Fencing Operation." *Justice Quarterly* 6(1):27–45.

Larson, R. 1972. *Urban Police Patrol Analysis.* Cambridge, Mass.: MIT Press.

Martin, S. 1985. *Catching Career Criminals: A Study of the Repeat Offender Project.* Washington, D.C.: Police Foundation.

Marx, G.T. 1988. *Undercover: Police Surveillance in America.* Berkeley, Calif.: University of California Press.

Moore, M. 1977. *Buy and Bust.* Lexington, Mass.: D.C. Heath.

Overly, D., and T. Schell. 1972. *New Effectiveness Measures for Organized Crime Control Efforts.* Washington, D.C.: U.S. Government Printing Office.

Packer, H. 1968. *Limits of the Criminal Sanction.* Stanford, Calif.: Stanford University Press.

Pate, T., R. Bowers, and R. Parks. 1976. *Three Approaches to Criminal Apprehension in Kansas City: An Evaluation Report.* Washington, D.C.: Police Foundation.

Raub, S. 1984. "Effects of Anti-Fencing Operations on Encouraging Crime." *Criminal Justice Review* 9(2):78–83.

Reiss, A., Jr. 1988. "Co-Offending and Criminal Careers." In M. Tonry and N. Morris, eds., *Crime and Justice: A Review of Research.* Vol. 10. Chicago: University of Chicago Press.

Reiss, A., Jr., and D. Bordua. 1967. "Environment and Organization: A Perspective on the Police." In D. Bordua, ed., *The Police: Six Sociological Essays.* New York: John Wiley and Sons.

Reuter, P. 1983. *Disorganized Crime: Economics of the Visible Hand.* Cambridge, Mass.: MIT Press.

_____. 1989. *The Organization of High-Level Drug Markets: An Exploratory Study.* Santa Monica, Calif.: Rand Corp.

_____. 1992. *On the Consequences of Toughness.* Santa Monica, Calif.: Rand Corp.

Rubinstein, J. 1973. *City Police.* New York: Farrar, Strauss, and Giroux.

Schack, S., T. Schell, and W. Gay. 1977. *Improving Patrol Productivity: Special Patrol.* Vol. II. Washington, D.C.: National Institute of Justice.

Sherman, L., ed. 1974. *Police Corruption: A Sociological Perspective.* Garden City, N.Y.: Anchor Books.

Sherman, L., P.R. Gartin, and M.E. Buerger. 1989. "Hot Spots of Predatory Crime: Routine Activities and the Criminology of Place." *Criminology* 27(1):27–55.

Skolnick, J. 1966. *Justice Without Trial.* New York: John Wiley and Sons.

Walsh, M. 1976. *Strategies for Combating the Criminal Receiver of Stolen Goods: Anti-Fencing Manual.* Washington, D.C.: U.S. Government Printing Office.

_____. 1977. *The Fence: A New Look at the World of Property Crime.* Westport, Conn.: Greenwood Press.

Whyte, W. 1955. *Street Corner Society.* Chicago: University of Chicago Press.

Wilson, J.Q. 1968. *Varieties of Police Behavior.* Cambridge, Mass.: Harvard University Press.

Chapter 5

Differential Police Response: Evaluation

Robert E. Worden
Stephen D. Mastrofski

Introduction

Differential police response (DPR) strategies are designed to maintain an optimum balance between too much and too little police resource allocation in responding to requests for police service. This is accomplished by differentiating systematically among requests for service, and varying who responds, in what form, and with what rapidity in accordance with a priority system established by department policy. For many decades following the widespread use of motorized patrol, the two-way radio and the telephone, police departments tended to dispatch a patrol unit as rapidly as possible to citizens' requests for service. A relatively high proportion of calls for service received an immediately dispatched officer, regardless of the situation's urgency. But rising demands for service and declining resource bases in the 1970s signaled a need for greater economy in the use of increasingly scarce police resources. DPR responded to demands for greater government efficiency and cutback management as it became clear that police could not respond quickly to all calls for service.

DPR emerged in the early 1980s as a means of instituting a more sophisticated set of response alternatives, grading the level and immediacy of the response to the particulars of the situation. In addition to the immediate dispatch of a patrol officer, DPR strategies include a variety of alternatives that either delay the dispatch of an officer or altogether relieve the patrol force of sending a sworn officer. The "delay" options can vary in the length of the delay, from a few minutes to several hours. "Relief" responses include dispatching civilian responders instead of sworn, taking reports by telephone, having citizens mail in reports or come to the station to complete them, routing requests directly to specialist police units (instead of sending a patrol officer first), referring requests to nonpolice service sources, and declining to provide service altogether. These alternative delay and relief responses are deemed appropriate for service requests for which an immediate mobile response is not essential for people's health and safety, property protection, evidence gathering, or offender apprehension. DPR is intended to enable an agency to cope efficiently with demands for service that outstrip available resources. It can also be used to expand officers' available time to engage in proactive police strategies (e.g., community and problem-oriented policing)—interrupted only by urgent calls. And ultimately, it offers an opportunity for top administrators to assert greater control over field operations by specifying through policies and procedures the priority of each type of service request and the response alternative appropriate for it.

The Context of DPR: Previous Writing and Research

Recognition of the need for DPR emerged as reformers and researchers began to acknowledge the extent to which American police were essentially *reactive*.   Researchers in the late 1960s and early 1970s noted that the vast majority of patrol officers' encounters with the public were the result of a citizen's request for service rather than an officer-initiated intervention (Reiss 1971; Wilson 1968). Researchers also found that most police time was spent on matters bearing little or no relationship to law enforcement, but rather on keeping the peace, taking reports, and providing an array of human services. Studies of the following decade or so repeatedly confirmed these findings, using a variety of measurement refinements.[1]

Evaluating the Reactive Model

On the heels of the research that described the reactive nature of policing, a number of studies began to *evaluate* it, concluding that its presumed benefits were far overrated.   Several studies found that, except for a small percentage of incidents, the rapidity of police response bore little relationship to the police capacity to apprehend criminals.   This is because there is a substantial delay between the commission of a crime and its report to the police, thus drastically reducing the chance of finding suspects and witnesses at or near the scene. The studies also found that citizen satisfaction with the police response time to a request for service was not solely a function of the rapidity of the response. Rather, satisfaction was best explained by the difference between the caller's expectations and the actual response time. Dissatisfaction is a consequence of response times that exceed citizen expectations, leading analysts to suggest that citizens be advised when delays are likely (Cordner et al. 1983; Kansas City 1978; Pate et al. 1976; Percy 1980; Spelman and Brown 1981; Tien et

---

[1]See Sumrall, Roberts and Farmer (1981) for a review of this literature. For a somewhat different interpretation, see Greene and Klockars (1991).

al. 1977). The research suggested that citizens' assessments of police performance might be malleable if call takers could change citizens' expectations.

Research also showed that reported crimes have a low probability of being cleared unless someone can give a description of the offender or give other leads (Greenwood and Petersilia 1975).   In cases for which this information is unavailable, many departments do not even assign detectives for follow-up investigation (Eck 1983).   It therefore seems reasonable to avoid dispatching a patrol officer by taking the crime report by telephone or having the citizen submit the report by mail or in person—with no reduction in information quantity or quality.

Research also suggests that crime victims' satisfaction would not necessarily suffer a precipitous drop if police failed to send a unit to the scene. Some research does indicate that victim satisfaction with police increases with the thoroughness of police work at the crime scene (Parks 1976; cf. Poister and McDavid 1978; Percy 1980).   But other research shows that victims' expectations of police depend on the type of crime (Brandl and Horvath 1991).   Sixty-nine percent of the victims of minor property crimes were satisfied with a low police investigative effort, while only 45 percent of the victims of serious property crimes (e.g., burglary) were satisfied with low-level effort.

Regarding the police practice of declining to provide service, but rather, referring the caller to another agency, research shows that by the late 1970s, police departments were already doing this at a significant level, but without benefit of much management guidance (Scott 1981:62).

The thrust of all of this research was that the immediate dispatch, incident-driven model did little to enhance police capacity to fight crime, and that moving away from this model would have little adverse effect on citizen satisfaction with police.

The Reformers' Call for an Alternative Model

Research on the reactive model of policing stimulated reformers to encourage police to reject immediate response as the defining feature of the police communications and patrol system: ". . . American policing has essentially become what the English call 'fire brigade' policing, an emergency response system" (Kelling 1983:160).   Reformers charged that police, burdened with the organizational imperative to be "in service" to handle the next call, "reject citizen requests for simple assistance" (Moore and Kelling 1983:50). Furthermore, they asserted that effective crime prevention and response efforts and peacekeeping activities suffered because of police inability to regulate the citizen-generated workload.   And the increased calls for service demand had made the dispatcher the *de facto* supervisor of patrol operations, relegating the sergeant to roll call, backup and report review (Sumrall et al. 1981).

This now traditional style of police response had come to be known as "incident-driven" policing (Eck and Spelman 1987:1–2). Goldstein (1990:20) summarized the case against it:

> In the vast majority of police departments, the telephone, more than any police decision by the community or management, continues to dictate how police resources will be used. These agencies are vulnerable to having all of their resources consumed in reacting to calls for help. This siphons personnel away from other equally important or perhaps more important tasks. It fosters the notion among operating personnel that policing consists simply of responding to little more than the most overt, one-time symptom or manifestation of a problem rather than to the problem itself . . . . Police are not part of the solutions to the problems they are called on to handle. They may actually make some problems more difficult to resolve . . . .
>
> Clearly, the reactive posture encourages superficial responses, placing a higher value on 'getting there' and on 'getting out' than on what actually happens in the handling of the incident. Officers frequently judge one another by the speed with which they handle a call . . . .
>
> The phenomenon, however, cuts even more deeply. It erodes the strength and self-image of the police. The agency commonly viewed by the outside world as so powerful, and frequently criticized as having too much autonomy, is often viewed by its own personnel as extraordinarily weak, as not having a direction of its own, as buffeted about and responding in a feeble fashion to the demands of every Tom, Dick and Harry. Operating almost exclusively in a reactive model results in the police resigning themselves to providing a very limited type of service; to responding repeatedly and inadequately to the same calls, often from the same persons or addresses. Officers become frustrated and cynical, and the public is left unsatisfied.

Sherman (1983:157) concluded that the reactive model of policing could be replaced by a more centralized and rational form of allocating police resources.

> The adoption of a call-screening system is the first step away from the maxim that 911 (the emergency police telephone number in many cities) runs the police department. It implies that police will no longer let individual complaining citizens— an unrepresentative sample of the population—decide how the police will spend their days. It commits the department to using analysis and planning to decide on crime prevention strategies and to carry them out on its own initiative. It is the

first step in transforming the public police from a primarily reactive force to a more goal-seeking organization.

Offering a different perspective on the reactive model, one commentator cautioned:

> With the possible exception of fire and emergency medical service, there is no more client-oriented local government undertaking than police patrol. For the cost of a phone call, virtually anyone can summon one of the state's most powerful agents. It is one of the few aspects of government service where both the poor and the wealthy have a roughly equal probability of getting public service at their doorsteps. The telephone has become the most powerful grassroots mechanism for shaping the allocation of police resources, because the bureaucratic decision rules for patrol assignment are designed in most departments to equalize the workload and thus distribute officers in direct proportion to demand. As the 'invisible hand' that parcels out police service, the reactive approach serves a far more diverse and 'representative' clientele than any of the alternative strategies proposed. To the extent that this clientele 'misrepresents' the general population, it does so on the basis of direct and more-or-less unambiguous expressions of need (Mastrofski 1985:30).

However, Worden (1993:7) argued that the demands citizens express through calls for service are not reliable reflections of need, since some needs are never voiced in this way, and calls vary in the extent to which they represent a 'need' for a sworn officer's presence.

The Development of Differential Response Models

While "incident-driven" policing faced increasing attention from commentators, a number of projects attempted to develop and field-test alternative approaches. Two nationwide surveys published in the early 1980s showed that police departments had for some time used a variety of devices to regulate demands for service, call screening and response prioritization being among the most frequent (Sumrall et al. 1981; Fennessy 1983). However, no single agency had used the full range of response alternatives that might give departments the greatest control over their workload.

Some preliminary studies sponsored by the National Institute of Justice focused specifically on demand management for patrol operations. The Police Executive Research Forum offered a differential response model composed of several elements: (1) an incident classification system not based on legal categories, but rather, on the needs of police in deciding how to respond; (2) the time between incident occurrence and reporting to police; and (3) a wide range of response alternatives (Sumrall et al. 1981). This model was not field-tested when presented, but the researchers performed some feasibility studies in Birmingham, Ala., and San Jose, Calif., concluding that the public would be receptive to the model's alternatives.

The first systematic evaluation of a demand management program was conducted in Wilmington, Del., as a follow-up to the Split-Force Experiment (Tien et al. 1977). The split-force plan provided for the division of the patrol force into two sections: a basic patrol force responsible for responding to calls for service, and a structured patrol force responsible for preventive patrol. The call intake process was reorganized with a greater emphasis on call screening by complaint takers, who were expected to divert a substantial proportion of the complaints from the traditional immediate dispatch to appropriate alternatives, such as delayed response, telephone response, walk-in, and specialist appointment. Using a pretest-posttest design (with no control group), the program evaluators concluded that although Wilmington's crime rate increased, it was within the range of similar cities, and that citizens continued to express high levels of satisfaction with police service after the program was implemented (Cahn and Tien 1981). Whether a citizen received the traditional response or one of the less costly alternatives bore no relation to satisfaction with the police response, and nearly half of the citizens surveyed indicated a willingness to accept a less costly alternative than the one they had received. The program was successful in diverting about 20 percent of the basic patrol force's workload to less costly response strategies (mostly telephone response), increasing overall response productivity by 16 percent. The evaluators noted that even greater efficiency might have been achieved if communications personnel had not underused the less costly response strategies.

Several other evaluations of alternative response strategies were conducted, producing similar findings: It is possible to increase police efficiency without reducing effectiveness—as measured by crime rates and citizen satisfaction.[2] However, these studies reported implementation problems, such as inadequate execution of the call classification system, failure to advise citizens of expected time delays, and underuse of less costly response options.

The Differential Police Response Field Test

In the early 1980s, the National Institute of Justice funded the Differential Police Response Field Test to provide a comprehensive and rigorous experimental evaluation of the DPR model in three sites: Garden Grove, Calif.; Greensboro, N.C.; and Toledo, Ohio. Although the precise plan implemented at each site varied somewhat, all three attempted to reduce resources committed to nonemergency calls

---

[2]See McEwen et al. (1984:43) for a review of these studies.

without the loss of citizen satisfaction (McEwen et al. 1984:3). Each site developed a new call classification system, revised call intake procedures, and conducted intensive training and pretesting. Each site implemented a unit for taking reports over the telephone, a delayed mobile response procedure (providing for delays up to 60 minutes), call referrals to other agencies, and at least one other alternative response method (scheduled appointments, walk-ins or mail-ins).[3] Emergency calls were excluded from the experiment and were handled with the traditional immediate response by mobile units. The experimental design varied somewhat among the three sites to accommodate differences in organization, procedure and record keeping.[4]

The evaluation team rated the DPR field test a success at all three sites. Each site experienced a notable decrease in the number of nonemergency calls handled by immediate dispatch. At all three sites, the nonmobile alternative responses accounted for 15 to 20 percent of the demands for police service, and up to 66 percent of the demands met the criteria for an alternative response (counting 15-minute delayed dispatches).

The delayed mobile dispatch was frequently used at all sites, ranging from 33 percent of all mobile dispatches in Greensboro, to 56 percent in Garden Grove. The types of calls handled this way varied among sites. Automobile accidents, public nuisances and suspicious activity complaints accounted for most of the delayed mobile responses in Greensboro; burglary and theft complaints accounted for most in Garden Grove; and theft, criminal damage, burglary, and traffic accidents accounted for most in Toledo. Responses that *actually* took over 30 minutes were infrequent, ranging from 5 to 21 percent of all delayed mobile responses. Patrol officers were not given alternative directed tasks, as they were in the Wilmington Split-Force Experiment. Had this been done, there would have been a much higher proportion of delays (McEwen et al. 1984:78, 101).

The most frequently used nonmobile alternative was the telephone report, accounting for more than two-thirds of the nonmobile alternative responses at all sites. The vast majority of these calls dealt with theft, vandalism and burglary, although some assaults, disturbances and suspicious circumstances were also handled by telephone. Only the use of mail-in reports was found unsuccessful, since their volume was so low that they accounted for an insignificant proportion of the workload.

---

[3]Greensboro and Toledo were already using a telephone response unit to handle some nonemergency calls; Garden Grove had to initiate one. Garden Grove and Greensboro used the mail-in alternative, Greensboro set up an appointment and referral system and Toledo used a communications callback procedure.

[4]See the section of this chapter on research design for a discussion of experimental designs. See also Chapter 4.

The delay and relief alternatives increased the amount of time available for other activities. For example, in Garden Grove, patrol unit calls for service decreased by 3 percent under experimental conditions, producing a net savings of six patrol officers' time. The new alternatives were less costly than the traditional approach. For example, the cost of the alternative response in Garden Grove was estimated to be only 27 percent of the cost of the immediate mobile response, while the productivity of alternative response personnel was three times that of patrol unit personnel. Response time to emergency calls was not compromised.

DPR's implementation at these sites showed little or no adverse impact on citizen satisfaction. At each site, citizens whose calls for police service were eligible for a delayed or relief response were interviewed by phone about their experiences with call takers and other department personnel. Some citizens had received an immediate mobile response by sworn officers, so their satisfaction levels provided benchmarks against which other citizens' responses could be compared. Citizen surveys conducted before the test phase showed high satisfaction levels, and there was little change when DPR was used. About 90 percent or more of the citizens expressed satisfaction with how their calls were handled across all forms of response: immediate mobile responses, delayed mobile responses, telephone reports, civilian responses, and walk-in reports. Satisfaction levels varied somewhat across forms of police response. Citizens receiving a delayed or relief response were less likely to be "very satisfied" and more likely to be merely "satisfied." They were also more likely to be dissatisfied, but they constituted a very small proportion of the citizens interviewed.

Unfortunately, the comparisons of pre-experimental and experimental phases in Greensboro and Toledo are not generalizable to departments that have little or no demand management procedures already in operation. Both of these sites had already implemented telephone report units to handle some calls for service *before* the project began. The question arises as to what extent the DPR program introduced a change in the use of alternatives, and suggests that DPR may be even more cost-effective for departments that currently have little or no demand management. According to the rough estimates in the report (p. 32), DPR increased the use of alternatives to two to three times the preexisting levels. Only in Garden Grove was the introduction of alternatives something entirely new, and a comparison of pre-experimental and experimental phases shows a small overall decline in satisfaction with the handling of calls designated for telephone and immediate mobile response.[5]

---

[5]Satisfaction with call takers declined 4.6 percent, and satisfaction with response time declined 6.7 percent from the pre-experimental levels. Pre-post comparisons of the delayed mobile, mail-in and walk-in alternatives were not presented.

The DPR field test evaluators concluded that DPR was the "new remedy" to deal with the problems of declining budgets, increasing demands for service, and public pressure to improve police performance (Cohen and McEwen 1984:4).   Following the publication of the study results, the three departments conducted technology transfer conferences for nearby police departments.   The International Association of Chiefs of Police and the National Institute of Justice sponsored training seminars on DPR.

The Aftermath of the DPR Field Test

Systematic data are not available, but it seems very likely that since the publication of the DPR field test study, there has been a significant growth in nationwide use of DPR in some form.   Unfortunately, there has been little additional research on this topic.   The report was criticized for a number of deficiencies, especially concerning its inadequate consideration of the equity issue—whether DPR altered the distribution of police services among different segments of the population (Mastrofski 1985).   When some types of calls receive delayed or relief responses, those who make those calls are given what is arguably reduced service.   If some income and racial groups are disproportionately represented among those who make those types of calls, then DPR may impose a greater burden on them than it does on others.

The DPR field test evaluation included pre-experimental surveys of people making nonemergency service requests in order to establish a benchmark satisfaction level.   The respondents' prospective willingness to accept alternatives was analyzed in terms of their age, income, sex, and length of residence, but not race (McEwen et al. 1984: Ch. 11).   Each characteristic showed a statistically significant relationship to the willingness to accept one or more of the alternatives in at least one site, although many of the differences were not substantively large.[6]   The omission of race from the evaluation is particularly unfortunate in view of the substantial evidence that blacks' evaluations of police are significantly lower than whites'—and that they would therefore probably be less receptive than whites to alternatives to immediate dispatch (see Jacob 1971; Furstenberg and Wellford 1973; Durand 1976; Flanagan 1985).   Furthermore, the respondents' retrospective satisfaction with alternatives during the experimental phase was not analyzed according to demographic characteristics, so one can only speculate about the extent to which

---

[6]One of the larger demographic differences found was in Toledo, where respondents' willingness to accept an alternative to immediate dispatch was sensitive to income: a respondent with more than $20,000 in annual income was about 1.6 times as likely to accept an alternative as one with less than $10,000.

different social groups evaluate their experiences with DPR differently.

Fortunately, a recent study of DPR in a different city corrects these methodological limitations. In Lansing, Mich., DPR strategies similar (though not identical) to those tested earlier were found to produce significant increases in efficiency without a decline in citizen satisfaction. Further, although there were differences among demographic groups in satisfaction with police services, the differences were *not* the results of DPR, suggesting that DPR did not contribute to inequities in service delivery (Worden 1993).

Despite the rather substantial empirical evidence of DPR's merits, there are still a number of unresolved issues about its utility.

First, to what extent, if any, are the quantity and quality of information gathered by alternative responses any different from those of information gathered by the dispatched officer? Do cold-crime reports taken over the phone or by mail produce less useful information than those taken by an officer responding to the scene? Do civilian report takers obtain information at the scene as well as (or better than) sworn report takers? Is it possible to motivate and train sworn officers to be better information gatherers in routine incidents than they have traditionally been, and if so, do they produce appreciably better information from being on the scene than the alternative responses produce? A major challenge in comparing the information gathered through various response methods is establishing criteria for what constitutes good information. Good information is that which contributes to the accurate identification of problems and points the way to solutions.

A second issue for future research is the extent to which reliance on alternative responses alters the officer's knowledge of people and places on his or her assigned beat. Diverting a significant proportion of incidents from beat officers to other response modes means officers are likely to have markedly reduced routine access to certain people and problems on their beats. Dispatch situations offer an opportunity for responding officers to get to know people, and often give them access to places where they would not ordinarily be. Whether DPR produces a significant decline in officers' knowledge of people and places will depend on how officers spend the time freed up by DPR. For example, do police-initiated, door-to-door, getting-to-know-you citizen surveys produce information as valuable to officers as simply responding to routine calls in the area? When officers are free to initiate encounters with the public, do they choose to deal with the same types of people they would encounter if they had spent that time responding to calls for service?[7]

---

[7]For example, a study of foot patrol officers in Edmonton showed that the officers—who were given far more discretionary time free of calls for service—were much more inclined to engage in contacts with people of higher, "white collar" socioeconomic status (Hornick et al. 1989:90).

A third issue for future research is the extent to which alternative responses alter the short- and long-term resolution of problems citizens ask police to handle. A now rather substantial body of research indicates that *immediate* response to calls produces an arrest in only a small proportion of in-progress incidents, but it is still possible that the presence of an officer (or other responder)—even if delayed—can produce more effective service than non-dispatch alternatives (e.g., telephone, mail report, walk-in). For example, evaluations of the various response alternatives have not examined other services police can (and do) provide in response to cold-crime calls. By examining the scene, the responder may be able to offer crime prevention tips to prevent future crimes of the same sort. The responder may also be able to offer a more realistic appraisal of the likelihood of property retrieval and offender apprehension than is possible via telephone. Further, if the responder is the beat officer for that location, he or she may obtain more detailed knowledge of the victim's vulnerability or the location and therefore pay closer attention in the future.

Assessing the capacity of various response modes to provide short- and long-term solutions is challenging. One promising alternative is to do a "repeat calls analysis" (Sherman, Gartin and Buerger 1989) on complainants and addresses. Such an analysis involves a comparison of subsequent complaints from the same person or address over a given period following the department's receipt of an initial call. If there is no difference between the effectiveness of a telephone response and a dispatch for a given type of problem (say burglary), then the rate of repeat calls should be similar between complainants receiving a telephone and a dispatch response.[8]

A fourth issue to be explored is the nature and extent of the "error" rate in the assignment of alternative responses by communications personnel. DPR increases the burden of complaint diagnosis on the call taker, because fewer calls will automatically receive a dispatched officer. Communications personnel can commit two types of errors:

- Type 1: assigning a response with a higher priority than the call deserves, and
- Type 2: assigning a response with a lower priority than the call deserves.

---

[8]Of course, to make this comparison meaningful, one would want assurance that the burglary calls receiving a telephone response were similar to those receiving a dispatch response. This can be accomplished by random assignment of calls, using an experimental design, which will be discussed later in this report.

The DPR field test did not conduct a thorough analysis of Type 1 and Type 2 errors, but it did report that communications personnel were inclined to "override" departmental guidelines in situations indicating a delayed or relief response, especially in Garden Grove (McEwen, Connors and Cohen 1984:80). This pattern may reflect the residue of the previous, more liberal dispatch practice, or it may reflect communications personnel's empathy for crime victims, as the researchers suggested. But the pattern is also consistent with a very rational personal strategy of self-protection. The consequences of "underresponding" can be catastrophic (e.g., severe injury or loss of life), increasing the vulnerability of the communications decision maker to sanctions (e.g., loss of job or lawsuit). The consequences of "overresponding" are, by comparison, minuscule, even if they contravene DPR's basic objective: to economize the use of police resources.[9]

Assessing the Type 1 and 2 error rates requires after-the-fact judgments about whether communications personnel did the right thing. This might be accomplished by examining departmental records on each call (including the audiotape), and conducting a follow-up survey of complainants. There are two criteria that might be applied: (1) compliance with departmental rules and guidelines, and (2) the demands of the particular situation. In the first case, the only question is whether the communications personnel complied with the call classification and response assignment directives set forth by the department. However, the real "bottom line" is whether the selected response was appropriate for the situation, regardless of whether the decision maker was in compliance, for in some cases, the directive may not be the best choice.

This higher standard is particularly important in light of recent developments in call management, which substantially reduce communications personnel's discretion in classifying calls and selecting responses. Some police departments have developed detailed protocols for call takers to follow in gathering information to select the best response. The call taker initially decides which of several classifications best characterizes the call.[10] Then the call taker asks a predetermined set of questions that are pertinent to calls falling into

---

[9]Overresponding on an occasional basis is unlikely to generate any negative consequence for the communications decision maker—or at most, a verbal cautioning. Even a more frequent pattern of overresponding is unlikely to produce more than a lower job performance evaluation.

[10]For example, the Peel Regional Police of Ontario use the following call classifications: crimes against persons, disturbance, assistance, crimes against property, traffic accidents/problems, suspicious circumstances, public morals, miscellaneous service, and alarms. The Houston Police Department is currently reviewing a classification system with the following categories: accidents, property crimes, auto thefts, patrol calls, crimes against persons, police transport calls, noncriminal service calls, assist the officer, and hospital checks.

the selected category. The questions vary according to classification, but there are several common items that facilitate response selection: time of occurrence (e.g., in progress, just occurred or cold); whether a suspect is at or near the scene; whether there are weapons present; and whether the situation is life-threatening. The nature of the "correct" response is specified by departmental rules, which indicate a particular priority code for each possible combination of responses in each call classification category.   Department policy also specifies which priority levels require an immediate dispatch (and under what level of urgency), and how many units will respond. Policy also stipulates which calls can be subject to delay and which can or must be diverted to alternative responses. Although some systems allow the communications personnel to use their own judgment to "override" the predetermined response priority for a given call, others do not. Given recent advances in computer-aided dispatch (CAD) systems, it is now possible for the call taker to serve only as an information gatherer, while the computer itself carries out the priority selection and unit assignment tasks.   Under these circumstances, it would be particularly important to assess the rate of Type 1 and Type 2 errors made by such a system.

Another new wrinkle in call management deserves evaluation: the callback. Callbacks are used on calls that are eligible for a dispatched unit but are lower priority and are placed on a pending or "stacked" delayed-response queue, awaiting the availability of an appropriate unit. Such calls are screened by telephone through a callback. By recontacting the complainant, the callback officer tries to determine whether it is feasible to divert, cancel or handle the complaint by alternative means (telephone report, mail-in, walk-in). On some occasions, the police will issue a warning by telephone to an offender or person believed to be responsible for a problem. Because the dispatch of units to these calls is delayed, the problems sometimes resolve themselves in the interim (or the presence of a police officer is otherwise unnecessary).

In 1987, the Cleveland Police Department conducted a test of the callback procedure for a one-month period (Cincinnati Institute of Criminal Justice 1988:10–15). Nearly all of the 1,133 referrals made to the department's telephone expeditor unit were handled by callback, and two-thirds of those resulted in the cancellation of a zone car assigned to take the call.[11] A one-day field test of the callback procedure in a Houston patrol district showed that almost 57 percent of all 330 callbacks in an eight-hour period resulted in the diversion or cancellation of the call.

---

[11]In 61 percent of the cases where the zone car was cancelled, the incident had been resolved without any police involvement; in 21 percent, advice was given by telephone to the complainant; in 18 percent, a referral was made to another agency or a specialist police unit; and in 1 percent, the offender was warned by telephone.

The callback approach would seem to have tremendous potential to reduce the demand for uniformed patrol response, which makes it all the more important to evaluate it through follow-up interviews with citizens who have experienced this method. It is also possible that an empirical assessment might reveal that refinements in the system of initial priority classification would result in fewer calls being assigned a delayed dispatch response at the outset—thus obviating the need for callbacks.

A final issue for future DPR evaluations concerns the problem of what experimental scientists call "dosage." The term *dosage* comes from medicine and has to do with the strength or amount of a drug given to a patient or research subject. The nature and extent of a patient's response to a drug will usually depend on the amount of the drug given. Usually, there is a range in which a drug will be optimally effective for a given patient. Too little or too much of the drug will produce less optimal, and even undesirable, effects. In a similar fashion, a DPR program's effects will depend in part on the *strength* of the program. A DPR program that produces a 25 percent reduction in the patrol division's response workload will probably have a significantly different set of impacts than one that produces only a 5 percent reduction in the patrol division's workload. For example, it is possible that with a 5 percent reduction, there is no significant decline in citizen satisfaction with police service delivery through alternatives to immediate dispatch, but a 25 percent reduction in immediately dispatched calls might be large enough to produce a substantial decrease in citizen satisfaction—because the latter program's scope cuts more deeply into services citizens cherish. It is dangerous to extrapolate the effects of higher dosage levels from those on which data are already available. For example, the trend line on citizen satisfaction levels established by 1, 5 and 10 percent reductions in workload might change at the higher reduction levels of 15, 20 and 25 percent.

The dosage of any DPR program is therefore critically important in terms of the expected consequences. A point to remember when developing a call management program is that the programs that have thus far been rigorously evaluated have been relatively modest in dosage—compared with the programs' *potential*. For example, in Greensboro's DPR field test, 46.4 percent of all calls could have received an alternative response to immediate dispatch, but, in fact, only 19.5 percent did (McEwen, Connors and Cohen 1984:10).   In Garden Grove, 22.3 percent of non-information calls could have received a non-dispatch alternative, and an additional 43.6 percent could have received a delayed response. In fact, only 12.4 percent received a no-dispatch alternative, and only 4.8 percent were actually delayed more than 30 minutes.[12] This dosage issue is particularly

---

[12]The underuse of alternatives to immediate dispatch at these sites was due in part to the requirements of the experimental design, which specified that half of

significant, given the citizens' reaction to the delayed mobile response. In general, the level of dissatisfaction with the response time for "delayed mobile" respondents was two to eight times that of immediate dispatch respondents, ranging from 16 percent in Garden Grove to 27 percent in Greensboro. Similarly, Worden (1993) found in Lansing that calls designated for a delayed response (up to 60 minutes) were rarely delayed that long, with about 60 percent receiving a response within 20 minutes. Further, calls diverted from dispatch for telephone report taking accounted for only about 3 percent of all calls.

Of course, dosage levels can affect other performance considerations, as well: quality of information gathered, apprehension of suspects, and long-term problem (repeat call) reduction. Thus far, researchers have paid little attention to DPR's impact at different dosage levels, but this will become very important for many departments that hope to make much greater reductions in mobile dispatch (both immediate and delayed) in their call management—through telephone response, mail-in/walk-in reports and callbacks.

Program Objectives and Unintended Effects

The previous section addressed a number of DPR objectives and discussed what research has shown about DPR's effects—both desired and undesired. This section offers a concise summary of DPR objectives and unintended effects.

OBJECTIVE 1: PROMOTE GREATER EFFICIENCY IN THE USE OF POLICE RESOURCES.

DPR attempts to avoid the use of more costly methods of response to requests for service in situations that can be handled satisfactorily by less costly means. This savings can be used in a variety of ways that are entirely independent of the decision to implement DPR: reducing police costs (e.g., personnel); handling an increased workload (e.g., more calls for service); or using personnel for other activities (e.g., community or problem-oriented policing).

The key to greater efficiency is minimizing Type 1 errors— assigning calls a higher response priority than they warrant. Thus, the

---

eligible calls be assigned an immediate dispatch and half be assigned an alternative response—for comparison purposes. One reason that actual delays were substantially less than the assigned category (15 minutes, 30 minutes or 60 minutes) was that the departments were not allowed to introduce changes in field operations that would have engaged officers in alternative activities, such as more on-scene investigations or directed patrol activities, thus increasing their availability to respond and reduce the *actual* delay. Departments that specify alternative activities (e.g., community policing and problem solving) for their officers should expect to experience much greater actual delay.

first step in achieving this objective is to identify the demands for police service and to differentiate among those demands according to their resource needs. This defines the limits of potential cost savings that a DPR system could optimally provide.

A DPR program's cost efficiency—compared with that of the previously used approach—can be measured in terms of

- the extent to which workload is transferred from more costly responses (e.g., dispatch) to less costly responses (e.g., telephone, referral or mail-in);
- the projected amount of patrol officer time saved by alternatives to dispatch;
- the estimated total dollar savings in handling calls by alternative means (including personnel, equipment, capital, and other operating expenses).

OBJECTIVE 2: PROMOTE (OR AVOID REDUCTIONS IN) SERVICE EFFECTIVENESS.

DPR attempts to help police departments accomplish many traditional tasks, such as responding to calls for service with a less costly allocation of resources. At the same time, it attempts to achieve these cost reductions without a significant decline in the quality of the service provided. For example, there is a concern that rapid response times *not* be compromised for true-emergency, high-priority calls, and that information gathered from cold-crime reports obtained by alternative means be as good as information that a dispatched officer would have obtained. Further, police departments *may* opt to use resource "savings" obtained through DPR to engage in other activities or programs, the objective of which is to increase the department's overall effectiveness (e.g., reducing crime, solving a host of non-crime problems).

Effectiveness goals relevant to DPR can be divided into five categories, each of which is briefly summarized below.

Quality/Quantity of Information Gathered

How good is the information the department gathers about a citizen's problem? How comprehensive is it? How accurate is it? Does it go into sufficient depth? To assess a DPR program, the evaluator is concerned about whether there are any differences in the quality/quantity of information gathered by *each* of the potential methods by which the department might collect information: immediate dispatch of a sworn officer, delayed dispatch, use of civilian report takers, telephone reports, mailed reports, and walk-ins. Different kinds of problems usually require different kinds of information, and the department often uses a different report form for each. To establish criteria regarding the quality/quantity of information provided by each method, the evaluator can draw upon the expertise of police officers and other personnel whose routine responsibility it is to use this information to deal with the problems citizens call about.

Officer Knowledge of Assigned Area

Because DPR affects how officers spend their time, and with whom they spend it, the evaluator must be concerned about how DPR affects what officers learn about the people, places and problems on their assigned beats (Mastrofski 1983). Does their knowledge change about crime suspects and, if so, what type? Does their knowledge change about victims, racial groups and people at risk to certain kinds of crimes and disorders? Does their "cognitive map" of places change? Given the wide range of information that is useful to police officers, it is impossible to state in a general way what constitutes better and worse knowledge. In large part, it depends on the department's expectations—given the community's needs. However, it is important to note that an officer's knowledge is a key tool in shaping how he or she practices policing (Mastrofski and Parks 1990; Muir 1977; Rubinstein 1973).

Precisely *how* DPR might be expected to change officer knowledge of the people and places on the assigned beat depends on how the officer spends the time freed up by call management. If DPR simply allows the department to keep the officers busy handling higher-priority calls, then the amount of change in knowledge may be modest. However, if DPR is used so that officers have greater discretion about how they spend their time, then there will undoubtedly be *increased* variation among officers in the quality and quantity of knowledge they have, since their contacts with the public will be more heavily influenced by their own predilections. Or if the department tries to structure the officers' freed-up time (e.g., with directed patrol), this will influence the changes to be expected.

Citizen Satisfaction With Police Service

Keeping the "customer" satisfied is as important to police as to any other service-oriented enterprise. In this case, there are two types of customers: those who have made a specific request of the police, and those who are *potential* requesters of police service, whether or not they have recently made such a request. In either case, citizens are concerned about a variety of things that help identify specific police objectives:

— Rapidity of response to the call for service
  Did the police address the caller's request in a timely fashion?

— Effort, concern and demeanor of police responder
Did the responder make a sufficient effort to deal with
the citizen's problem? That is, did the responder *try*
hard enough?
Did the responder show appropriate interest in or
concern about the citizen's problem?
Was the responder's demeanor appropriate for the
situation?

— Outcome of effort
How satisfactory was the outcome of the responder's
effort? Did the police effort contribute to the reduction
or elimination of the citizen's problem?

Citizens may weigh each of these factors differently in assessing
the overall quality of the police response to their requests. In every
case, however, it is important to remember that the citizen's
satisfaction level is strongly affected by his or her expectations. This
was one of the major lessons of the response time studies reviewed
earlier in this chapter. If two citizens with identical problems receive
the exact same response, their evaluations of the response will
probably differ if their expectations differ. Those with low
expectations are easier to satisfy than those with high expectations.
One of the ironies of consumer satisfaction surveys is that a service
provider who has a reputation for high-quality service will be held to a
higher performance standard by the regular clientele than one who
has a weaker reputation. This makes it all the more essential to learn
the police personnel's performance expectations when assessing their
levels of satisfaction with service delivery.

Problem Reduction or Elimination

The reduction or elimination of citizens' problems is the "bottom
line" of a results-oriented police department (Goldstein 1990).
Citizens who receive a police response are in a unique position to
offer *their* perspective on the impact of the police effort to deal with
their problem, but they are not the sole source, and they are often not
the most objective source. For a variety of reasons, police cannot
assume that a problem has been reduced or eliminated simply because
a citizen expresses satisfaction with the police response (see earlier
comments regarding the impact of citizens' expectations on their
evaluations). The objective of a DPR evaluation regarding the
recurrence of a problem is that—at a minimum—the recurrence rate
for DPR be at least *no worse* than that for the previous method of
handling citizens' demands for service.
The ways in which citizens' problems can be reduced or
eliminated are as varied as the problems themselves. Goldstein (1990)
offers some useful examples of problem reduction. Here it is noted
only that an evaluator can assume the reduction or elimination of a

problem, once identified, by the extent to which it recurs following the police response. This can be measured by the frequency and intensity with which the problem reemerges in a specified period following the police response (e.g., a day, week, month, or year). Another way to measure recurrence is to determine the "time to failure." During a specified period—say, a month—how much time elapsed before the problem occurred again? The longer the time to recurrence (or "failure"), the greater the reduction of the problem.

Measures of this objective are possible from a number of police data sources. Calls for service data permit the department to assess the recurrence of calls from a given complainant or address during a specified period. Crime reports allow the department to determine the recurrence of reported crime for a given complainant or address. It is also possible to conduct follow-up surveys of complainants to ask them detailed questions about the nature and extent of a given problem's recurrence during a set period. This methodology was used in the Minneapolis Domestic Violence Experiment (Sherman and Berk 1984), and in later replications at other sites. In this case, citizen respondents were *not* asked to give their assessments of police service, but only to report whether they had experienced domestic violence again following the police intervention.

Minimization of Type 2 Errors

Recalling the earlier discussion, a Type 2 error occurs when the police give a request for service a lower priority than it actually deserves. Because DPR is designed to reduce the frequency with which requests are given *more* resources than they need (Type 1 errors), vigorous pursuit of this objective increases the risk of Type 2 errors. Examples of Type 2 errors are numerous:

— failure to dispatch a sworn officer to a life-threatening situation,
— failure to dispatch a sworn officer soon enough to a life-threatening situation,
— failure to dispatch *enough* sworn officers to handle a given situation,
— failure to dispatch a civilian report taker to an incident where useful information could have been obtained, and
— referring a citizen complaint to another agency when the police could have handled it more effectively.

These types of errors occur because of (1) diagnosis failures of individual call takers, (2) system or procedural breakdowns in the execution of directives, or (3) weaknesses in the policies and directives themselves.

An example may be instructive. Domestic and neighborhood disturbances account for a large proportion of most departments' calls for service workload.   Many of these calls prove to be nonemergencies and are therefore good candidates for an alternative to an immediate dispatch: delayed dispatch or callback (with the subsequent possibility of handling by telephone or referral).   As police are well aware, however, such interpersonal disturbances *can* generate incredible violence with catastrophic results.   Consequently, even if the risks of a Type 2 error in these cases are small (because so few actually develop into life-threatening situations), the costs of making such an error are tremendous.   By forcing police response decision makers to screen these calls and assign them different response levels, the department creates a need to consider explicitly the risks *and* costs of making a Type 2 error.   The department must then make a conscious choice about what level of risk of a Type 2 error is acceptable, and how to organize its management of disturbance calls to ensure that that risk level is not exceeded.

Type 2 errors reduce the department's capacity to apprehend criminals (when there is a chance of catching them), save lives or otherwise deal with the situation most effectively.   When Type 2 errors occur, aside from the degradation of service to the individual citizen-client, the department is also highly vulnerable to bad publicity and civil suits.   In some ways, a department may be willing to accept the costs of certain kinds of Type 2 errors due to DPR (e.g., a modest reduction in the quality of information obtained on minor auto accidents via telephone and mail-in reports).   However, Type 2 errors in the high-priority categories (involving serious threats to life and property) are matters no department wishes to take lightly.   That is why departments engaging in DPR must continue to be concerned about response times to high-priority calls, and whether adequate police backup was present.

OBJECTIVE 3: PROMOTE (OR AVOID REDUCTIONS IN) EQUITY OF SERVICE DISTRIBUTION.

DPR programs are designed to increase police efficiency by altering call management practices and introducing new, less costly methods of response.   Although DPR is not *intended* to affect the distribution of police services among different groups of citizens, it is quite possible that distributional changes will be an unintended consequence—which may or may not be desired.   On the one hand, it may be desirable to have people with the most serious high-priority problems receive the highest-priority police response, while those with less pressing problems receive lower levels of response.   On the other hand, such a shift may also reallocate resource delivery to the community's different social, economic and demographic groups in ways that will seem unfair to those who "lose" in the reallocation.

Judging the equity of police resource distribution depends on how equity is defined.   It might be defined as everyone being treated the same.   If Citizen Jones calls for assistance, he is as entitled to a dispatched officer as Citizen Smith is.   This has obvious appeal on the surface, but clearly falls short when one considers that all the problems police confront are not equally *needful* of police attention. Some are, indeed, more worthy of attention than others—hence, the need for setting priorities according to need. Most DPR programs appear to be designed to define equity as deploying police resources according to the apparent level of need, treating all similar levels of need the same.[13]

If "need" is the definition of equity used by a department, then an examination of the equity of service distribution might take the following form. First, the evaluator would want to be sure that the department's need (priority) categories for call classifications were indeed appropriate. That is, the evaluator would want to know that all of the types of calls falling in the Priority 1 category are indeed a higher priority than those falling in the Priority 2 category, and so on. Next, the evaluator would examine the extent to which all calls falling within the same priority category receive the same level of response. Consider this example: 25 percent of all top-priority calls are handled in under five minutes, 25 percent are handled in five to 10 minutes, 25 percent are handled in 11 to 15 minutes, and 25 percent are handled in 16 to 20 minutes. This amount of variation might be cause for concern, particularly if it was correlated with certain "suspect" categories: race, socioeconomic status or residence in particular parts of town. If low-income neighborhoods were more likely to have slower response times for high-priority calls than middle-income neighborhoods, there is some evidence to suggest an inequitable distribution of service delivery, and it would certainly bear further investigation.

OBJECTIVE 4: INCREASE MANAGEMENT'S CONTROL OF PATROL RESOURCE ALLOCATION.

An appealing aspect of DPR for many police administrators is its capacity to empower them to set policy about how police resources will be allocated. DPR attempts to impose top-down rules, guidelines or constraints on the discretion of low-ranking decision makers in the call-response process. For many years, police communications personnel have received little attention from administrators in terms of call management policies, training and supervision (Percy and Scott 1985). Thus, police administrators' capacity to influence resource allocation was limited mostly to establishing shift schedules and beat boundaries. But once the officers reported for duty, when and to whom they were dispatched was left largely to the discretion of the people answering telephones and operating the two-way radio.

---

[13]See Worden (1993) for a brief discussion of equity relating to DPR. For more general discussions of equity and police service distribution, see Mastrofski and Wadman (1991), Ostrom (1983) and Whitaker et al. (1982).

Assessing the degree of control administrators exercise through DPR is relatively straightforward: To what extent do the people responsible for receiving and handling calls actually comply with departmental directives? If a directive specifies that *all* Priority 1 calls assigned to a single-officer unit will *automatically* receive a backup, how often does that happen?

Of course, assessing administrative control becomes more complex when directives are vague or more complex.   Simple compliance is difficult to determine; what the administrator (and evaluator) is looking for is whether the judgment of the call-management decision makers is what the administrator wants. This requires a careful review of the decision-making situations themselves. Fortunately, calls for service are readily taped, so that *post hoc* evaluations of individual choices are possible, with the unusual (for police) added benefit of being able to consider virtually the same information that was available to the decision maker.

Implementation Considerations for Evaluation

Many police programs fail to achieve their goals, not because the ideas and theories underlying the programs were faulty, but because the programs were not implemented properly.   Implementation failures occur when a program was not operated as planned: (1) sufficient resources were not provided; (2) the operational plan (policies, rules and guidelines) was inadequate; (3) program personnel were not adequately prepared to fulfill their responsibilities; or (4) program personnel failed to carry out their responsibilities (intentionally or unintentionally).   In short, implementation concerns are the "practical" concerns of seeing that the program as operated closely resembles the program as planned.   When evaluators try to assess the impact of a program that had serious implementation problems, they are placed in the position of a football coach who wants to assess the effectiveness of a new offensive play, but is unable to do so because his team does not execute it as planned. Unless the team finds a way to execute the play properly, the coach will never learn just how useful the play could be.   And unless a police department implements a program properly, evaluators will never learn just what kind of impact the program could have.

DPR, like any program, is subject to implementation problems that interfere with the execution of the call-management plan.   The number of such problems is phenomenal, so only a few of the more likely ones will be discussed in this section.

Instituting Feasible Call-Management Protocols

The heart of the DPR program is its call classification and priority system, which sets forth precisely *how* each type of call is to be treated. No matter how elegant this system may appear on paper, if those charged with using it cannot easily do so, the DPR program is virtually guaranteed to produce unexpected, and usually undesirable, results. First and foremost, the call classification system must make sense to the people who have to use it. Call takers who make the initial classification decision must translate what callers tell them into a "language" that the police organization understands and has routines for handling. A department may develop a detailed list of "incident" or "problem" codes with more than a hundred categories (Cincinnati Institute of Criminal Justice 1986), but for the purposes of deciding what immediate response to choose, it makes sense to group these many detailed categories into a few. Eight or nine general categories seem popular among police agencies using DPR. These categories usually reflect the substantive nature of the problem the police must handle: crime against person, traffic accident, disturbance, or miscellaneous service, for example.

Categories that describe the problem's substantive nature are not enough, however, since they provide little information about the situation's urgency. Situations that are "in progress" are generally thought to be more urgent than those where the "damage" has already been done. And those problems that have "just occurred" are thought to be more urgent than those that have occurred less recently. When the problem source (e.g., the suspect) is still at the scene, it is thought that there are greater prospects for an immediate and urgent dispatch to be effective than when there is no problem source present. And of course, anything that indicates a life-threatening situation (especially the presence of weapons) increases the urgency for immediate police intervention.

Thus, the two major urgency considerations appear to be (1) the scope of the harm that has occurred or might occur, and (2) the likely impact that immediate police presence will have on preventing, reducing or ameliorating the harm. Naturally, calls that rank high on both those dimensions (e.g., in-progress rapes) will be assigned a high priority according to the protocol, and those ranking low on both dimensions will receive a low priority. But calls that rank high on one category but low on another (e.g., dead-body calls, motorists in distress) have priorities that are not so obvious. Still others rank somewhere in the middle on both dimensions (e.g., missing juveniles, noise disturbances, shots fired, indecent exposure, customer trouble). One way to systematize this is to create a matrix with one dimension arrayed in rows and the other in columns, arranged from high to low. Then a priority number is assigned to each, again usually limiting the priorities to a small number, since most departments cannot effectively discriminate among more than six priority levels in responding to calls.

Once priorities have been established for each type of call, then response protocols can be specified. Some will be mandatory. For example, all departments require an immediate emergency dispatch (of usually more than one unit) to an "assist officer" call. Similarly, a cold auto theft call might always be routed to a telephone report unit or some other designated alternative response. But there might be some calls for which the dispatcher is given an option, depending on the details of the situation and the availability of units to respond. For example, some DPR programs allow communications personnel to override the normal protocol if the caller insists on a dispatched officer instead of a non-dispatch alternative. It is particularly important to make clear what priorities *require* a given response, and what priorities (if any) allow the dispatcher some discretion. In the latter case, it is important to set forth guidelines for the exercise of discretion.

It is easy to see how, in designing such a system, a department could generate an enormously complex set of rules and procedures. Departments must always balance the need to cover a wide range of contingencies with a response plan, while maintaining a system that is simple and efficient enough to be used under real-life work pressures.

Computer-aided call classification and dispatch can help reduce the number of things communications personnel must remember, but heavy reliance on the computer to make judgment calls is risky, since the computer's decision can be no better than the software installed to handle calls. It has long been a precept of street-level police officers that those who are at the scene or in the situation are almost always in the best position to judge what to do about it, since it is exceedingly difficult to write rules and guidelines that specify in advance what should be done. That should be kept in mind for call classification and dispatch, as well. So if the department envisions the use of a highly automated system of initial call screening and dispatching, then it is *especially* important for evaluators to monitor the system's capacity to assign incoming calls as they should be.

Whether or not the department uses a CAD system, it would be useful to appoint a task force to develop or review the call classification and priority assignment protocols. This task force should include experienced communications personnel and patrol officers, since these are the people who will be using the system.

Selecting and Training Personnel to Conduct DPR

In the past, relatively little attention was paid to selecting and training police communications personnel, since it was (erroneously) thought that they exercised little discretion. DPR now makes obvious the importance of selecting the right people and adequately preparing them for the work. Communications personnel are to police officers what physicians' assistants have become to medical doctors: they perform the initial diagnosis and, in many routine cases, treat the patient, as well. Furthermore, as DPR innovations continue to expand alternative response modes, the nature of alternative responders diversifies as well. Of course, DPR requires initial call screeners and dispatchers. But it may also involve a wide range of other positions: telephone report takers, callback operators, staff to handle walk-in and mail reports, staff to handle dispatched report takers, and so on.

Departments must decide which (if any) of these positions will be handled by civilians, and which by sworn personnel.

The nature and extent of training will depend on the kind of DPR system the department sets up. It is not the purpose here to provide a how-to manual on training and selection, but it will be noted that, as with the development of the call-management protocols, it would be best to include some of the people who will be receiving the training in the development of training curricula. If the department will use callbacks as a way of reducing dispatches, the authors believe that the people who make the calls will require exceptional judgment. They will be dealing with calls that have been initially determined to warrant a dispatched unit. The callback operator must be able to determine over the telephone whether—upon subsequent examination—a dispatch is really necessary. This requires a strong knowledge of police work (whether or not the operator is sworn), and creativity in seeking alternative solutions to dispatch. Type 2 errors in the callback situation seem a special risk.

Training funds for the DPR system should also be used for police officers, especially those assigned to patrol. If officers do not understand or appreciate the new DPR system, it will matter little how good the communications and alternative response personnel are. To the extent that it is possible, *all* department personnel should see DPR as a joint team effort—not just the responsibility of a few specialists.

Supervising DPR Personnel

As with selecting and training DPR personnel, it is also important to ensure that they have adequate supervision. Supervisors should monitor their subordinates' performance, and fortunately for call-management functions, this task is relatively easy due to the availability of audiotapes that record much of the process.[14] Thus, it is possible to routinely conduct "quality control" checks on the decisions made by call takers, dispatchers and alternative responders who use the telephone. However, supervisors should monitor more than their subordinates' performance; they should also monitor the system's performance. For example, a number of departments have reported that after a DPR program has been in effect for a while, communications personnel tend to stop referring calls for alternative responses, suggesting the possibility of an escalation of Type 1 errors. Careful inquiry into this situation has shown that, in some cases, it was due not to problems with the personnel, but rather, to the policy and procedures.

---

[14]Audiotapes do not cover alternatives such as mail-ins, walk-ins and dispatched responses.

Developing an Adequate Internal and External Referral System

Much of the DPR system's cost-reduction benefit is possible because the system enables the department to avoid sending an initial responder to the scene and, instead, refers the citizen immediately to an appropriate department unit or person/agency outside the department. If this referral system is to work properly, the department needs two things: (1) a thorough knowledge of available community referral resources, and (2) a good working relationship with those resources, so that when referrals are made, there is a reasonable chance that they will be productive. In general, the larger the community, the more numerous and complex the potential referral resources—and thus, the more challenging the task of developing a systematic "encyclopedia" of resources. Some departments are now developing very elaborate referral files on people and agencies that might be able to help with the incredibly wide variety of problems that come to police attention. These files can be organized by type of problem and can include agency names, key agency personnel, telephone numbers, addresses, and other important information that would help a police telephone operator or other responder identify the best referral source for a given problem. For those departments with the capability, such files can be automated, which makes them easy to expand, update and make accessible to a large number of department personnel. The department may publicize its search for referral agencies, but it will be important to carefully check out those they are unfamiliar with, to ensure they are indeed likely to provide the type and quality of service they indicate.

It is one thing to compile such an encyclopedia, but it is a much greater challenge to develop and maintain a good working relationship with these referral resources. Interorganizational cooperation is a two-way street, so many of these organizations may well place demands, both appropriate and inappropriate, on the police. Also, police should monitor the referrals' impact on these agencies' workload. Anticipated changes in referral procedures should, whenever possible, be discussed in advance with those agencies likely to be affected. Finally, police should monitor what happens after the referrals are made. It would be impossible to follow up on *each* referral, but some sampling of referrals will help the department decide if changes should be made. Ultimately, referrals that do not turn out well will likely come back to haunt the department in the form of additional calls for service, complaints against the department, or a general decrease in support for the department. If referrals are viewed strictly as a way to relieve workload—and not help citizens solve their problems—the DPR program will probably get a bad reputation among the public.

Making Logistical Decisions

A number of logistical decisions must be made in the planning stages of DPR and carefully executed during implementation: physical plant and equipment, staffing levels, and deployment. The authors cannot offer specific do's and don'ts regarding these important decisions, since they will depend on the particular departments and the DPR systems they want. However, in all cases, a careful analysis of past call patterns must precede a *projection* of what the workloads are likely to be for each of the new response alternatives, as well as for the patrol force. Many departments have found it useful to implement each response option on a short trial basis (perhaps in only a part of the jurisdiction, if it is large) to get some estimate of how it will perform and how its performance will affect other units. For example, Cleveland and Houston have been able to estimate the likely effects of using callbacks by employing this approach on a short trial basis. And just as it is important to ensure that patrol staffing levels correlate with variations in the work demand by time of day, so is it important to ensure that the staffing of alternative responders is similarly arranged.

Departments will also confront the rather down-to-earth but important decisions regarding whether to centralize or decentralize alternative response options, such as walk-in reports, mobile civilian police service officers, and telephone report units. Larger departments may opt to decentralize some or all of these functions in precinct stations and mini-stations.

Finally, given the potentially profound effects of DPR on where and how patrol officers spend their time, departments will want to carefully consider the designation of patrol shifts and beats, particularly because these designations will affect response times. Indeed, any change in the call-management system is likely to require a thorough integration with policies on shift and beat structures.

Managing Information

DPR programs diversify the sources of information on what the police department is being asked to do and what the department and other agencies are doing about it. In the past, the patrol officer was the primary service provider for a given area, and he or she was considered the most likely to know what was going on in that area. DPR is intended to relieve the patrol officer of a significant proportion of the initial response workload, but that does not mean that the officer—and others in the department—do not need to know what those requests are and what is being done about them. Indeed, the information requirements of community and problem-oriented policing are even more demanding than ever. For example, if telephone operators start handling a significant proportion of the minor-disturbance calls, police officers assigned to the areas may still want to know where those problems are, who is causing them, and who is complaining about them. Minor disturbances can escalate into larger problems. So the challenge for departments implementing DPR is to find ways to make useful information about "relief" alternative responses accessible to beat patrol officers and others who need it.

Details on how to set up an information management system to accomplish this objective will not be given here, but it should be noted that rapid advances in police automated record keeping and user-friendly direct access to data files by the rank and file (through mobile-digital terminals, for example), now make it feasible for departments to effectively use information.

Preparing the Public for DPR

The final, but perhaps most important, implementation challenge is preparing the public for DPR. DPR has many technical facets that are beyond most citizens' knowledge or interest, but citizens do need to understand its objectives and how and why some of their routine requests may be handled differently. News stories and public service announcements are important ways to get the word out. It may also be a good idea to provide more details through various community-contact outlets (crime prevention groups, business associations, churches, neighborhood organizations).

To secure the public's cooperation, the most important thing is for citizens to know what DPR is intended to accomplish and how it will affect them. If some groups come to perceive DPR as a reduction in service quality, they will undoubtedly complain. That is why it is also particularly important that all of the jurisdiction's relevant elected officials be fully informed about the DPR program. Their understanding and support may help to assure others about DPR, and at least provide a "grace" period for the department to show what DPR can do.

Research Designs

Evaluations of DPR's impacts could be designed as experiments or as quasi-experiments; an evaluation could include components of both, depending on the questions being addressed. This section describes the elements of each design in general and with reference to evaluating DPR programs' impact on the satisfaction of citizens who call for service. The section then addresses how each design could be applied in evaluating DPR's impacts on the following: the quantity and quality of information collected by the police; the short- and long-term effects on the problems that generate calls for police service; the amount and distribution of time available to patrol officers for proactive work; and officers' knowledge of the people and problems on their beats.

Outcome Evaluations:
Experiments vs. Quasi-Experiments
Citizen Satisfaction

An experimental design provides both for treatment and control groups—the program or "treatment" is applied to the treatment group and withheld from the control group—and for random assignment of subjects to those groups. In this case, the subjects are calls for service. Treatment group calls are handled according to DPR procedures, while control group calls are handled by "normal" agency procedures.[15] (By normal, the authors mean whatever procedures predate the program under evaluation; for example, in most agencies, a normal procedure would be to dispatch a patrol officer rather than use a relief response, i.e., use an immediate rather than a delayed dispatch.) The *random* assignment of subjects to treatment *and* control groups permits a comparison to be made between groups that are truly comparable—that is, the groups are the same except that one receives the treatment, and the other does not. Provided that the experiment has been properly designed and successfully executed, it usually provides a firm basis for assessing the program's effects, because if the outcomes for the groups are different, i.e., if one group is less satisfied than the other, the program is probably the only factor to which the different outcomes can be attributed. That is what is meant by "internal validity": one can say with confidence whether the outcomes are caused by the program, rather than by some other factor.

The virtues of experimental designs are clear when one considers the shortcomings of quasi-experimental designs. One form of quasi-experiment provides for no conventional control group; the program is withheld from no one.   A survey of citizens who call for service before implementation forms the basis for the "pretest" measure of outcome; a survey of citizens who call after implementation forms the basis for the "posttest" measure of outcome.   Thus, the only comparison is made across time, before and after the treatment is

---

[15]For simplicity's sake, the discussion will describe experimental and quasi-experimental designs with only one treatment group and one control group. Depending on the program and the scope of the evaluation, the design might provide for several treatment groups—one for each response alternative, such as delayed response by sworn personnel, telephone reporting, civilian response, etc.—and several control groups—one for each treatment group. Comparisons would be drawn between corresponding treatment and control groups. Alternatively, an evaluation could provide for, and draw comparisons among, two (or more) treatment groups and a control group. For example, for cold crimes, the control group might be calls to which patrol officers were dispatched, one treatment group might be calls referred to a TRU, and a second treatment group might be calls to which officers trained and motivated to conduct thorough investigations are dispatched (as described previously).

introduced. This makes it difficult to isolate the program's impact because, over time, other events could affect the outcomes. For example, say that between the pretest and the posttest, allegations of corruption or brutality are made and publicized, affecting citizen's satisfaction. A decrease in satisfaction levels between the pretest and the posttest could be the result of the program, or it could be the result of the negative publicity; this quasi-experimental evaluation would not enable one to distinguish between these effects. If the posttest for the treatment group could be compared with the posttest for a control group, then one could ascertain whether (a) both groups showed equal declines in satisfaction, indicating that both groups were affected by the publicity and the program had no negative effect; (b) satisfaction declined in both groups, but declined more in the treatment group than in the control group, indicating that the program and the publicity had negative effects; or (c) satisfaction declined in the treatment group but not in the control group, indicating that the program (but not the publicity) had a negative effect. However, in the absence of a control group, no such inferences are possible.

Another form of quasi-experiment provides for treatment and control groups, but not for random assignment to the groups. When subjects are assigned by some other mechanism, e.g., by having the police call taker assign calls for service to groups, there is a greater likelihood that the groups will differ in some respect other than the treatment. This, too, makes it difficult to isolate the program's impact. Randomization ensures that any differences are the result only of chance and not of some other factor that could affect the groups' compositions and hence the outcomes. Moreover, even though the groups might not be identical, randomization enables one to use the laws of probability to estimate the likelihood that the groups are different by chance.

A third form of quasi-experiment provides for neither a control group nor a pretest; the outcomes are measured only after the program has been implemented. This design provides the weakest basis for assessing the program's impact, because no comparisons are possible. For example, the evaluation finds that 60 percent of callers are satisfied; one cannot determine whether satisfaction increased, decreased or stayed the same as a result of the program because there are no callers whose calls were handled in some other way and with whom the treatment group can be compared. The only recourse is to come up with a "nonequivalent" control group; e.g., people whose calls are handled by a TRU could be compared with people whose calls are dispatched to patrol officers. The latter is a nonequivalent control group in that the calls concerned different sets of problems, and thus it is not directly comparable with the treatment group. Differences in the two groups' satisfaction could be due to the differences in how their calls were handled, or to differences in the nature of the problems and in callers' expectations (or to other, unknown differences).

For the purpose of drawing conclusions about a DPR program's impact, an experimental design is the strongest possible design. But the ease with which an experimental design can be adopted depends on whether the evaluation is undertaken prospectively—focusing on a still-to-be-implemented program or on modification of an existing program—or retrospectively—focusing on a program that is and has been in operation. How an experimental design could be executed in each case is discussed below.

Consider an agency that responds on a first-call-first-served basis, and that plans to implement a DPR program for the first time. An experimental evaluation should be undertaken *before* the program is implemented, and the control group should consist of calls for service that are handled according to the first-call-first-served rule, while the treatment group should consist of calls that are handled according to the new procedures. To illustrate, for an experimental evaluation of procedures whereby some types of offense reports are taken by a TRU, all calls eligible for telephone reporting would be randomly assigned to either the TRU—the treatment group—or to the dispatcher for "normal" handling—the control group. If the assignment of calls to the groups is random, then the two groups' satisfaction levels can be compared directly.

An experimental evaluation could also be conducted by an agency that already has a DPR program in place but plans to modify or extend it. For example, an agency might already have a TRU that handles some types of calls for service, but it plans to increase the range and number of calls diverted to the TRU from the dispatch queue. Calls for service in the newly designated categories could be randomly assigned to the treatment group (i.e., handled by the TRU) or to the control group (i.e., handled by traditional procedures), and the two groups' satisfaction levels could be compared. The results would indicate whether more extensive use of the TRU would adversely affect citizen satisfaction.

Finally, an experimental evaluation of an existing DPR program could be conducted. But it would require that the agency randomly assign some calls to be handled as usual under DPR, while DPR is withdrawn from other calls by assigning them to receive upgraded responses (e.g., a delayed dispatch rather than a telephone report). This is the only way to compose a control group to which calls could be randomly assigned.[16] If an agency is unwilling to upgrade responses to a subset of calls for an evaluation, then it must turn to a quasi-experimental design lacking a control group.

The relative merits of experimental vs. quasi-experimental designs for examining citizen satisfaction turn largely around the feasibility of having an equivalent control group. Whenever a control group can be included in a DPR evaluation, randomization is a fairly simple matter

---

[16]If calls were nonrandomly assigned to a control group, then the design would be a quasi-experiment with a control group.

that greatly improves the quality of the results. One way to randomize is to designate some call takers as the treatment group, and the remainder as the control group (so long as the routing of calls to call takers is random); calls received by the former are processed according to DPR procedures, and calls received by the latter are processed as they would have been in the absence of DPR. Another way to randomly assign calls for service is to designate some randomly selected days of the month as those on which DPR procedures will be used, so that calls received on those days constitute the treatment group, and calls received on other days constitute the control group. For those agencies with CAD systems, still another method of achieving random assignment is to reprogram the system to route a randomly selected fraction (say, one-half or one-third) of eligible calls to the treatment group, and the remaining calls to the control group (see McEwen et al. 1984).

If circumstances make it impossible or unduly difficult to have a control group, it does not mean that an evaluation is not worth undertaking. However, it does mean that conclusions about the program's impact must be drawn more cautiously. Even so, a survey of citizens who call for police service can nevertheless provide information on which a DPR program can be assessed, and on which modifications may be considered. For example, whatever the proportion of citizens who expressed dissatisfaction with the way their calls were handled, if those citizens are asked *why* they are dissatisfied, their answers may indicate something about the program's impacts. The content of citizen surveys is discussed in more detail below.

Information

The design considerations that arise in examining citizen satisfaction also arise in examining the information collected for police reports. An experimental evaluation would provide for the random assignment of calls for service to treatment and control groups. For example, calls that concern cold crimes might be referred to a TRU, or they might be dispatched to patrol units; the former would constitute the treatment group, and the latter, the control group. The outcome—the quality and quantity of information—might be measured by asking citizens about the information that they had and the information that they gave to police, or by analyzing the content of the police reports (e.g., those reports written by patrol officers on the scene, compared with those reports prepared by TRU officers). Still better, both means of measuring the outcome could be used. But any assessment of a DPR program's impact on the quality and quantity of information collected rests on the strongest possible base when the evaluation is designed as an experiment.

However, when attention is focused on the outcome of information collection, an experimental design may not offer the same margin of superiority over a quasi-experimental design. A same margin of superiority over a quasi-experimental design. A quasi-experimental evaluation that provides for only pre- and posttest comparisons, with no conventional control group, is always vulnerable to changes over time in factors external to the program; in the example above, publicity over incidents of brutality or corruption was such a factor. But compared with citizen satisfaction, the content of police reports is more within the agency's control and less likely to be influenced by external factors. If the implementation of the DPR program does (or did) not coincide with other organizational changes that would affect the content of reports, then this form of quasi-experiment may enjoy a high degree of validity. Furthermore, such a quasi-experiment could be undertaken to evaluate a program that had been in place for some time. Current police reports (which would form the basis for the posttest) could be compared with reports that predated the program (which would form the basis for the pretest). If posttest levels of information were lower than pretest levels, this would indicate that less, or less useful, information was collected as a result of the DPR program. If posttest levels were the same as pretest levels, then the program probably had no detrimental impact.

Short- and Long-Term Problem Resolution

When evaluation focuses on the satisfaction of people who call for police service, or on the information collected by police, then the "subjects" to which the program is applied are individual calls for service, and calls for service can easily be randomly assigned to treatment and control groups. But for evaluations that examine police success in solving problems, which could, as we suggested above, analyze repeat calls and/or subsequently reported crimes from the same address (or, for some purposes, the same person), the subjects must be either addresses or some larger geographic unit (such as a beat).[17] This complicates the implementation of an experimental design. Some CAD systems permit call takers to retrieve information about previous calls from the same address, and those systems could be reprogrammed to store information about the assignment of addresses to treatment or control groups. Agencies that use such systems could randomly designate individual *addresses* to receive treatment and control responses for the duration of the evaluation. If, say, addresses in the treatment group generated more repeat calls or crime reports, on average, than addresses in the control group, then

---

[17]If the subjects for such an evaluation were calls for service rather than addresses or police beats, then it would be possible that an address from which one call was assigned to the treatment group might generate a later call that is assigned to the control group (or vice versa). As a result, the small number of addresses that generate a disproportionate number of calls would likely appear in both the treatment and control groups, and inferences about the treatment's impact would be muddled indeed.

the evaluation would indicate that the program had a negative impact on problem resolution. If the average numbers of repeat calls or crime reports were the same in the treatment and control groups, then the evaluation would indicate that the program had no negative effect on problem resolution.

However, few agencies likely have the technical capacity to assign *addresses* to treatment and control groups. In most agencies, the only feasible evaluation design would be an experiment or quasi-experiment in which reporting areas or police beats were assigned to treatment or control groups; the addresses in those areas would thereby also be assigned to groups. All eligible calls originating in areas designated as treatment areas would be assigned to the treatment group for, say, some form of relief response. All similarly eligible calls originating in areas designated as control areas would be assigned to the control group. If addresses in the treatment areas were found to generate a larger (or smaller) number of repeat calls or crime reports than addresses in the control areas, then the evaluation would provide evidence of a program effect.

Officers' Time, Knowledge and Activities

When an evaluation examines the time available to patrol officers, or the activities in which they engage, then the subjects of analysis are neither calls for service nor the addresses from which the calls originate, but rather, individual patrol units. In principle, patrol units could be assigned to treatment and control groups. In a city with 20 patrol beats, 10 could be designated as treatment beats. Calls originating in those beats could be handled according to DPR procedures while calls originating in the remaining 10 beats (the control beats) could be assigned as they would be in the absence of DPR. Then the amount and distribution of time available to those units and the levels of activity in which they engaged could be compared to determine DPR's impacts.[18] If DPR is successful in restructuring the time available for proactive policing, then the evaluation would show that the units assigned to treatment beats (a) had more time that was not occupied with calls for service, (b) had larger blocks of time that was not occupied with calls for service, and

---

[18]In this case, the subjects of analysis are beats or areas, and not the addresses within them. Thus, whether the design is experimental or quasi-experimental depends not only on whether the assignment to groups is random or nonrandom, but also on the numbers of areas. One rule of thumb holds that for an experiment, the number of subjects in each group should be no fewer than 20 (Langbein 1980:69); below that threshold, with or without randomization, the evaluation is fundamentally quasi-experimental. Many small and medium-sized jurisdictions have too few police beats to support an experiment, so any evaluation would need to consider differences between the groups as possible explanations for outcomes.

(c) engaged in more officer-initiated activity. (Time and activity could be coded from dispatch records and activity logs, as discussed below.)

Such an evaluation design is feasible provided that eligible calls from control beats do not frequently result in cross-beat dispatching. If officers assigned to treatment beats must often respond to calls originating in control beats, then the integrity of the groups is compromised, and so, too, is the validity of the results; the patrol units that would be expected to have more time and to be more active as a result of DPR would instead be responding to calls in control beats.

An examination of officers' knowledge of their assigned beats could in principle follow a similar design, with the outcome—officers' knowledge—measured through a survey of officers assigned to the treatment and control beats. This design is technically feasible provided, again, that cross-beat dispatching is not commonplace, and provided also that officers' assignments to (treatment or control) beats are stable for the duration of the evaluation. Therein lies a rub. A DPR program's impact on officers' knowledge of their beats is unlikely to be felt in the short run, and the evaluation period for any control-group design would probably be so lengthy that most agencies would find it unworkable. The only alternative would be a quasi-experiment with pre- and posttests (and no control group), for which officers' knowledge some time after the implementation of DPR would be compared with their knowledge before DPR. Needless to say, agencies that already have DPR programs cannot avail themselves of this design either.

Process Evaluation

A process evaluation of DPR implementation is fundamentally descriptive; for all or most purposes, the choice between experimental and quasi-experimental designs need not be made. Nevertheless, a process evaluation can be not only valuable but also critical for assessments of DPR programs. A process evaluation would address questions of program coverage—how many and what types of calls for service were actually assigned alternative responses, and what types of citizens placed those calls—and of program implementation—how accurately were calls assigned to call categories, how many Type 1 and Type 2 errors did call takers make, how often did call takers fail to advise citizens of likely delays, and what were the lengths of actual delays of different kinds (e.g., delays in mobile responses, delays in callbacks). A process evaluation could also address the issue of how communications, patrol and other police personnel reacted to DPR procedures. Each of these matters will be taken up as they arise in connection with evaluation data and evaluation analysis.

The sources of data that might be exploited or developed for an evaluation of a DPR program, the forms of data that could be collected from those sources, and the ways those data could be collected are discussed below.

Police Department Records

Data culled from police department records are integral to any evaluation of DPR. The records that are available, the form in which they are stored, and the data that can be derived from them all vary to some extent from agency to agency, and the data that will need to be collected for any particular evaluation will depend on the questions posed. Thus, any discussion of these data must be couched in somewhat general terms if it is to have broad applicability. Discussed below are the different possible sources of data and the evaluative questions to which the data are relevant.

Call and dispatch records. Call and dispatch records provide some of the most basic information for an evaluation of (delayed) mobile responses by sworn or civilian personnel. Records of calls for service may also be a source of information about calls that are referred to non-dispatch alternatives such as telephone reporting, or mail- or walk-in reporting, depending on individual agencies' record-keeping practices. Calls for service records may also be a source of information on callbacks, depending on the allocation of responsibilities for that function (in some departments, it is performed—if it is performed at all—by call takers) and/or the record-keeping procedures.

Call and dispatch records may include the date and time at which a call was received, the incident or problem category into which the call was placed, the location of the incident, the number of the phone from which the call was placed, and (in many cases) the name of the caller; they may also include the times of dispatch, arrival and completion. These data can be used to assess program coverage—i.e., the numbers of each type of call that are eligible for each alternative response—and program implementation—i.e., the actual delays in responding to eligible calls.[19] These data can also be used to describe the amount and distribution of time that is not consumed by calls for service; these data enable one to calculate, for each unit, the time during which the unit was occupied by calls and, by implication, the time left over after calls, as well as the amount of time between calls

---

[19]The information on times of arrival and completion must be used with some caution, since they are likely to be incomplete and somewhat unreliable. The data may be missing because field personnel sometimes fail to signal their arrival at the locations to which they are dispatched, and sometimes even fail to indicate when they are back in service after they complete a call. The data are unreliable to the extent that field personnel misreport the times of arrival and completion. Under some circumstances—certainly if the call records are not computerized—it may be necessary or desirable to select a sample of calls. See the discussion of sampling below, in connection with citizen surveys.

for service.[20] Finally, these data obviously are essential for surveying citizens whose calls were eligible for one of the alternatives.[21]

Records of calls would also be the principal source of data on repeat calls from specific addresses or people, for an examination of short- and long-term problem resolution. Relevant information would include the dates of calls and the types of incidents that the calls concerned. Analysis (described below) would address the length of the interval between the original call (i.e., the first call from an address or person during the evaluation period) and the first subsequent call, as well as the volume of repeat calls. It might focus only on repeat calls that concern the same (or similar) types of incidents as the original call, or it might include all subsequent calls.

Recordings of calls. Tape recordings of conversations between citizens and call takers could be examined for a process evaluation.[22] These recordings could form the basis for assessing call takers' compliance with DPR procedures, and the accuracy with which call takers classify incidents. Many coding categories would correspond to the dimensions of call classification: the time of the incident, the amount of property damage or loss, the presence of suspects, the availability of evidence, and other information, as appropriate. In addition, information on call takers' compliance with other procedures—e.g., advising callers of likely delays—could be coded. (Records of calls would probably be the source of information on the actual classification of the incident.)

For the purposes of evaluation, coding need not and probably should not include the call takers' identities. The process evaluation is intended to assess the extent of implementation and to aid in diagnosing any problems in implementation.

Collecting data from recordings is necessarily labor-intensive, and therefore cannot be done for more than a fairly small sample of calls. The discussion of sampling for a citizen survey applies equally well to

---

[20]As indicated above, if DPR is successful in restructuring the workload by providing time for proactive policing, then the average amount of time between calls for service should be greater under DPR. But the same caveat about the quality of this information, as discussed above, applies here as well.

[21]If calls for service records include information on calls that were referred for non-dispatch alternatives, then they should be used to select respondents for a survey; if respondents are drawn from the reports taken over the phone, walked-in, or mailed-in, then the survey would exclude those who were not recontacted by the TRU or who did not walk- or mail-in their reports.

[22]An alternative to reviewing tape-recorded conversations is to listen to them in real time. Depending on the agency's communications facilities, this could be accomplished more or less unobtrusively. For example, some agencies have a supervisory console from which call takers' stations can be monitored, and from which "observations" can be made. Collecting data from recordings is less time-consuming (especially during less-busy times), however, and suffers no disadvantages.

sampling calls for this purpose (whether or not a citizen survey is part of the evaluation). If a citizen survey is done, it can serve to identify calls that may have been misclassified (as discussed below), and so it will enable an evaluator to economically collect data from selected recordings.

Offense/incident/accident reports. Reports generated through non-dispatch alternatives—telephone, mail-in or walk-in reporting— may include information on the nature of the event; the date, time and location at which the event occurred; the date and time of the report; and the name, address and phone number of the reporting party. These data can serve to describe the scope of these response alternatives—the total volume of calls diverted from the dispatch queue, and the numbers of different types of calls—and the length of any relevant delays (e.g., in recontacting citizens for telephone reports). Some of the data may also be necessary for surveying citizens served by these alternatives.

For an examination of the quality and quantity of information collected through alternative response modes, the contents of these reports and comparable reports written by patrol officers (or by civilians in the field) could be coded for analysis. The coding categories would depend on the kinds of events on which the reports were prepared—burglaries, assaults, automobile accidents—and so could vary markedly from one evaluation to another. These categories should be developed with a view toward what information is pertinent to the classes of events on which the evaluation focuses, and toward the kinds of information that the agency itself considers important.

Finally, these reports could be used in much the same way calls for service would be used to examine problem resolution. Relevant information would include the types and dates of the events. Analysis would parallel an analysis of repeat calls, described above.

Patrol activity logs. Patrol activity logs may include more-or-less detailed information on the number and types of activities in which officers engage on their own initiative. The specific activities that can and should be coded for any evaluation will depend on the questions the agency addresses and the quality of the information the logs contain. Even under the best of circumstances, the accuracy of that information is suspect. But in the absence of either extensive (and expensive) observations or onerous reporting requirements, there are no other options.

Survey of Citizens

One of the more important forms of data that can be collected for a DPR evaluation is information on how such procedures are received by the public, and particularly by citizens who request service.[23]   A carefully designed and executed survey can be a valuable source of feedback on an agency's performance in general, and on a DPR program's impact in particular.   By conducting a survey, an agency can solicit the opinions of citizens who are, as a group, representative of the public, rather than relying on opinions volunteered in the form of complaints (or, less commonly, in the form of compliments). Citizen surveys can also serve as a source of other information that could be used for evaluative purposes, as discussed below.

Whether a survey is conducted by in-house or external evaluators, the development of the survey instrument should be based on a careful assessment of what information the agency wants and what information survey respondents can be expected to provide. A survey might include questions about a citizen's satisfaction with the police response generally, and with how his or her call was handled, first by the call taker, and later by other personnel, such as patrol officers, community service officers (or analogous civilians), evidence technicians, telephone report unit personnel, and so on; citizens who are dissatisfied could be asked why. A survey could also include items of a more objective nature, concerning (as appropriate) the length of response delays, and the actions of police (e.g., whether certain questions were asked by call takers or others). Surveys should not include items that extend beyond the scope of citizens' experiences; for example, they probably should not ask whether citizens would be willing to accept response alternatives with which they have no experience (see McEwen et al. 1984).

A survey of citizens could be conducted through face-to-face interviews, telephone interviews or a mail questionnaire.[24] Generally, face-to-face interviews provide better and more complete information—larger proportions of those contacted complete the interview, the survey instrument can include items for which some kind of visual aid is necessary, and interviewers can both explain items that are not self-explanatory and ask respondents for clarification— but at much higher cost. Mail questionnaires are, for most purposes, the least expensive form of survey, but response rates are often very low, so there is good reason to question whether respondents are representative of citizens more generally. A telephone survey is

---

[23]This discussion will dwell on surveys of citizens whose calls for police service are eligible for some kind of alternative response.   Where resources permit, an evaluation of DPR would do well to undertake a general survey of citizens, and not just those who call for service during the evaluation period. Such a survey could indicate (where DPR has been in operation for some time) whether citizens have been discouraged from calling for service, as a result of either their own experiences with DPR or those of friends or neighbors.

[24]For more detailed discussions of the construction and administration of surveys, see Dilman (1978), Groves and Kahn (1979), Schuman and Presser (1981), and Converse and Presser (1986).

probably optimal: response rates are fairly high, and interviewers can explain the meaning of questions and ask for clarification as necessary.[25]

No matter which medium is used, each interview should be conducted a short time—that is, within a few days—after the citizen's call for service is received. The more time that elapses between the call and the interview, the more dimly respondents will recollect their experiences; for those who call frequently for police service, a long interval may make it difficult for them even to determine the call with which the interview is concerned. Furthermore, as time goes by, citizens are more likely to mentally reconstruct events as they think about them and talk about them with others. Consequently, the shorter the interval between the call and the interview, the better the information collected in the survey.

Respondents are, in general, more likely to be candid if the interviewers are civilians who are not employed by the agency. In effect, then, the authors recommend that an agency contract with a private or nonprofit firm to administer the survey, even if the instrument is developed in-house. If police officers conduct the interviews, then one can expect some inflation in the level of measured satisfaction, inflation for which one should account in interpreting the results.[26]

Sampling. A survey will require that respondents be sampled from the population of citizens whose calls for service are eligible to receive the alternative response that is the subject of the evaluation. The sample should be selected randomly, so that the laws of probability can be used in drawing generalizations about the population from the sample. The selection of a sample is not the same as the assignment of calls to treatment and control groups; randomization is not random sampling. For example, an evaluation is to focus on having civilians respond to noise complaints. The population of calls, then, consists of all noise complaints—the eligible calls in Figure 1. For an experimental evaluation, these calls would be randomly assigned to treatment and control groups. To select a

---

[25]More than one survey medium could be used in a single evaluation. For example, cost considerations may make it necessary to conduct most interviews by phone, but it may be possible to conduct face-to-face interviews with a smaller sample; together, the two surveys could provide the breadth needed for representativeness (within resource constraints), and the depth afforded by face-to-face interviews.

[26]For a recent survey in Jersey City, N.J., some interviews were conducted by officers, and others by civilians. Responses to most items were similar across the two sets of interviews, which suggests that respondents were not, for the most part, affected by having an officer conduct the interview. But on one item—citizens' satisfaction with police—respondents who were interviewed by officers reported higher levels of satisfaction (Weisburd and Green 1994: fn 5).

random sample for a survey, calls would be randomly selected from each of these groups.

ELIGIBLE
CALLS

TREATMENT   Randomization   CONTROL
GROUP   GROUP

Random Sampling

NONSAMPLED   SAMPLED   SAMPLED   NONSAMPLED
TREATMENT   TREATMENT   CONTROL   CONTROL
CALLS   CALLS   CALLS   CALLS

Figure 1

Randomization and Random Sampling

The selection of random samples is straightforward. Some procedures are more complex than others, but all follow the same principle: each call must initially have some chance of being included in the sample. The simplest approach is to list the calls in the treatment and (if any) control groups and, using a coin, a die or a table of random numbers, select a subset of the calls in each group. Such a list could be produced every day, or every few days, depending on the numbers of calls; in any case, it should be done often enough to ensure that interviews can be completed in a timely fashion.

If the numbers of calls are large, a list of eligible calls in each group need not be prepared every day; it would be more economical to first sample days, and to then sample calls from the selected days. One could select the days randomly, or one could randomly select a specified number of different days of the week (e.g., two each of Mondays, Tuesdays, etc.) to ensure the inclusion of the range of problems and service conditions (such as backlogs of calls at busy times).[27] Continuing the above example to illustrate, one could

---

[27]The selection of days for inclusion in the sample would be constrained if the procedures for randomization used days as the basis for assignment to treatment and control groups, as described above. If, for example, eligible calls received on even-numbered days were assigned to the treatment group, and

randomly draw two Mondays of the coming month on which noise complaints will be randomly selected for the sample, two Tuesdays, two Wednesdays, and so on (see Figure 2). If the number of calls on selected days is not too large, then all calls on those days can be included in the sample.

	M	Tu	W	Th	F	Sa	Su
First Week	X		X			X	
Second Week		X	X	X			X
Third Week		X			X	X	
Fourth Week	X			X	X		X

Figure 2

Sampling Calls for Service by Days

The representativeness of the sample will inevitably be compromised to some extent by problems in reaching citizens who have relevant information. Many agencies have call takers routinely record the number of the phone from which calls are made (and some have 911 systems that make it unnecessary for call takers to ask for the number), but many calls are made from numbers at which the callers cannot subsequently be reached. Consequently, if the survey is done by telephone, then those who are too poor to have phones in their homes and who call from elsewhere are underrepresented among the respondents, as are those (poor or not) who call about certain types of incidents—such as automobile accidents, calls about which are often made from pay phones or from businesses at which the caller does not work. In some cases, a modest effort to locate the caller—by looking up his or her name in the phone book—is all that is needed, but in other cases, it will not be possible to complete an interview. Face-to-face interviewing presents problems of equal or greater magnitude, since even if careful efforts are made to record callers' addresses (in addition to the addresses of the incidents about which they call), it is sometimes difficult (and expensive) to contact and meet would-be respondents.

Furthermore, some citizens will decline to be interviewed, and if those who refuse are different from those who do not, then the sample

---

eligible calls received on odd-numbered days were assigned to the control group, then the sample of treatment group calls would have to be drawn from those received on even-numbered days, and the sample of control group calls would have to be drawn from those received on odd-numbered days.

will be biased to the degree that they differ. For example, if those who refuse are, on average, less satisfied than those who participate, then the survey will overestimate the level of satisfaction. The nature and extent of the bias can be (roughly) estimated by comparing those who refuse with those who participate, at least in terms of the available information, such as the types of incidents about which they called, and the areas from which they called.

Content. The heart of a citizen survey is citizens' satisfaction with the police services they receive, but at marginal cost, the survey could encompass other matters relevant to an assessment of a DPR program. This section discusses the more important categories of content and their relationship to the evaluative questions raised above. The appendixes include survey instruments that could be adapted to conform with individual agencies' specific procedures, along with some instructions for interviewers. Experience with instruments very similar to these indicates that they typically take five to 10 minutes to complete.

Before respondents are asked how satisfied they are with how their calls were handled, they should be asked, first, to *briefly* describe the incident about which they called and, second, some specific questions about delays in discovering the problem and calling the police, about the amount of property loss or damage, and about any information (e.g., about perpetrators) that they had. These items serve to refresh the respondent's memory so that responses to later items about satisfaction are more likely to represent thoughtful assessments rather than spontaneous judgments; they can also identify cases in which call takers may have made Type 1 or Type 2 errors, i.e., misclassified the call.[28] Items about information could be used to assess the nature and amount of information lost.

Respondents could also be asked whether the call takers advised them of any likely delays in responding to their calls (e.g., by patrol units, by civilians or by TRU officers), how long the delays were, and whether the delays were longer than, shorter than, or about the same as they expected. The first of these items addresses what has reportedly been an implementation problem in many DPR programs: call takers have often failed to inform callers when delays were likely. An analysis of responses to these items could also reveal whether call takers can shape or influence callers' expectations discussed below in the section on data analysis.

Respondents should be asked about their satisfaction with how their calls were handled by each of the units with which they had contact—call takers, patrol officers, TRU officers, and so on.

---

[28]Respondents' answers to these items cannot be taken at face value, of course; there may be discrepancies between what callers told call takers and what they later tell interviewers. But for those calls for which the survey data indicate a potential error, the survey data could be cross-checked against recordings of conversations between the respondents and the call takers.

Satisfaction items can be preceded by items that focus on some aspect of the police-citizen interaction. For example, the survey instruments in the appendixes include questions about the communication "style" of communications personnel (call takers and TRU officers): their concern, their precision in conversation, their attentiveness, and their apparent emotional state. These items are based on previous research that suggests that these characteristics are related to citizen satisfaction (Glauser and Tullar 1985). Unless the evaluation—and hence, the survey—focuses on a specific and fairly narrow category of calls for service, it may be difficult to formulate a set of closed-ended items about the actions of some police personnel. At a minimum, in those cases, respondents should also be asked to briefly describe what the personnel did; this not only refreshes the respondent's memory, but also, the account itself can be content-analyzed to identify DPR-related sources of positive or negative evaluations.

Finally, the survey should include items on respondents' characteristics: wealth, race, age, length of residence, sex. These data are useful for a process evaluation, describing the clientele who receive alternative responses. They are also useful for an analysis of satisfaction, which would indicate whether any demographic groups are particularly unreceptive to specific forms of police response.

Surveys of Police Personnel

Police personnel can also be surveyed. The attitudes of call takers, dispatchers and patrol officers toward DPR procedures and toward those procedures' implications for their working environments are important in their own right. Moreover, systematic surveys of police personnel can identify unexpected problems.

For a process analysis of a DPR program, perhaps the most valuable survey data would come from semi-structured interviews consisting of open-ended questions, i.e., items that do not provide a restricted set of response options, but rather, allow respondents to answer in their own words. Such a survey provides more detailed information than one consisting of closed-ended questions, and is particularly useful for identifying unexpected program effects (which are, by nature, difficult to detect through closed-ended questions). When samples must be large to be representative, open-ended surveys provide so much unstructured information that analysis is unmanageable. But the numbers of police personnel to be surveyed need not be large, so the information can be analyzed without an enormous investment of time.

The survey could consist of a few general questions about the program, and perhaps a few more specific questions tailored to the roles of different respondents (e.g., call takers, patrol officers, TRU officers). General questions might include the following: What are the advantages, as you see it, of the differential response program? What are the disadvantages, as you see it, of the program? What are the advantages of using [response alternative—e.g., delayed response, telephone reporting]?   What are the disadvantages of using [response alternative—e.g., delayed response, telephone reporting]?   Each question should be followed up with additional questions, as necessary, to elicit the respondents' reasoning for their answers. Specific questions for call takers might include the following: How does the call classification system affect the way you do your job? How does the availability of response alternatives affect the way you do your job?   Additional questions might touch on whether the call classification system and response alternatives help or hinder call takers in their jobs, and what, if any, problems call takers have experienced in using them.   Specific questions for field personnel might include the following: How adequate is the information the dispatchers provide?   Do you sometimes have time to [conduct follow-up investigations/conduct surveillance/conduct field stops/ contact citizens, going door to door/etc.]?   In addition, questions posed to officers might include items designed to assess their knowledge of their beats, if that is an outcome of interest for the evaluation.   Officers might be asked to describe the makeup of the people on their beats; the economic conditions on their beats; the nature and locations of the serious police problems on their beats; the names of repeat offenders on their beats; and the names of, contact persons for, and activities performed or services provided by, community associations, block clubs and service agencies on their beats.

Analysis

This discussion focuses on the more fundamental kinds of analysis that would be central to an assessment of program impact.   If the evaluation is based on an experimental design, then the analysis is straight-forward.   Mean outcome scores (e.g., repeat calls for service) can be computed for the treatment and control groups, respectively, and compared with one another; any difference in the means can be examined to determine the likelihood that it is merely the result of chance fluctuations.[29]   In addition, for outcomes that are measured in terms of discrete categories—e.g., citizen satisfaction is typically measured in terms of four or five categories of response—it would also be revealing to compare the frequency distributions of outcomes for the two groups in a cross-tabulation.   Figure 3 illustrates such an analysis of citizen satisfaction, but analogous analyses could be performed on, say, the information contained in police reports.   The numbers in the cells of the table represent the numbers and percentages of each group (treatment and control) that were very satisfied, satisfied, etc.   These hypothetical results show that the treatment group is less satisfied: a smaller proportion of the treatment group is very satisfied (10% vs. 20%), and a correspondingly larger

---

[29]An explanation of statistical inference is well beyond the scope of this chapter. For a lucid treatment, see Langbein (1980).

proportion of the treatment group is merely satisfied (70% vs. 60%), while there are also small differences in the proportions dissatisfied (favoring the treatment group) and very dissatisfied (favoring the control group). The mean satisfaction scores are also different (2.85 vs. 2.98), but the means do not reveal the patterns that can be observed in the cross-tabulation.[30]

	Treatment	Control
Very Satisfied (4)	30 10%	60 20%
Satisfied (3)	210 70%	180 60%
Dissatisfied (2)	45 15%	54 18%
Very Dissatisfied (1)	15 5%	6 2%
Totals	300 100%	300 100%

Figure 3

Cross-Tabulation of Satisfaction by Group

The same kinds of analyses can be performed if the design is quasi-experimental, but conclusions based on the comparisons must be drawn more cautiously, because factors external to the program are not experimentally controlled. Efforts to statistically control some of these factors (e.g., characteristics of the incidents about which citizens have called, or characteristics of the citizens) should be made, if

---

[30]Separate analyses would be conducted for each satisfaction item on the survey instrument—e.g., satisfaction with the call taker and satisfaction with the TRU officer.

possible, through three-way cross-tabulations or through more sophisticated multivariate techniques of analysis, such as regression. If the design provides for a pretest but no control group, then the analyses would be conducted as above, substituting the pretest for the control group.

Whether the design is experimental or quasi-experimental, if the evaluation encompasses multiple categories of calls for service, then the analyses should be repeated for each category separately. This would represent one approach to the issue of "dosage" raised above. If the DPR dosage is too heavy, i.e., if citizens find the provision of alternative responses to some types of calls especially objectionable, or if alternative responses to certain types of calls have especially pronounced effects on the information collected, then for those types of calls, the analysis will show especially low outcome levels. This fact might not be apparent in an analysis that includes several types of calls. For example, Figure 4 shows a hypothetical cross-tabulation

	Treatment	Control
Very Satisfied (4)	3 5%	10 17%
Satisfied (3)	22 37%	25 42%
Dissatisfied (2)	23 38%	20 33%
Very Dissatisfied (1)	12 20%	5 8%
Totals	60 100%	60 100%

Figure 4

Cross-Tabulation of Satisfaction by Group
for One Type of Call

that includes only one of the several categories of calls in Figure 3; the results in Figure 4 indicate that most of the dissatisfaction found in Figure 3 can be attributed to citizens whose calls concern one type of incident. By breaking satisfaction down by categories of calls, it may be possible to locate pockets of dissatisfaction and thus determine whether the DPR dosage is too heavy.

Analyses could also be conducted to examine the equity of a DPR program. As explained above, the issue of equity concerns the receptivity of different population subgroups (e.g., high- vs. low-income, minority vs. white) to alternative responses. One way to examine this issue is to compare the treatment vs. control satisfaction levels across population subgroups. For example, one might find that, among high-income respondents, 84 percent of the treatment group was satisfied, and 86 percent of the control group was satisfied, while among low-income respondents, 60 percent of the treatment group was satisfied, and 75 percent of the control group was satisfied. That the difference between the treatment and control group is larger among low-income respondents suggests that low-income citizens are affected (negatively) more than high-income citizens.

Summary

Evaluations are meant to provide information to policymakers and others with a "stake" in public programs. Any evaluation of a DPR program will be tailored to the program elements and questions of most concern, all within resource constraints. This chapter addressed a variety of evaluative components. All or most of the more important components were discussed, but even so, some additional issues will inevitably arise in designing and executing an evaluation. However, police agencies should not be discouraged from conducting evaluative research. In the absence of sales figures and profit-and-loss statements, evaluative research can provide valuable information on what works (and what does not work) in policing. The most challenging step, perhaps, is asking questions to which the answers are unknown.

Selected Bibliography

Brandl, G., and F. Horvath. 1991. "Crime Victim Evaluation of Police Investigative Performance." *Journal of Criminal Justice* 19:293–305.

Cahn, M.F., and J.M. Tien. 1981. *An Evaluation Report of an Alternative Approach in Police Response: The Wilmington Management of Demand Program.* Cambridge, Mass.: Public Systems Evaluation Inc.

Cincinnati Institute of Criminal Justice. 1986. *Cleveland Police Department's Communication Center: Report on Differential*

Response Study. Cincinnati: Cincinnati Institute of Criminal Justice.

_____. 1988. *Cleveland Police Department's Communication Center: Final Report on Telephone Expeditor Unit Test.* Cincinnati: Cincinnati Institute of Criminal Justice.

Cohen, M., and J.T. McEwen. 1984. "Handling Calls for Service: Alternatives to Traditional Policing." *NIJ Reports* (September):4–8.

Converse, J.M., and S. Presser. 1986. *Survey Questions: Handcrafting the Standard Questionnaire.* Beverly Hills, Calif.: Sage.

Cordner, G., J.R. Greene, and T.S. Bynum. 1983. "The Sooner the Better: Some Effects of Police Response Time." In R.R. Bennett, ed., *Police at Work: Policy Issues and Analysis.* Beverly Hills, Calif.: Sage. Pp. 145–164.

Dilman, D.A. 1978. *Mail and Telephone Surveys: The Total Design Method.* New York: John Wiley.

Durand, R. 1976. "Some Dynamics of Urban Service Evaluations Among Blacks and Whites." *Social Science Quarterly* 56:698–706.

Eck, J.E. 1983. *Solving Crimes: The Investigation of Burglary and Robbery.* Washington, D.C.: Police Executive Research Forum.

Eck, J.E., and W. Spelman. 1987. *Problem Solving: Problem-Oriented Policing in Newport News.* Washington, D.C.: Police Executive Research Forum.

Fennessy, E. 1983. *Police Directed Patrol Programs: An Initial Assessment.* Washington, D.C.: National Institute of Justice.

Flanagan, T.J. 1985. "Consumer Perspectives on Police Operational Strategy." *Journal of Police Science and Administration* 13:10–21.

Furstenberg, F.F., and C.F. Wellford. 1973. "Calling the Police: The Evaluation of Police Services." *Law and Society Review* 7:393–406.

Glauser, M.J., and W.L. Tullar. 1985. "Communicator Style of Police Officers and Citizen Satisfaction With Officer/Citizen Telephone Conversations." *Journal of Police Science and Administration* 13:70–77.

Goldstein, H. 1990. *Problem-Oriented Policing.* New York: McGraw-Hill.

Greene, J.R., and C.B. Klockars. 1991. "What Police Do." In C.B. Klockars and S.D. Mastrofski, eds., *Thinking About Police: Contemporary Readings*, 2nd ed. New York: McGraw-Hill. Pp. 273–284.

Greenwood, P.W., and J. Petersilia. 1975. *The Criminal Investigation Process—Volume I: Summary and Policy Implications.* Santa Monica, Calif.: Rand.

Groves, R.M., and R.L. Kahn. 1979. *Surveys by Telephone: A National Comparison With Personal Interviews.* New York: Academic Press.

Hornick, J.P., B.A. Burrows, I. Tjosvold, and D.M. Phillips. 1989. *An Evaluation of the Neighbourhood Foot Patrol Program of Edmonton Police Service.* Ottawa: Ministry of the Solicitor General of Canada.

Jacob, H. 1971. "Black and White Perceptions of Justice in the City." *Law and Society Review* 6:69–89.

Kansas City Police Department. 1978. *Response Time Analysis: Executive Summary.* Washington, D.C.: U.S. Department of Justice.

Kelling, G.L. 1983. "On the Accomplishments of the Police." In M. Ponch, ed., *Control in the Police Organization.* Cambridge, Mass.: MIT Press. Pp. 150–168.

Langbein, L.I. 1980. *Discovering Whether Programs Work: A Guide to Statistical Methods for Program Evaluation.* Glenview, Ill.: Scott, Foresman and Co.

Mastrofski, S.D. 1983. "Police Knowledge of the Patrol Beat: A Performance Measure." In R.R. Bennett, ed., *Police at Work: Policy Issues and Analysis.* Beverly Hills, Calif.: Sage. Pp. 45–64.

_____. 1985. "The New Autonomy of American Police: Review and Critique of a Contemporary Reform Program." Paper presented at the annual meeting of the American Society of Criminology, San Diego.

Mastrofski, S.D., and R.B. Parks. 1990. "Improving Observational Studies of Police." *Criminology* 28:475–496.

Mastrofski, S.D., and R.C. Wadman. 1991. "Personnel and Agency Performance Measurement." In W.A. Geller, ed., *Local Government Police Management*, 3rd ed. Washington, D.C.: International City Management Association.

McEwen, J.T., E.F. Connors, and M.I. Cohen. 1984. *Evaluation of the Differential Police Response Field Test.* Alexandria, Va.: Research Management Associates Inc.

Moore, M.H., and G.L. Kelling. 1983. "To Serve and Protect: Learning From Police History." *The Public Interest* 70:49–65.

Muir, W.K., Jr. 1977. *Police: Streetcorner Politicians.* Chicago: University of Chicago Press.

Ostrom, E. 1973. "On the Meaning and Measurement of Output and Efficiency in the Provision of Urban Police Services. *Journal of Criminal Justice* 1:93–112.

_____. 1983. "Equity in Police Services." In G.P. Whitaker and C.D. Phillips, eds., *Evaluating Performance of Criminal Justice Agencies.* Beverly Hills, Calif.: Sage. Pp. 99–125.

Parks, R.B. 1976. "Police Response to Victimization: Effects on Citizen Attitudes and Perceptions." In W. Skogan, ed., *Sample Surveys of the Victims of Crime.* Cambridge, Mass.: Ballinger.

Pate, A., A. Ferrara, R.A. Bowers, and J. Lorence. 1976. *Police Response Time: Its Determinants and Effects.* Washington, D.C.: Police Foundation.

Peel Regional Police Force. 1991. "Joint Administration/Operations Review Committee on Communications/SPR Issues." Brampton, Ontario: Author.

_____. 1991. "User's Manual: Strategic Police Response." Brampton, Ontario: Author.

Percy, S.L. 1980.   "Response Time and Citizen Evaluation of Police." *Journal of Police Science and Administration* 8:75–86.

Percy, S.L., and E.J. Scott.   1985.   *Demand Processing and Performance in Public Agencies*. University, Ala.: The University of Alabama Press.

Poister, T.H., and J.C. McDavid.   1978. "Victims' Evaluation of Police Performance." *Journal of Criminal Justice* 6:133–149.

Reiss, A.J., Jr. 1971. *The Police and the Public*. New Haven, Conn.: Yale University Press.

Rubinstein, J. 1973.   *City Police*.   New York: Garrar, Straus and Giroux.

Schuman, H., and S. Presser.   1981.   *Questions and Answers in Attitude Surveys: Experiments on Question Form, Wording and Context*. New York: Academic Press.

Scott, E.J. 1981. *Calls for Service: Citizen Demand and Initial Police Response*. Washington, D.C.: National Institute of Justice.

Sherman, L.W. 1983. "Patrol Strategies for Police." In J.Q. Wilson, ed., *Crime and Public Policy*. San Francisco: ICS Press. Pp. 145–163.

Sherman, L.W., and R.A. Berk.   1984.   "The Specific Deterrent Effects of Arrest for Domestic Assault." *American Sociological Review* 49:261–272.

Sherman, L.W., P.R. Gartin, and M.E. Buerger. 1989. "Hot Spots of Predatory Crime: Routine Activities and the Criminology of Place." *Criminology* 27:27–55.

Spelman, W., and D.K. Brown.   1981.   *Calling the Police: Citizen Reporting of Serious Crime*. Washington, D.C.: Police Executive Research Forum.

Sumrall, R.O., J. Roberts, and M.T. Farmer. 1981. *Differential Police Response Strategies*.   Washington, D.C.:   Police Executive Research Forum.

Tien, J.M., J.W. Simon, and R.C. Larson. 1977. *An Evaluation Report of an Alternative Approach to Police Patrol: The Wilmington Split-Force Experiment*. Cambridge, Mass.:   Harvard University Press.

Weisburd, D., and L. Green. 1994. "Defining the Street-Level Drug Market." In D.L. MacKenzie and C.D. Uchida, eds., *Drugs and Crime: Evaluating Public Policy Initiatives*. Thousand Oaks, Calif.: Sage. Pp. 61–76.

Whitaker, G.P., S. Mastrofski, E. Ostrom, R.B. Parks, and S.L. Percy. 1982.   *Basic Issues in Police Performance*.   Washington, D.C.: U.S. Department of Justice.

Wilson, J.Q. 1968. *Varieties of Police Behavior: The Management of Law and Order in Eight Communities.* Cambridge, Mass.: Harvard University Press.

Worden, R.E. 1993. "Toward Equity and Efficiency in Law Enforcement: Differential Police Response." *American Journal of Police* 12(1):1–32.

Appendix A—Citizen Survey

Delayed Sworn Response
or Civilian Response

Respondent's Name_____

Respondent's Phone Number _____ID #_____

(circle one)

	Business Residential	(circle one)
Initial Call	Date_____Time_____	AM PM
First Callback	Date_____Time_____	AM PM
Second Callback	Date_____Time_____	AM PM
Third Callback	Date_____Time_____	AM PM
Fourth Callback	Date_____Time_____	AM PM

HELLO. MAY I SPEAK TO _____? MY NAME IS _____. I AM A MEMBER OF A RESEARCH TEAM STUDYING POLICE SERVICES IN [CITY]. WE ARE TRYING TO LEARN WHAT [CITY] RESIDENTS THINK ABOUT HOW EFFECTIVELY THE POLICE DEPARTMENT HANDLES CALLS FOR SERVICE, AND WE UNDERSTAND THAT YOU CALLED THE [CITY] POLICE ON [DATE]. I WOULD LIKE TO ASK YOU A FEW QUESTIONS ABOUT YOUR EXPERIENCE WITH THE POLICE. THE INTERVIEW WILL TAKE ONLY FIVE TO 10 MINUTES. YOUR PARTICIPATION IS VOLUNTARY. YOU MAY CHOOSE NOT TO PARTICIPATE OR NOT TO ANSWER CERTAIN QUESTIONS WITHOUT PENALTY, AND YOUR REFUSAL TO PARTICIPATE WILL IN NO WAY AFFECT FUTURE LAW ENFORCEMENT SERVICE PROVIDED TO YOU. **YOUR RESPONSES WILL BE COMPLETELY CONFIDENTIAL.** SO, ARE YOU WILLING TO PARTICIPATE?_____

BEFORE I BEGIN, LET ME EXPLAIN THAT WE OBTAINED YOUR NAME FROM THE [CITY] POLICE DEPARTMENT'S RECORDS OF CALLS FOR SERVICE. BUT YOUR NAME WILL NOT BE ASSOCIATED WITH YOUR RESPONSES IN ANY REPORT, AND THE POLICE DEPARTMENT WILL NOT BE ABLE TO IDENTIFY YOUR RESPONSES WITH YOU.

IF THE RESPONDENT HESITATES, BE PREPARED TO EXPLAIN THAT
- **RESPONSES TO THE SURVEY WILL NOT BE IDENTIFIED WITH HIM/HER INDIVIDUALLY IN ANY REPORTS OF THE RESULTS,**
- HE/SHE CAN CALL XXX-XXXX BETWEEN 8 AM AND 5 PM TO VERIFY YOUR IDENTITY, AND
- THE INFORMATION GIVEN MAY HELP IMPROVE POLICE SERVICES._____

IF RESPONDENT INDICATES THAT HE/SHE DOESN'T HAVE THE TIME, ASK IF THERE IS A MORE CONVENIENT TIME AT WHICH YOU MAY CALL BACK.   CALL BACK

Date _____Time _____

Detach here.

		Column
Date of Call _____	(1)____	
Time of Call _____	(5)____	
Event Code _____	(9)____	
Priority _____	(12)____	
Time of Dispatch _____	(13)____	
Time of Arrival _____	(17)____	
Time Back in Service ____	(21)____	
Reporting Area _____	(25)____	
Respondent ID # _____	(28)____	
Time Interview Started __	(31)____	

1. First, would you briefly describe the incident about which you called the police? _____ (35)_____
    _____ (38)_____
    _____ (41)_____

    [code up to three types]

1A. **IF INCIDENT WAS NOT IN PROGRESS WHEN REPORTED TO POLICE:**
    About how long after the incident occurred did you become aware of the problem?
    _____ Days / _____ Hours / _____ Minutes   (44)_____
    [code minutes]

2. **IF PROPERTY WAS DAMAGED OR STOLEN:**
    What was the approximate value of the property damaged or stolen?
    $_____   (48)_____
    [Code dollar value. If unknown, code 9. If too large, code all 9s.]

3. (Once you discovered or became aware of the incident), how long was it before you called the police?
    _____ Days / _____ Hours / _____ Minutes   (52)_____
    [code minutes]

4. Did the call taker tell you how long it would take for an officer to arrive?
    1____Yes   (53)_____
    2____No
    9____Don't remember

4A. [If yes]:   ____Hours   (54)_____
    How long did the   ____Minutes   [code minutes]
    call taker say it   9____Don't remember
    would be?

5. Would you say that the call taker seemed very concerned about your problem, somewhat concerned, or not at all concerned?

    1_____Very concerned   (57)_____

    2_____Somewhat concerned

    3_____Not at all concerned

    9_____Don't know

6. Would you say that the call taker was very accurate and clear in your conversation, somewhat accurate and clear, or not at all accurate and clear?

    1_____Very accurate and clear   (58)_____

    2_____Somewhat accurate and clear

    3_____Not at all accurate and clear

    9_____Don't know

7. Would you say that the call taker listened very carefully to what you had to say, somewhat carefully, or not at all carefully?

    1_____Very carefully   (59)_____

    2_____Somewhat carefully

    3_____Not at all carefully

    9_____Don't know

8. Would you say that the call taker was very calm and collected, somewhat calm and collected, or not at all calm and collected?

    1_____Very calm and collected   (60)_____

    2_____Somewhat calm and collected

    3_____Not at all calm and collected

    9_____Don't know

9. How satisfied were you with how the call taker handled your call? Would you say that you were very satisfied, satisfied, dissatisfied, or very dissatisfied?

    1_____Very satisfied } GO TO   (61)_____

    2_____Satisfied   } ITEM 10

    3_____Dissatisfied

    4_____Very dissatisfied

    9_____Don't know

9A. [If dissatisfied]: Why were you dissatisfied?

    _____

    _____

    [DON'T READ]

    1_____Had to argue to get desired response   (62)_____

    2_____Call taker seemed unconcerned/disinterested   (63)_____

    3_____Call taker asked too many questions   (64)_____

    8_____Other   [code up to three]

10. After you called, how long did it take for the police to arrive?
    _____Hours / _____Minutes [if necessary, probe for rough estimate]
          [or]

	1_____Came next day	(65)_____
GO TO ITEM 14	2_____Never came	[code minutes]
GO TO ITEM 12	9_____Don't know	

11. Was the response slower than, faster than, or about the same as what you expected?
    1_____Slower   (68)_____
    2_____Faster
    3_____About the same
    9_____Don't know

11A. If response time exceeded one hour:
     Did the call taker call you back to tell you that an officer would be there as soon as possible?
     1_____Yes   (69)_____
     2_____No
     9_____Don't remember

12. When the police arrived, what did they do?
    _____
    _____

12A. How many officers responded to your call?
     _____Officers   (70)_____

12B. About how long were the police there?
     _____Minutes   (72)_____

13. Overall, how satisfied were you with the way the officer(s) handled your complaint? Would you say that you were very satisfied, satisfied, dissatisfied, or very dissatisfied?
    1_____Very satisfied } GO TO   (75)_____
    2_____Satisfied   } ITEM 14
    3_____Dissatisfied
    4_____Very dissatisfied
    9_____Don't know

13A. [If dissatisfied]: Why were you dissatisfied?
     _____
     _____

[DON'T READ]
1_____Officer was not courteous   (76)_____
2_____Officer could not solve problem   (77)_____
3_____Officer was incompetent; didn't know what
         he or she was doing   (78)_____
4_____Officer used poor judgment; did the   [code up to three]
         wrong thing
5_____Officer did not care; was not understanding
6_____Response time was poor
8_____Other

NOW I HAVE SOME GENERAL QUESTIONS. YOUR ANSWERS WILL
BE USEFUL FOR COMPARING DIFFERENT NEIGHBORHOODS.

14. How long have you lived in your neighborhood?
    _____Years   (79)_____
    _____Months   (81)_____

15. In what kind of housing do you live? Is it a single-family home, a duplex,
    an apartment, a mobile home, or another type of residence?
    1_____Single-family home
    2_____Duplex
    3_____Apartment   (83)_____
    4_____Mobile home
    8_____Other

16. Including the occasion that I've asked you about, how many times have you
    called the police during the past year?
    1_____Once
    2_____Twice
    3_____Three times   (84)_____
    4_____Four or more times
    9_____Don't recall

17. How would you rate the overall quality of police services in your immediate
    neighborhood, that is, in the two or three blocks right around your home?
    Are police services outstanding, good, adequate, inadequate, or very poor?
    1_____Outstanding
    2_____Good
    3_____Adequate   (85)_____
    4_____Inadequate
    5_____Very poor
    9_____Don't know

18. In what year were you born? 19 _____   (86)_____

19. What is your race or ethnic background?
    1_____White
    2_____Black
    3_____Hispanic   (88)_____
    8_____Other

20. Was your total family income for last year less than $20,000 or more than $20,000?

    _____Less than $20,000   _____More than $20,000
    [IF LESS]   [IF MORE]
    Was it less than $10,000?   Was it more than $30,000?
    1_____Yes [less than $10,000]   4_____Yes [more than $30,000]
    2_____No [$10,000–$20,000]   3_____No [$20,000–$30,000]
                                                             (89)_____

21. [DON'T READ]
    Respondent's Sex
    1_____Male
    2_____Female
    9_____Don't know   (90)_____

THOSE ARE THE QUESTIONS I HAVE. THANK YOU VERY MUCH FOR YOUR HELP. MY SUPERVISOR MAY CALL YOU TO VERIFY THAT THIS INTERVIEW WAS COMPLETED.

TIME INTERVIEW ENDED _____   (91)_____

Appendix B—Citizen Survey
Telephone Report Union (TRU)

Respondent's Name_____
Respondent's Phone Number _____ID #_____

	(circle one) Business Residential	(circle one)
Initial Call	Date_____Time_____	AM PM
First Callback	Date_____Time_____	AM PM
Second Callback	Date_____Time_____	AM PM
Third Callback	Date_____Time_____	AM PM
Fourth Callback	Date_____Time_____	AM PM

HELLO. MAY I SPEAK TO _____? MY NAME IS _____. I AM A MEMBER OF A RESEARCH TEAM STUDYING POLICE SERVICES IN [CITY]. WE ARE TRYING TO LEARN WHAT [CITY] RESIDENTS THINK ABOUT HOW EFFECTIVELY THE POLICE DEPARTMENT HANDLES CALLS FOR SERVICE, AND WE UNDERSTAND THAT YOU CALLED THE [CITY] POLICE ON [DATE]. I WOULD LIKE TO ASK YOU A FEW QUESTIONS ABOUT YOUR EXPERIENCE WITH THE POLICE. THE INTERVIEW WILL TAKE ONLY FIVE TO 10 MINUTES. YOUR PARTICIPATION IS VOLUNTARY. YOU MAY CHOOSE NOT TO PARTICIPATE OR NOT TO ANSWER CERTAIN QUESTIONS WITHOUT PENALTY, AND YOUR REFUSAL TO PARTICIPATE WILL IN NO WAY AFFECT FUTURE LAW ENFORCEMENT SERVICE PROVIDED TO YOU. **YOUR RESPONSES WILL BE COMPLETELY CONFIDENTIAL.** SO, ARE YOU WILLING TO PARTICIPATE?

BEFORE I BEGIN, LET ME EXPLAIN THAT WE OBTAINED YOUR NAME FROM THE [CITY] POLICE DEPARTMENT'S RECORDS OF CALLS FOR SERVICE. BUT YOUR NAME WILL NOT BE ASSOCIATED WITH YOUR RESPONSES IN ANY REPORT, AND THE POLICE DEPARTMENT WILL NOT BE ABLE TO IDENTIFY YOUR RESPONSES WITH YOU.

IF THE RESPONDENT HESITATES, BE PREPARED TO EXPLAIN THAT
- **RESPONSES TO THE SURVEY WILL NOT BE IDENTIFIED WITH HIM/HER INDIVIDUALLY IN ANY REPORTS OF THE RESULTS,**
- HE/SHE CAN CALL XXX-XXXX BETWEEN 8 AM AND 5 PM TO VERIFY YOUR IDENTITY, AND
- THE INFORMATION GIVEN MAY HELP IMPROVE POLICE SERVICES.

IF RESPONDENT INDICATES THAT HE/SHE DOESN'T HAVE THE TIME, ASK IF THERE IS A MORE CONVENIENT TIME AT WHICH YOU MAY CALL BACK.   CALL BACK
                                               Date _____Time _____

Detach here.

                                                        Column
Date of Call _____(1)_____
Offense Category _____(5)_____
Reporting Area _____(8)_____
Respondent ID # _____(11)_____
Time Interview Started _____(14)_____
                                                        [24-hour time]

1. First, would you briefly describe the incident about which you called the
    police? _____(18)_____
    _____(21)_____
    _____(24)_____
                                        [code up to three types]

2. **IF PROPERTY WAS DAMAGED OR STOLEN**:
    What was the approximate value of the property damaged or stolen?
    $_____   (27)_____
    [Code dollar value. If unknown, code 9. If too large, code all 9s.]

3. (Once you discovered or became aware of the incident), how long was it
    before you called the police?
    _____Days / _____Hours / _____Minutes   (31)_____
                                                        [code minutes]

4. Did you have any information about who did this?
    1____Yes   (35)_____
    2____No } NEXT PAGE   GO TO ITEM 5
    8____Refused to give it }
    9____Don't know }

4A. [If yes]: What type of information did you have?
    _____
    _____

    [DON'T READ]
    1____Saw persons and knew who he or she/they   (36)_____
         was/were
    2____Saw persons and could give description
    3____Didn't see anyone, but had some idea of who did it
    4____Knew of a similar thing happening to a neighbor
    8____Other

4B. What information did you give to the police call taker?
BE SURE RESPONDENT REFERS TO CONVERSATION WITH CALL
TAKER.

_____

_____

[DON'T READ]
1_____Told call taker I didn't know anything   (37)_____
2_____Gave call taker some information, but not all I had
3_____Gave call taker all the information I had }GO TO ITEM 5
4_____Didn't tell the call taker anything, because the call taker did not ask}
8_____Other

4C. Is there any particular reason that you didn't give the call taker all the
information you had?

_____

_____

[DON'T READ]
1_____Call taker didn't ask [GO TO ITEM 5]   (38)_____
2_____Forgot at the time
3_____Didn't want to embarrass friend, neighbor, family
4_____Was afraid of consequences, retaliation
8_____Other

4D. Did the call taker ask if you had any information about who did this?
1_____Yes   (39)_____
2_____No
9_____Don't know

5. Would you say that the call taker seemed very concerned about your
problem, somewhat concerned, or not at all concerned?
1_____Very concerned   (40)_____
2_____Somewhat concerned
3_____Not at all concerned
9_____Don't know

6. Would you say that the call taker was very accurate and clear in your
conversation, somewhat accurate and clear, or not at all accurate and clear?
1_____Very accurate and clear   (41)_____
2_____Somewhat accurate and clear
3_____Not at all accurate and clear
9_____Don't know

7. Would you say that the call taker listened very carefully to what you had to say, somewhat carefully, or not at all carefully?

    1____Very carefully   (42)_____
    2____Somewhat carefully
    3____Not at all carefully
    9____Don't know

8. Would you say that the call taker was very calm and collected, somewhat calm and collected, or not at all calm and collected?

    1____Very calm and collected   (43)_____
    2____Somewhat calm and collected
    3____Not at all calm and collected
    9____Don't know

9. How satisfied were you with how the call taker handled your call? Would you say that you were very satisfied, satisfied, dissatisfied, or very dissatisfied?

    1____Very satisfied } GO TO   (44)_____

    2____Satisfied   } ITEM 10
    3____Dissatisfied
    4____Very dissatisfied
    9____Don't know

9A. [If dissatisfied]: Why were you dissatisfied?

    _____

    _____

    [DON'T READ]
    1____Call taker didn't send an officer   (45)_____
    2____Call taker seemed unconcerned/disinterested   (46)_____
    3____Call taker asked too many questions   (47)_____
    8____Other   [code up to three]

10. Your call was referred to the telephone report unit. After you finished talking with the call taker, how long did it take for an officer from the telephone report unit to call you back?

    ____Hours / ____Minutes [if necessary, probe for rough estimate]
    [or]
                           1____Called next day   (48)_____
    [GO TO ITEM 18]   2____Never called   [code minutes]
    [GO TO ITEM 12]   9____Don't know

11. Did the officer call sooner than, later than or about the same as when you expected?

1____Sooner   (51)_____
2____Later
3____About the same
9____Don't know

[IF ANSWER TO ITEM 4 WAS YES]:
12. What information did you give to the telephone report unit officer? BE SURE RESPONDENT REFERS TO CONVERSATION WITH TRU OFFICER.

_____
_____
_____

[DON'T READ]
1____Told officer I didn't know anything
2____Gave officer some information, but not all I had   (52)_____
3____Gave officer all the information I had } GO TO
4____Didn't tell the officer anything,   } ITEM 13
       because the officer didn't ask
8____Other

12A. Is there any particular reason that you didn't give the officer all the information you had?

_____
_____

[DON'T READ]
1____Officer didn't ask [GO TO ITEM 13]   (53)_____
2____Forgot at the time
3____Didn't want to embarrass friend, neighbor, family
4____Was afraid of consequences, retaliation
8____Other

12B. Did the officer ask if you had any information about who did this?
1____Yes   (54)_____
2____No
9____Don't know

13. Would you say that the officer seemed very concerned about your problem, somewhat concerned, or not at all concerned?
1____Very concerned   (55)_____
2____Somewhat concerned
3____Not at all concerned
9____Don't know

14. Would you say that the officer was very accurate and clear in your conversation, somewhat accurate and clear, or not at all accurate and clear?
    1_____Very accurate and clear   (56)_____
    2_____Somewhat accurate and clear
    3_____Not at all accurate and clear
    9_____Don't know

15. Would you say that the officer listened very carefully to what you had to say, somewhat carefully, or not at all carefully?
    1_____Very carefully   (57)_____
    2_____Somewhat carefully
    3_____Not at all carefully
    9_____Don't know

16. Would you say that the officer was very calm and collected, somewhat calm and collected, or not at all calm and collected?
    1_____Very calm and collected   (58)_____
    2_____Somewhat calm and collected
    3_____Not at all calm and collected
    9_____Don't know

17. How satisfied were you with how the telephone response unit handled your call? Would you say that you were very satisfied, satisfied, dissatisfied, or very dissatisfied?
    1_____Very satisfied } GO TO   (59)_____
    2_____Satisfied   } ITEM 18
    3_____Dissatisfied
    4_____Very dissatisfied
    9_____Don't know

17A. [If dissatisfied]: Why were you dissatisfied?

_____

_____

[DON'T READ]
    1_____An officer wasn't sent   (60)_____
    2_____Officer seemed unconcerned/disinterested   (61)_____
    3_____Officer asked too many questions   (62)_____
    8_____Other   [code up to three]

17B. Would you have preferred to have an officer meet with you?
    1_____Yes   (63)_____
    2_____No
    9_____Don't know

18. If the same type of incident were to happen in the future, would you call the police to report it?

1_____Yes   (64)_____

2_____No

9_____Don't know

NOW I HAVE SOME GENERAL QUESTIONS. YOUR ANSWERS WILL BE USEFUL FOR COMPARING DIFFERENT NEIGHBORHOODS.

19. How long have you lived in your neighborhood?

_____Years   (65)_____

_____Months   (64)_____

20. In what kind of housing do you live? Is it a single-family home, a duplex, an apartment, a mobile home, or another type of residence?

1_____Single-family home

2_____Duplex

3_____Apartment   (66)_____

4_____Mobile home

8_____Other

21. Including the occasion that I've asked you about, how many times have you called the police during the past year?

1_____Once

2_____Twice

3_____Three times   (67)_____

4_____Four or more times

9_____Don't recall

22. How would you rate the overall quality of police services in your immediate neighborhood, that is, in the two or three blocks right around your home? Are police services outstanding, good, adequate, inadequate, or very poor?

1_____Outstanding

2_____Good

3_____Adequate   (68)_____

4_____Inadequate

5_____Very poor

9_____Don't know

23. In what year were you born? 19 _____   (69)_____

24. What is your race or ethnic background?

1_____White

2_____Black

3_____Hispanic   (71)_____

8_____Other

25. Was your total family income for last year less than $20,000 or more than $20,000?

_____Less than $20,000   _____More than $20,000

[IF LESS]   [IF MORE]

Was it less than $10,000?   Was it more than $30,000?

1_____Yes [less than $10,000]   4_____Yes [more than $30,000]

2_____No [$10,000–$20,000]   3_____No [$20,000–$30,000]

                                                        (72)_____

26. [DON'T READ]

    Respondent's Sex

    1_____Male

    2_____Female

    9_____Don't know   (73)_____

THOSE ARE ALL THE QUESTIONS I HAVE. THANK YOU VERY MUCH FOR YOUR HELP. MY SUPERVISOR MAY CALL YOU TO VERIFY THAT THIS INTERVIEW WAS COMPLETED.

TIME INTERVIEW ENDED _____   (74)_____

About the Authors

David L. Carter is a professor in the School of Criminal Justice and director of the National Center for Community Policing, both at Michigan State University. He is formerly a research fellow with the Police Executive Research Forum. He received his bachelor's and master's degrees in criminal justice from Central Missouri State University, and his doctorate in criminal justice administration from Sam Houston State University in Huntsville, Texas. He has provided community policing training and technical assistance nationwide and has also conducted research on a wide range of policing issues in the United States, Europe, and Asia. Dr. Carter's most recent book (with the late Louis Radelet) is *The Police and Community*, fifth edition, Macmillan Publishing Co.

Gary W. Cordner is a professor in the Department of Police Studies at Eastern Kentucky University and director of its Regional Community Policing Institute. Previously, he taught at both Washington State University and the University of Baltimore. He has also served as a police officer and police chief in Maryland. He received his doctorate from Michigan State University. Dr. Cordner has coauthored textbooks on police administration and criminal justice planning, coedited the volumes *What Works in Policing?*, *Managing Police Organizations*, *Managing Police Personnel*, and *Police Operations: Analysis and Evaluation*; edited the *American Journal of Police* from 1987 to 1992; and coedited the *Police Computer Review* from 1992 to 1995. He is currently working with Abt Associates on the national evaluations of Weed & Seed and the Youth Firearms Violence Initiative, and with the Police Executive Research Forum on the development of problem-oriented policing.

John E. Eck is the evaluation coordinator for the Washington/ Baltimore High Intensity Drug Trafficking Area, where he assesses the performance of local, state and federal drug enforcement groups. Dr. Eck is also an associate research scholar at the University of Maryland, where he teaches police management and environmental criminology. He is a vice president of the Crime Control Research Corporation, where he conducts research for expert witness testimony. He is the former research director for the Police Executive Research Forum, where he pioneered the development and implementation of problem-oriented policing. In 1984, Dr. Eck served as a consultant to the London Metropolitan Police on investigations productivity. He has conducted research on crime mapping, retail drug markets, problem-oriented policing, and criminal investigations. He is the co-editor of *Crime and Place* and the author of numerous other publications on police effectiveness, drug markets and the geography of crime. Dr. Eck received his doctorate from the University of Maryland, College Park, and his master's in public policy from the University of Michigan.

Larry T. Hoover received his bachelor's, master's and doctorate degrees from Michigan State University and has been on the criminal justice faculty at Sam Houston State University since 1977. He previously taught at Michigan State University, served on the staff of the Michigan Law Enforcement Officers Training Council, and held assignments in the patrol, communications and personnel divisions of the Lansing, Mich., Police Department. A past president of the Academy of Criminal Justice Sciences, Dr. Hoover now directs the Police Research Center at Sam Houston State University. Since 1980, he has been coprincipal of Justex Systems, a personnel relations consulting firm that conducts promotional examinations for public safety agencies and publishes the newsletters *Police Labor Monthly* and *Fire Service Labor Monthly*. His publications include articles in the *Journal of Criminal Justice, American Journal of Police, Public Personnel Management, Monthly Labor Review, Security Administration*, and *Liberal Education*, as well as a research monograph for the National Institute of Justice. He is also coeditor of the *Encyclopedia of Police Science* and editor of *Police Management: Issues and Perspectives* and *Quantifying Quality in Policing*, both anthologies published by the Police Executive Research Forum.

Clifford Karchmer is director of program development for the Police Executive Research Forum, where he has been since 1986. He is currently directing a number of projects, including developing a New England-area automated gang information system, convening a conference on police traffic services in the 21st century, and developing a homicide investigative model. His areas of expertise include white-collar crime, traffic safety and technology, among others. His previous positions include project director at the Battelle Human Affairs Research Centers, director of operations for the National Center on White-Collar Crime, director of the Massachusetts Organized Crime Control Council, and several assignments with the Massachusetts Committee on Criminal Justice. Karchmer earned a master's in public administration from the John F. Kennedy School of Government at Harvard University, a master's in political science from the University of Wisconsin, and a bachelor's degree in politics from Princeton University.

Dennis J. Kenney has over 24 years of experience in varied aspects of criminal justice—as a Florida police officer; as a director of research and planning in Savannah, Ga.; as a project director for the Police Foundation; and as a university professor at both the Western Connecticut State University and the University of Nebraska at Omaha. Currently, he is an associate director and director of research for the Police Executive Research Forum. He is the author or coauthor of numerous articles and books, including *Crime, Fear and the New York City Subways* (1986); *Organized Crime in America* (1995); *Police Pursuits: What We Know* (1997); *Crime in the Schools* (1997); and *Managing the Police: An Historical Look at the Future* (1997). Additionally, Dr. Kenney has provided consulting services to police agencies around the country, has managed federally sponsored research and technical assistance projects, and is the past editor of the *American Journal of Police.* At present, he is completing funded research projects on police performance evaluations, police fatigue and its effects on officer performance, and the nature and extent of abortion-related violence. Dr. Kenney holds a doctorate in criminal justice from Rutgers University.

Stephen D. Mastrofski is a professor in the School of Criminal Justice at Michigan State University and a former visiting fellow with the National Institute of Justice. Dr. Mastrofski has done research on a number of police-related topics, such as program evaluation and performance measurement, police reform, police agency consolidation, accreditation, and drunk driving enforcement. He served on the editorial boards of the *American Journal of Police* and *Criminology.* In addition to scholarly journals, his work has appeared in police professional journals and the International City Management Association's *Local Government Police Management.* Dr. Mastrofski has written several essays and articles on community policing and coedited a volume titled *Community Policing: Rhetoric or Reality.* He has provided technical assistance on community policing to a number of departments in the United States and Canada. He is currently conducting a National Institute of Justice-sponsored observational study of patrol officers engaged in community policing.

Allen D. Sapp is a professor in the Department of Criminal Justice at Central Missouri State University and formerly a research fellow with the Police Executive Research Forum. He received his bachelor's degree from the University of Southern California, master's degree from the University of Nebraska and doctorate in criminal justice theory from Sam Houston State University. He has provided training and technical assistance to a wide range of police agencies on issues related to strategic planning, forecasting and policy analysis. His latest work has been with the FBI Academy on arson research.

Robert E. Worden is an associate professor of criminal justice and public policy at the Rockefeller College of Public Affairs and Policy, University of Albany and State University of New York. He holds a doctorate in political science, with a specialization in public administration and policy analysis, from the University of North Carolina at Chapel Hill. He previously served on the faculties of the University of Georgia and Michigan State University. His research on the police has appeared in a number of scholarly journals, including *Justice Quarterly*, *Law & Society Review*, *Criminology*, the *American Journal of Police*, and others. He is currently one of the four principal investigators of the Project on Policing Neighborhoods, a study of police patrol funded by the National Institute of Justice.

About Sam Houston State University (SHSU)

Sam Houston State University (SHSU) enrolls approximately 13,000 students. The 211-acre campus is located in Huntsville, Texas, a picturesque community of 30,000 residents. Established in 1965, SHSU's Criminal Justice Center has evolved into one of the largest criminal justice education and training programs in the world. The university's Criminal Justice Center houses the College of Criminal Justice and the Institute of Criminal Justice. The center contains a courtroom, auditorium, dining facility, classrooms, seminar rooms, computer laboratories, and offices for faculty members and graduate assistants. A 98-room hotel provides accommodations for visiting faculty and seminar participants. The college offers both baccalaureate and master's degrees in criminal justice and is one of 20 institutions in the United States that offers the Ph.D. in criminal justice. Institute programs include the Bill Blackwood Law Enforcement Management Institute of Texas supported by a $3 million annual appropriation from the Texas legislature, the Correctional Management Institute of Texas, the Police Research Center, and the newly established Texas Community Policing Institute.

About The Police Executive Research Forum (PERF)

The Police Executive Research Forum (PERF) is a national professional association of chief executives of large city, county and state law enforcement agencies. PERF's objective is to improve the delivery of police services and the effectiveness of crime control through several means:

1. the exercise of strong national leadership,

2. the public debate of police and criminal justice issues,

3. the development of research and policy, and

4. the provision of vital management leadership services to police agencies.

PERF members are selected on the basis of their commitment to PERF's objectives and principles. PERF operates under the following tenets:

1. Research, experimentation and exchange of ideas through public discussion and debate are paths for the development of a comprehensive body of knowledge about policing.

2. Substantial and purposeful academic study is a prerequisite for acquiring, understanding and adding to that body of knowledge.

3. Maintenance of the highest standards of ethics and integrity is imperative in the improvement of policing.

4. The police must, within the limits of the law, be responsible and accountable to citizens as the ultimate source of police authority.

5. The principles embodied in the Constitution are the foundation of policing.

Related Titles

The following publications also address issues related to police research and program evaluation. PERF also offers a free publications catalog listing its nearly 60 publications on police management and practice. To request a free catalog or order PERF publications, call the toll-free PERF publications line at **1-888-202-4563**.

Information Management and Crime Analysis: Practitioners' Recipes for Success
(Melissa Miller Reuland, ed., 1997)
152 pp., Product #819
ISBN #: 1-878734-48-2
Member Price: $18.95
Nonmember Price: $21.00
In *Information Management and Crime Analysis: Practitioners' Recipes for Success*, police practitioners from around the country discuss ways to manage police information to meet a variety of needs, from crime analysis to community awareness. Chapters cover crime information, database structures, administrative crime analysis, use of information technologies to assist investigations and tactical planning, how crime analysts can use computer mapping to identify "hot spots," and decentralization of information to beat officers and citizens.

Using Research: A Primer for Law Enforcement Managers
(John E. Eck and Nancy La Vigne, 1994)
180 pp., Product #045
ISBN #: 1-878734-33-4
Member Price: $19.95
Nonmember Price: $22.00
Using Research, now in its second edition, remains the only research text specifically tailored to police audiences. Authors John Eck and Nancy La Vigne provide a comprehensive introduction to the research process, from defining the problem to designing the research, from analyzing the data to reporting the findings. They also provide criteria for judging others' research and a listing of information sources. The second edition is updated to reflect changes in technology and in the nature of policing itself. Anyone interested in evaluating police practices will want to add this book to his or her collection.

Quantifying Quality in Policing
(Larry Hoover, ed., 1995)
280 pp., Product #804
ISBN #: 1-878734-40-7
Member Price: $19.95
Nonmember Price: $22.00
In *Quantifying Quality in Policing*, police professionals and social scientists identify those elements of total quality management (TQM) that may be used to assess effectiveness in police performance. In the past, police performance has primarily been evaluated in terms of numbers, such as crime statistics and arrest rates. The authors of *Quantifying Quality in Policing*, however, suggest that other indicators such as citizen satisfaction and crime prevention, although hard to quantify, are also important in fairly assessing police services. Routinely used as required reading for classes and promotional exams, this book features such noted experts as George Kelling, Gary Cordner, John Eck, Darrel Stephens, and David Bayley.